SEE NAPLES

SEE
NAPLES

A MEMOIR

Douglas Allanbrook

A Peter Davison Book

HOUGHTON MIFFLIN COMPANY

Boston • New York

1995

For information about permission to reproduce
selections from this book, write to
Permissions, Houghton Mifflin Company,
215 Park Avenue South, New York,
New York 10003.

Library of Congress Cataloging-in-Publication Data
Allanbrook, Douglas.
See Naples : a memoir / Douglas Allanbrook
p.   cm.
"A Peter Davison book."
ISBN 0-395-74585-3
1. Allanbrook, Douglas. 2. Americans — Italy
— Naples — Biography. 3. Naples — Social life
and customs. 4. Americans — Italy — Naples
— Social life and customs. 5. Naples (Italy) —
History — 1945–   6. World War, 1939–1945 —
Campaigns — Italy. 7. Italy — History — Allied
occupation, 1939–1947.   I. Title.
DG850.A55A3 1995   95-21202
945'.73092 — dc20   CIP

Printed in the United States of America

Book design by Robert Overholtzer

QUM 10 9 8 7 6 5 4 3 2 1

For information about this and other
Houghton Mifflin trade and reference books
and multimedia products, visit The Bookstore
at Houghton Mifflin on the World Wide Web
at http://www.hmco.com.trade/.

TO MY TWO SONS

Timothy and John

ACKNOWLEDGMENTS

I should like to thank several persons for their help in bringing this book to completion. Miss Beate Ruhm Von Oppen was a careful reader with invaluable suggestions. My first wife, Candida Allanbrook, gave it her scrupulous attention and let no Italian references escape unchecked. My younger son, John, drove me to a computer and insisted that the manuscript be in proper shape. A student of mine, Christopher Kurfess, checked all of the galleys with me with great good cheer. Most particularly I am grateful to Peter Davison, who was unstinting both in his enthusiasm and in his determination to see the book through to its finished state.

Staff Sergeant Douglas Allanbrook, 1945

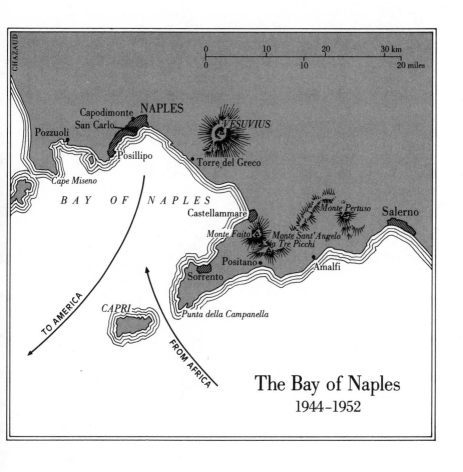

The Bay of Naples
1944–1952

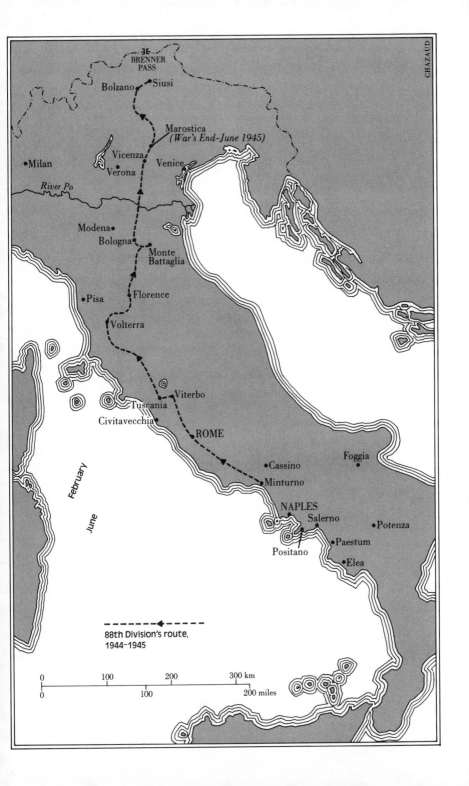

SEE NAPLES

1

"I HATE VESUVIUS," said Mrs. Picabia, stroking her favorite hen, whose broken leg she had splinted that morning, and addressing herself to the two of us standing with her on the terrace of the villa at Capodimonte. The sun was sinking over the city and the gulf beyond reflected its ambient rays. The famous volcano was etched in violet, clear against the darkening sky. I recalled the first time I saw Vesuvius, standing with Leonard on the deck of the dirty British transport which had brought us up from Oran. The mountain was in eruption, with the funicular burning a diagonal on its slope and a crisscross of anti-aircraft fire searching out a rather desultory German air raid. That was six years ago in January.

Paul and I shivered in the evening breeze and Mrs. Picabia pulled a shawl over her scrawny shoulders more to warm the hen, it seemed, than to bring any comfort to herself. The villa, a mile down the ridge from the royal palace at Capodimonte, was perfectly positioned on the edge of the famous hill, at the apex of a triangular lot, a lot which opened up and spilled down over the hill in a ramshackle garden of grapefruit, lemons, and decaying palms. On the left of the property the road descended precipitously toward a particularly squalid quarter of the city, the Sanità. It was one of those roads seen throughout Campania, a road which had sunk as much as six feet below the surrounding

fields, the volcanic tufa having crumbled under countless generations of feet and hoofs. You could lean on the wall at the edge
of the garden, below a decaying fountain which stood in front of
the façade of a crumbling chapel, and watch people passing
below and hear the soft voices of trysting couples finding sexual
solace in the penumbra of the sunken road.

Earlier that fall I had become disturbingly aware of the presence of caves, dug into the tufa below the very bottom of the
garden. They were inhabited. During the war they had functioned as air-raid shelters; they functioned now as places of
abode for the many homeless in the poor and eternally ramshackle city. The villa's façade, which could be seen as one
peered through the iron grillwork of the entrance gate, bore the
symmetrical impress of the eighteenth century. It was a reflection of the architectural taste of not only the late Bourbon court,
but more poignantly, of the Neapolitan enlightenment and its
abortive revolution, an uprising brutally stamped out when the
court returned from Palermo under the aegis of Admiral Nelson,
sitting out in the bay on his British flagship while Cardinal Ruffo
hanged the enlightened members of the educated class in the
square downtown now known as the Piazza dei Martiri. The
executions were welcomed with enthusiasm by the mob, some
of whom would assist the executioner by hanging on the heels
of the victims.

It is only in hindsight that I can speak of such things for at
that time I knew very little of the history of the ancient kingdom
of Naples; indeed I was engulfed in my own particular memories of the war I had been in and with the impact upon me of the
shattered and coruscating Naples I felt so near to. The nexus of
my attention then was upon my life in the villa and upon my
relations with its bizarre landlady, a Hungarian woman married
to an Italian from Parma, Mr. Picabia. His Spanish name carried
more Italian history with it than I was then aware of. He, poor
man, was lost in the quick-witted world of Neapolitan jurispru-
dence. By profession a lawyer, by nature slow and pleasant, he

had many years before married the wealthy Hungarian lady who was the proprietor of the villa. By her he had had two handsome children. This I learned from my old Luisa, who cooked and cleaned for my friend and me. She was an aging inhabitant of Capodimonte and she detested the present mistress of the villa just as the present mistress detested all Neapolitans and, even more, the locals. Mr. Picabia, despite his good nature, carried in his bones the ancient prejudice of the North toward Naples and Neapolitans, that terrible breach which had only become wider when the Piedmontese united Italy. Luisa recounted with relish the story of the slow, wasting illness of the original Ungherese and the arrival from Budapest of a nurse, the present *padrona*. "The new one had him in her bed long before the old one was in her coffin," she cackled.

The villa retained many of the accouterments of its prewar prosperity: modern plumbing and bathrooms, a gleaming range in the kitchen. All of these bespoke more than modest wealth in the Naples of the twenties and thirties. Now all was in decay: money had disappeared; plumbing, even if functional, was doubtful; the city was not to repair the gas lines for years to come. The villa was the only asset of poor Mr. Picabia, whose legal wits were not up to Neapolitan quickness; he had no professional life nor hope for one. He lived, in quiet desperation, high up above the teeming city with his two handsome children and his shabby witch of a wife. His only two suits were shiny and the cuffs of his shirts frayed. Mrs. Picabia took little care of anything, delighting in bewailing her fate to her two new American tenants and devoting herself to her hens and to her cocker spaniel, an aging creature with the unlikely English name of Flash. The two children were, of course, not hers, but "the first one's," the now long-deceased rich one. All of us up in the villa were foreigners, strange folk adrift on our hilltop, with the cherished or hated city stretched out below, remote from us.

It was this very remoteness which had attracted Laura to Capodimonte. I had been leaning toward finding a place in Pozzuoli, that fervid little port just north of Naples which had struck me, then caught up in my away-from-home sickness, as even more Neapolitan than Naples. It took me a bit of time to realize that this meant it would be even more public than the larger city and would make private life remote from prying eyes well-nigh impossible. Seeking privacy, one warm afternoon in late September Laura and I had gone to a remote beach up toward Cape Miseno, north of Pozzuoli. In the midst of our underwater amours Laura spotted a priest on top of a bluff watching us through a pair of binoculars.

Walking through the corridors of the conservatory with Laura it seemed, according to her vivid accounts, that everyone who passed by, students and teachers alike, had a known lover, or was intriguing to gain one, and the entrancing quickness of the glances seemed to substantiate the presence of a world of passion and sexual awareness. Eyes are everywhere in Naples and a Spanish severity censures a girl's every move. Where to go? While poor lovers from Capodimonte frequented the sunken road, the villa above, far from the gaze of the city and owned by non-Neapolitans, was the very haven that Laura was looking for. She had read the notice which Mrs. Picabia had posted downtown at the United States Information Office and had been quick to act upon it. That very afternoon we took the bus up the Via Roma, twisting around the hairpin curves underneath the shockingly extravagant new church being erected in the midst of the misery of the city by the archdiocese. We arrived at the top of the hill by the royal palace, turned left along the ridge and got off at Salita dello Scudillo a Capodimonte. What an address! I always wrote it with a baroque flourish on my letters home.

My deal with the Picabias was quickly struck, the unusable splendors of the modern bathroom examined, the balcony, the terrace, the decaying chapel with its ruined fountain in front, and the famous view all admired. The rent seemed a proper amount to me and I accepted it despite wary glances from Laura. The Picabias were more than happy; they knew that no Neapolitan would live so far from the center of town and even more to the point they calculated that an American student wouldn't know enough to complain.

Laura found me a servant, Luisa. She was an aging woman, disfigured with a pendulous goiter. She lived nearby, supporting her six children as best she could, her husband having been killed during the Allied bombardments. He had worked for the municipal streetcar company and his minuscule pension left Luisa in abject poverty. Laura and she bargained together, speaking in the deepest dialect. A price was agreed upon to their mutual satisfaction: Luisa was to cook, clean house, shop, and wash my clothes for what struck me as an appallingly meager sum. The agreement made between Laura and Luisa was one made between two women who, despite vast differences of money and station, inhabited the same world, the world of Naples; they spoke the same language and inhabited the same moral realm. Mrs. Picabia, no part of that world, would constantly complain to me that Luisa was carrying food away with her every afternoon, never understanding that that was part of the implicit pact. What the young master did not need she certainly did. She never stole anything — something that soon turned out not to be true of the Ungherese.

A particular world exists in a particular way at a certain place and at a certain time. One seemed to be emerging for me that fall at Capodimonte and I sometimes wonder if it is not now realer as I look back over the span of forty years and remember scenes, loves, and particular sunlit days, all colored with the careful shading of regret. Certainly Capodimonte stands clear in my imagination and the more clearly I resurrect it the more disturbing become the shades of time behind and before it: Naples in wartime, disembarkation at the bomb-shattered port, north up the Via Appia to our position in the line, and Leonard's death. As I write about it it takes on the character of a fixed rendezvous.

Salita dello Scudillo a Capodimonte was part of Naples; and Naples obstinately, even stupidly, insists upon itself as being a very world of its own. The city has its own language, its own poetry, its own music, its own brand of melancholy — all framed by the glory of the bay and the blessed islands and haunted by the sleeping volcano. Boston, where I was brought up, is a kind of world for me, but never present to me with the vividness expressed by a quick-witted (and bright-eyed!) street boy who knew something about grand and splendid things. "Picasso, yes," he said. "Picasso is the greatest painter in Naples!"

I remember one period when Luisa had seemed increasingly restive and even a bit annoyed with me. She would come into the room where my piano and my desk were, muttering to herself, and regarding with suspicion the manuscript paper and the scribbling. After a week or so of this she burst into my studio late one morning with a freshly ironed shirt in her hands. "Oh, Signore," she exclaimed with all of her Neapolitan élan, "you're wasting the goods of God (*il bene di Dio*)! You have money in your pocket and I give you this fresh shirt. Get down off this dreary hillside and take a *passeggiata* at Santa Lucia; sit in a café, find your Donna Laura!" Neapolitan dialect has the entrancing habit of addressing ladies as "Donna," a habit that is natural to Neapolitans but full of overtones to a literary ear from abroad. There was a special minor pleasure involved in my calling Luisa "Donna Luisa" and in hearing her say "Donna Laura." It brought with it echoes of Petrarch.

How easy it is to be a lover of a foreign place, to be a Francophile or a "philo-Neapolitan": to mask the harsh reality of a place with one's fancy. At the bottom of my garden were entire families squatting in damp misery in caves scooped out of the volcanic tufa; half a mile away on the twisty curves of Via Roma the archdiocese of Naples was squandering millions on an immense and ugly neo-Baroque basilica; the mayor and his cronies were shifty and corrupt, crafty crooks perfectly at ease with Lucky Luciano, who, exiled from the United States, could be seen whiling away pleasant afternoons on the terrace of the Hotel Vesuvius. In an earlier century, when the Spanish viceroy received complaints concerning the dangers of the dark alleys of his capital city and the crying need for illumination, he had ordered statues of the Madonna to be placed in all of the darker corners of the town. "The faithful will take care of the rest with their votive candles," he said. How grand and how chilling cynics can be when they are in command! The most terrifying third-person imperative ever uttered came from the mouth of Pope Alexander VI when he was informed that a lady of the Vatican court was pregnant by one of the castrated members of the Sistine Chapel choir. "Let them be better castrated," he pronounced.

Laura loved me. Did I love her? I had early on at the villa persuaded my friend Paul to come down from the Academy in Rome to share my hilltop eyrie. On his arrival he had immediately dubbed Laura my Neapolitan Bette Davis, studying us both with his gray haddock eyes. Her eyes *were* like Bette Davis's and they were intent upon me the first time we saw each other. She was obsessed with me just as later I became obsessed with her successful rival when first I spotted her (Candida — my pale and placid nymph!) on the beach at Forte dei Marmi. Is that first electric flash the primal *"stupor,"* which can never be extirpated?

It certainly was something akin to that *stupor* which struck Laura when first she saw me the summer of 1949 at the Accademia Chigiana in Siena. There were four other members of the harpsichord class, all of them women: a piano teacher from Bergamo, a bright and talented little French girl from Paris, and two Neapolitan girls from Maestro Gerlin's winter *scuola* at the conservatory in Naples. One of the girls from Naples was Laura and the other was Maria della Cave, a thin and querulous girl whom Laura not so much detested as pitied. "Of course she's difficult," explained Laura. "She's a thin little thing and has no breasts."

In Gerlin's mind I was the true musician of the group as I was a pupil of the famous Nadia Boulanger. He was both delighted and flattered to have me. All of Gerlin's musical roots were in

Paris. He had gone there from Venice at the age of twenty-one and had left only when the Germans were about to appear and his teacher and goddess, Wanda Landowska, had to leave. He had been her principal assistant and willing slave for most of his grown-up life.

"Calma, figlio mio," he would say, "calma," and he would place my hand properly on the keyboard with each finger prepared to play with the precision and relaxation of a dancer's foot. "A curve, a curve," he would say as I reached for an interval. "You must never play in a straight line. Curve up and over!" He wrote Landowska's adroit fingerings into all the volumes of Bach that I studied with him: fingerings designed not so much for facility (although often they did facilitate) as for proper articulation: discourse for the fingers! For two winters in Naples I was the only serious member of the harpsichord class and would meet with Gerlin in the damp ground-floor room at the conservatory (San Pietro a Majella) to which the exalted piano maestros of the upper floors had relegated him. Maestro Gerlin was a solid little man, a Venetian, a bit frightened of Naples: another stranger, out of his element yet hypnotized by the quick glances and muscular limbs of the street boys. It was always a secret, well kept by him, as to where he lived.

That first year I would often walk downtown from the villa, making the sharpest descent on the sunken Salita dello Scudillo beneath the villa's garden, passing through the squalor of the Sanità quarter, on down the Via Roma for a bit, left at Piazza Dante and under the arch into Spaccanapoli — the straight Greek street which cuts the town in half — finally taking a right on down to the conservatory. What a morning's walk! — families peering out of their caves up on the sides of the Salita, narrow alleys which served as living rooms for the hordes of families ensconced in one room; peddlers and beggars and sidewalk stalls with fast food; restaurants, street fairs, side shows with fire-eaters; and everywhere quick eyes and supple flesh: such riches and such poverty! Other mornings I would take the bus down to Piazza del Plebiscito, walk past San Carlo, up through the shabby Galleria and on through a tangle of streets to Santa Chiara, stopping at a *tabaccaio* for cigarettes and condoms (a bit shamefacedly — my Boston heritage).

Maestro Gerlin drew me to Naples as much as did Laura's eyes. Forty years later his words remain: "You will see, figlio mio," he would say. "You will see. You will remember how to use your fingers, how to play Bach. It goes inside and matures there." The doing and the making and the playing of music, so intimately entangled with time, remain in our memory in a way that differs radically from the eyes and the loves and the legions of regret that are astir in our souls. Past time is vividly present, without editing, when it is involved in actual doing, as in playing and making music. It is a necessary fiction when it is tied to our own histories, immersed, in our fervid imagination of places and times, in the larger history of a particular world. Was my time in Naples an infinitesimal fragment of a more or less modern history? Except for the accident of Gerlin's being there, holding the position of harpsichord maestro at the Naples conservatory, my time spent in learning to perform keyboard music, which always remains unchanged and can be made actual by my fingers at any time, had little to do with Naples. It's impossible, on the other hand, to detach my Neapolitan Bette Davis from her city; any recollection of her implies that city's history, tying the person, the love, and the memory to a singular spot with its own singular history. In black self-scrutiny I often conjecture if it was Naples more than the eyes that caught me. The eyes, after all, looked like Bette Davis's.

Is it a literary question? If Dante was so struck with *stupor* at the sight of Beatrice's eyes as a boy in Florence, was that a Florentine moment? There is a certain doubt as to the existence of Petrarch's Madonna Laura and her two shining orbs, encountered, as the story goes, in Avignon. Why was it such an intimate delight to go into a shirtmaker's shop near Laura's house at Piazza Amedeo, accompanied by my Laura, and to have the lady measuring and cutting my shirts examine me closely, then turn to Laura and ask, "Fidanzato?" When I shook my head she retaliated with full dialectical relish, "What's the matter with you? Isn't she a handsome creature?"

Certainly the bishop of Pozzuoli must have thought I was Laura's *fidanzato* when she brought me to his palace for tea one afternoon. He studied me for a minute when we were introduced and then proceeded to gossip avidly with Laura as to who was doing what to whom in all of the many families they both knew in Neapolitan society. I was entranced; it was the first time I had ever had tea with a bishop, let alone a Neapolitan one; that he was a consummate gossip was an unexpected dividend. It was so unlike the First Congregational Church of Melrose where I had played the piano for the Christian Endeavor Society. It was not unlike the shock I received on another afternoon as we were passing in front of the cathedral. I was struck by the sight of the carabinieri in full dress uniform flanking the great doors of the church. "Why the cops all dressed up in front of the church?" I demanded of Laura. "Why?" she replied. "Why indeed! The cardinal-archbishop of Naples is a Prince of the Church."

Did I want to belong to a foreign place, my cherished Naples? There's always a bit of snobbery in choosing a foreign place and making that place one's vocation, in larding the conversation with references to it, in introducing a compatriot to it, and, God knows, in writing about it. Composing music is a more honest endeavor than putting words down on paper. The notes must be right but, thank God, they are not symbols; they only stand in entrancing relation one to another without all the shaggy illusions and history that words carry in their train. Notes don't lie — they either work or they don't work. A composer may write "national" pieces: witness Bach's English and French Suites or my own Naples and Venice music or my deliberate imitation of American jazz pianists. None of this implies being sentimental or daffy about some foreign or local habitat. All music has to have some particular affect, some idiomatic measuring of the feet and the breath. The tarantella is certainly Neapolitan and pulses through lots of the city's songs; it is enjoyed, as is a polonaise, without engendering the slightest wish either to visit Naples or to envisage Warsaw.

It is an old American habit to live abroad and to write about it, and the love affair that may accompany this living away from home is always fraught with intense self-consciousness: identity doubts itself. Is there an identity which is cosmopolitan? — as if the whole world were one city — and if that did turn out to be so, would an idiomatic "self" survive it? Can it exist without its shell, a nautilus without its chambers, exploring memory's fictional counterparts, appreciating all cultures, savoring all climes, and exploring all the vagaries and varieties of love?

Are my Neapolitan worlds fictional now that I write about them? They seemed real then in their vividness and in the completeness of that particular world encompassed by that very real city. Naples was not a country or a nation, though once it had been and had had its own very special and very Neapolitan kings. It certainly wasn't Italy, which had repudiated it. It encompassed every profession I needed, from shirtmakers to music copyists adept at extracting orchestral parts from my scores. It had its philosopher, whose daughters I would visit in their palazzo on Spaccanapoli, around the corner from the conservatory; it had its resplendent opera house, and it had brothels for all purses and all persuasions. It had my poor Luisa and, as its centerpiece, it had Laura and her close-knit family.

Paul's view of Naples was tinged with his constant contrasting of our life up at the villa with life back in his family's house in the Chicago suburbs. The vista from our terrace would arouse in him the recollection of the dreariness of rows of back yards stretching away into an Illinois perspective. He was a French Canadian, Catholic of course, an only son and most devoted to his parents. After the first year of his fellowship in Paris he had taken what cash remained to him and traveled all the way back home to Chicago by ship and train to visit his parents before returning to spend the second year of his fellowship in Italy. I stayed abroad almost five years, happy to be away from home with never a tinge of remorse. Paul's constant contrasting of his home life back in Chicago with our life up at the villa gave a voluptuous twinge to his pleasure as we would sit out on the terrace after dinner, being served our coffee by old Luisa. He was a tall skinny man with big gray eyes, a beak of a nose, and a prominent Adam's apple. I always sensed an enormous amount of repressed sexual tension in him and he loved to eat and to drink. Many people up at the Academy in Rome and back in Cambridge imagined we were lovers. We weren't. We had both been pupils of Mlle Boulanger before the war, and both of us went to Harvard on the GI Bill when we left the army. We were so often together: we played two-piano recitals, we were the best composers of our day in Cambridge, and we both received fellowships to Paris. Though Paul's face and figure remain perfectly clear to me and his music still sounds when I listen inwardly, his presence in my memory has no immediacy, a fact accounted for most probably by the absence of any erotic strain. Instead he became the backdrop against which my sexual life ran its course.

On Christmas day Laura's family invited both of us down to dinner. On the bus Paul said, "I'm really amazed that the Venutis are inviting the two of us to such a closed family celebration; do you realize that even the maiden aunt who teaches school up in the Veneto is going to be there!" I could understand his puzzlement; I had been strangely affected by the invitation. At home we never invited strangers to holiday dinners and Neapolitan families were more passionately knit entities than any I had encountered in Boston.

The Venutis occupied the second floor of an apartment building (what the Italians call a palazzo) which faced onto Piazza Amedeo. This square was at the bottom of an ascent which rose through Parco Margherita and the Via Tasso to the heights of the Vomero. A few paces from their door was the *funicolare* up to the

Vomero, and a few steps in the other direction was the entrance to the Metropolitana, the Neapolitan subway, which went in one direction over to the central railroad station and in the other direction under the escarpment of Posilipo and on out to Pozzuoli. During the bombardments the families in the neighborhood used it as an air-raid shelter. Visiting the Venutis' house always seemed to me like penetrating a fortress. There was a massive entrance door, opened for the visitor by a little maid who came from the family's country property out near Avellino. The visitor entered a large, dark entrance room, hermetically sealed off from the rest of the house. There one waited while the maid informed the family of the visitor. This was partly to be explained by the fact that Laura's father was a doctor with an office in his home, though he spent most of his time down at Torre del Greco where he was the director of a sanatorium situated on the lower slopes of Vesuvius. The mother also had a medical degree.

It was a most substantial family, substantial in a way which I came to realize only gradually. They owned properties not only out near Avellino but also north of the city, properties which they administered in a way foreign to my American experience. The peasants from these properties would come to town on Saturday mornings not only to settle their accounts with the doctor but also to talk over their family affairs or to arrange a marriage. Dr. Venuti felt responsible for both their health and their welfare; he treated them gratis as part of his obligations as a *padrone* and a doctor. Laura sometimes would talk of her *fratellini di latte*, her "milk-brothers." It had to be explained to me as if I were the denizen of another planet that they were the children of her wet nurse and that often, when older, she would go to stay with them in the country.

The Venutis' house was a fortress not only as it appeared to one after ringing the bell and being ushered into the ponderous waiting room; it took me a while to realize that the house was the center of a network of responsibilities which encompassed both the extended family (what the Italians call the *parentela*) and all of the dependents who worked the land. This kind of bulwark against the world was more ancient and deep-seated than any mere political bond; it took care of its own with a fervor no state could ever match, particularly such a place as Italy, which, following its unification under the northern kingdom and its years under Mussolini, has never gained the trust of its inhabitants. (At the time of the unification of Italy a southern peasant was heard asking, "Who is this 'Italia' — the daughter of the king?")

Laura's father and mother were substantial in appearance and in girth, heavy with large brown eyes which took in everything; they accepted the world as it presented itself to them. They saw that Laura was in love with me but doubted, as I now conjecture, that I would ever marry her. "You should have known Maria, Laura's older sister," said Mrs. Venuti to me that Christmas day, after our dinner. "She had such a good character!" — all the while glancing with both love and shrewdness at her daughter Laura. I had heard about Maria's death from Laura. It had occurred toward the end of the war. Dr. Venuti had been out at the country house in Avellino and had been taken by the Germans. For all that his family or anyone else knew, he had been shipped off to Germany. It was never understood why this had happened and the family was unclear as to the details of his capture.

One day, a month after Dr. Venuti's disappearance, the family were all out at Avellino when Maria noticed a truck at the end of the long lane leading up to the house. Out of it stepped her father, and in a kind of ecstasy she ran down the lane, leapt into his arms and fainted. The rest of the family — Laura, Paula, Giacomo, and Mrs. Venuti — all clung to the father as he carried Maria up to the house, thinking only that the poor girl had been stricken with emotion at his return from what had seemed to all of them a probable death. It was Maria who died three weeks later of a massive heart attack, a death for which Dr. Venuti never forgave himself. "I, a doctor," he would say. "Not paying attention to the poor creature's condition, so overcome by the emotion of my own homecoming that I made no proper diagnosis!"

Laura's younger sister, Paula, was engaged to a pleasant and serious fellow, Elio Colucci. She was not a beautiful girl, but rather handsome, dark, and straight. Her manner of speaking was both prosaic and enlightened, and she harbored no illusions concerning herself or the world. Paul and I both thought of her as an *honnête femme*, a woman of eminent good sense. She laughed when I asked her if she loved Elio, implying that it was up to me to state what that had to do with marriage. She respected and liked her fiancé, became a good wife to him, bore him children, took loving care of her father and mother in the long years of their old age, and put up with long years of residence down in the Basilicata where Elio was employed as director of the gas company of Lucania, that wretched province whose arid hills have been eroded since the days of the Roman Empire. (Both the emperors and Mussolini used its towns as places of exile. I remember sitting in a box at San Carlo, Naples' resplendent opera house, and chatting with a dear old lady who was accompanied by a sallow-looking youth whom I took to be her son. "Are you Neapolitan?" I asked. "Ah yes," she replied with some fervor, "but as God would have it I married down there in the Basilicata." She sighed and glanced at her son. She was delighted to be back in her city of light, released at least for a few days from her abode of matrimonial exile.)

What bound me to Laura was not only Naples but just as much an obligation I felt toward her family. They had opened their doors to me and when I peremptorily dropped Laura at the end of that first year in Naples, their very closeness and perspicuity made me feel shabby. Not that Laura hadn't often challenged the nature of my attachment to her. The subject of marriage lurked in the shadows when we were together and my lack of money was an easy alibi.

I was worried. Money, or rather the lack of it, had fixed me for three long years after high school in a menial job as handyman at the piano in a girls' finishing school in Providence, teaching Cadillac granddaughters and Mrs. Whitney's ward for the sum of fifty dollars a month plus room and board. The three years I spent in the infantry had at least given me the GI Bill and made Harvard possible. Professor Piston had then guaranteed me my Paris years with the traveling fellowship he had secured for me, and the U.S. government was now keeping me as a Fulbright fellow in Naples. My prospects for a job were grim, however, for a fussy old professor back in Cambridge had informed me in no uncertain terms that they had no desire to see me return as an assistant while gaining another degree. "The place for you, dear Allanbrook," he had written, "is living on a private income in Europe." "True enough," I had said to Paul when the letter arrived. "True enough, old Tilly!" It was a blow, nevertheless, as almost all the other Fulbright fellows drifted back to the dreary routine of more degrees and subsequent academic jobs.

Laura would not rest content but pushed the subject further. Her obsession with me, her love, was the content of her being for two years; she was constantly under its goad. I once said to her lamely, "I'm with you because I'm so fond of you." Her eyes darkened and she said, "Do you think I sleep with you because I'm fond of you!" Her English was perfectly fluent; she did not confuse my "fond of" with the fervid Italian expression "Ti voglio bene!"

My Roman friends, when they descended upon Naples, found her not only bourgeois but also a bourgeoise from what was for them another world. She was Neapolitan. I suppose at the time I had sensed that she was not my type, and the very passion she bore me, framed in its Neapolitan setting, made me hold her at a certain aesthetic distance. I was playing with fire, taking one part of my foreign domain and placing it, in my judgment, against the imaginary worldliness of Rome and Paris.

Sophistication was a mask of sophistry, a kind of casuistry, an argument (at that time) against commitment, even though the terms of the argument are only now clear to me. (Eliante says it most lucidly in Molière's *Misanthrope:* "Cela fait assez voir que l'amour dans les coeurs, / N'est pas toujours produit par un rapport d'humeur.") If it had not been for Candida, however, I might very well have married Laura, and then, obviously, would never have married Candida — an event which occurred a year later.

It was in June 1951 that Paula married Elio, several weeks after Laura discovered that Candida was ensconced in the place I had found for the summer down in Positano. I edged my way into the back of the church, unseen (I presumed) by the Venuti family and followed the ceremony, which was conducted by a fashionable young priest (a cousin of Candida's, as it later turned out), blond and refined. The day before I had sent off to Paula my wedding present, an Epithalamion for piano — long, stately and, as I felt, rather sublime. (My truest wedding music is contained, however, in the finale of my comic opera after Peacock's *Nightmare Abbey*. It occurs when the assembled cast all sing a hymn to convention as the hero's two best friends marry the two women he loves.)

Paul left for Rome, Paris, Chicago, and eventually Cambridge at the end of March, leaving me alone up at Capodimonte. I was nearing the end of an enormous work that spring: an opera based on Edith Wharton's *Ethan Frome*. Its lines and cadences galvanized all my psychic interests, and while Laura was being gradually effaced by Candida, Candida was generally far away touring with her acting company. My operatic lovers were trapped in the Siberian winter of their hopeless love, while outside, the Neapolitan sunshine and the glitter of the bay made a frame for the bleak intensity of the make-believe world I was crafting out of Edith Wharton's fictional New England. There is a rightness, a propriety even, in writing opera in Naples. The spiritual center of the place is not so much centered upon the cathedral as upon San Carlo, the Bourbons' grand opera house, a theater which dwarfs the royal palace in such a way that the palace seems merely an adjunct. (In the eighteenth century, when the kings reigned in all their particularity, the back doors of the stage would be thrown open to reveal a show of fireworks erupting from barges in the bay: a fitting finale to a royal entertainment!) I attended every production that year, at first with Paul, and later, when he had left, alone. Late at night, at the end of each performance, decrepit buses awaited us in front of the opera house. I would board the appropriate one, which would then climb the Via Roma to Capodimonte. It was crowded with Neapolitans in all their finery, the men in "smoking" and the ladies in their gowns. As we wended our way up the hill they would descend at the various little streets which traverse the Via Roma, shedding their operatic costumes when they reached their poor family rooms, most of which faced directly onto the teeming alleys of the city.

One time the Cunninghams, a well-to-do Boston and New York family, went to the opera with me. Their daughter was a member of our coterie at Cambridge and in Paris, and her parents kept close watch over her. The mother and father were great travelers, bred-in-the-bone old-style Americans. Something of the atmosphere of Edith Wharton's novels adhered to them. The opera we went to see was a flamboyant and raucous performance of *The Girl of the Golden West*, Puccini's most ridiculous work. Maria Caniglia, aging but potent, defeated the sheriff at poker with a gleaming high C, and Mario del Monaco, at that moment the youngest and loudest of tenors, shook the rafters. There was plenty to laugh at, but the Cunninghams, from the height of their American provincialism, laughed instead at the costumes of the Neapolitans, all dressed up for the opera.

The first time I went to San Carlo, when the war was still on, was very different. I had a weekend pass, my first since arriving in Italy. It was a scruffy, knocked-together production of *Bohème*, and I was surrounded in the theater by GIs, fumes of bad cognac, and shabby whores who offered quick blow jobs in the gloom at the back of the boxes. Sitting in that opera house, in the midst of the battered city of Naples, in the midst of war, caught up in the terror of my own life in a dugout just north of the Garigliano, I wept for poor Mimi. Ahead of all of us lay so many deaths; we all knew that. Leonard's was but the first and I was washing away its memory with my tears for Mimi. Soon there would be an avalanche of dead and wounded, whose memory was best left entombed by the day they died though Leonard's went underground for me. Like Lazarus he would arise again, never to be exorcised!

I invited the Picabias' daughter, Lodovica, to a performance of *Traviata* that spring; it was just before the unpleasant occurrence up at the villa which caused my leaving it forever. Renata Tebaldi had been snubbed up at La Scala, and Naples retaliated by booking her for an unprecedented eight *Traviata*s in a row. They were all of them sold out. I was to meet Lodovica a half-hour before the performance in front of San Carlo. What with one thing and another I was nearly ten minutes late. As I pushed through the crowd in front of the entrance to the theater I suddenly caught a glimpse of Avvocato Picabia and his daughter. He had a look so worn and worried, so shabby but so decent that I felt abashed. He expressed enormous relief when I pulled up beside them. "It is so important for her to see a *Traviata* and especially this one with Tebaldi," he murmured to me. It was only later that I understood the importance of what he had said. He was speaking as a Parmigiano, a native of Verdi's home ground; but he spoke as a foreigner in the jungle of Naples, a stranger isolated from his roots, a poor man at the end of his resources even though he was blessed with a splendid daughter and a handsome son who was a cadet at the aeronautical academy at Caserta. He was ashamed of his own stature in the eyes of these children; he could do little for them and had given them as a stepmother a creature full of gall, more devoted to her animals than to them.

The performance was splendid but, looking intently at the daughter, I was sorry I had not invited the father instead. Parma loved opera in a more knowledgeable fashion than Naples: connoisseurs as opposed to lovers. Lodovica was dutiful and appreciative but not thrilled, I fear, as were the Neapolitans and as I was. The memory of Tebaldi's upper register shaped certain telling phrases for my poor Mattie Silver, the doomed heroine of my opera *Ethan Frome*.

I was sometimes careless with the money I had. I was paid in lire by my Fulbright fellowship and would cash in the whole lot at the beginning of the month, not bothering with checks as they were such a bother to negotiate in the Neapolitan banks. It made quite a large wad, as the 10,000-lire notes were enormous in those days. I kept a fair amount tucked away in the upper right-hand drawer of a commode in my bedroom. I was nearing the end of my first year's fellowship and though I had applied for a renewal I had heard nothing at this juncture, though it was already the first of May. I arrived up at the villa after a particularly good session at the conservatory with Maestro Gerlin and accompanied Luisa's good lunch with an appropriate amount of wine. I had cashed my fellowship check a few days before and so had a considerable bundle of lire, some in my wallet and the rest in the commode tucked underneath my winter pajamas. I went in for my afternoon siesta, full of food and contentment. (I had played the Italian Concerto really well that morning!) As an extension of this mood I decided to count my money, to handle it, to add security to my sense of well-being. Money had always been in short supply. In Naples, I had played with the fatalistic thesis that money was simply what Luisa and Laura had told me it was, another facet of God's bounty, on a par with good looks and good health, their implication being that it was to be enjoyed with no second thoughts. (Luisa had bought fireworks with the Christmas bonus I had given her and had shot them off on New Year's Eve.)

I fumbled under the pajamas in the top right drawer and drew forth what at first glance seemed to be the accustomed wad of bank notes, topped by a 10,000-lire note. Under that top pristine bill, alas, were no more big ones. The pile had been stacked with miserable 500- and 1,000-lire notes. I had not only been robbed, I had been tricked with the very trick the money-changers used when they cheated the tourists who streamed ashore from their cruise ships down at Piazza Municipio. Though the thought passed quickly through my head that Luisa might have taken the money, I found it hard to believe. When my glance rested on the coverlet of my bed I knew the truth, or what I immediately took to be the truth, since in the eyes of the law I would never know it absolutely. On the coverlet were the pawprints of Flash, Mrs. Picabia's wretched cocker spaniel. I was seized with money panic, a panic which had as its immediate backdrop the sure knowledge that I was not welcome back in Cambridge, that I had no assured future, no source of funds, that I was still awaiting a renewal notice of my fellowship, that I was stranded and alone up in my fool's paradise on the edge of the hill at Salita dello Scudillo a Capodimonte.

With this baggage bunched up in my soul I proceeded to commit a major folly. I acted as if I were in the United States: I expected Naples to behave in a way that I felt was proper. If my sentimental education had reached a crisis that spring it was now time for my political indoctrination. With considerable indignation and a modest amount of bravura I went down to the police station at Capodimonte, located just under the royal palace. My heart sank the moment I entered. Two sad-eyed policemen glanced warily up at me. They were seated at a table reading comic books. A glimmer of uncertainty flecked their large black eyes as I explained to them that I had been robbed. I took ridiculous care not to let them know I was American though it soon fell out that everyone in the neighborhood knew about the American musician who lived at the Ungherese's: Luisa had given a complete account of all of my comings and goings, and, as I was to realize later, all there was to be known about my apparent *fidanzata*, Laura.

There was a pause when I finished my account. No emotion

was registered. People in Naples, so often voluble and vivid in their gestures and their speech, have all of them in their bones an instinct for a poker face when matters of justice and law are at stake. They thanked me for informing them about the robbery. (I had not told them about Flash's pawprints.) There was another pause while the two of them looked at each other. "Well," one of them said, "we'll put your *donna di servizio*, Luisa, inside for a while."

Then I, in my worst Italian so far, spurred on by my sense of justice, blurted out the whole story. "Signora Picabia was the miscreant; her dog's footprints were on my bedspread, she must have been in my room and she must have taken the money."

There was another long pause, longer than the second one, long enough for several flies to amble across the dirty blotter on the table, which bore the remains of some bread and salami. I looked closely at the room for the first time; it was replete with poverty and apathy. The second and fatter of the two policemen finally spoke: "U Signor'," he said in his guttural dialect, "U Signor', do you want a *perquisizione*?" I had no notion of what they were talking about except that it had an official ring to it and I did want something to be done, and I certainly did not want poor Luisa to be shut up wherever they shut people up, which, if it were like the police station, must be miserable indeed — a Neapolitan prison! I had seen a Mexican prison once down by the Rio Grande in Matamoros, and the Capodimonte police station had a Latin American air about it. Strange stirring of being an American trapped south of the border assailed me. My agreement to a *perquisizione* seemed a grave moment for the two of them in that sordid room; something was afoot whose prosecution was soon to reverberate from Capodimonte to the villa at the top of Salita dello Scudillo.

Several evenings later while I was strolling down from the bus stop toward the villa I was tapped on the shoulder. I turned and was face to face with Salvatore, Luisa's eldest, a dark and somewhat sleazy boy with flashing eyes. From my eyrie at the back of the garden I had often descried him down below in the sunken road, where he had found quiet and privacy for his amours. He drew his fingers across his throat and said, "Signor Douglas, if they put my mother away, pay attention!" He was unsure of himself but resolved to play his part. I tried to assure him that the police would find the truth though I was loath to tell him my suspicions of the Ungherese.

In the next weeks my world became unsure and Capodimonte full of shadows. The *perquisizione* (investigation) unfolded; it took on a life of its own. The two policemen plus a cadaverous *maresciallo* (marshal) showed up at the villa, inspected my bedroom, talked to the *avvocato,* Mr. Picabia, but not, to her infinite regret, to his wife. There were two weeks of increasing tension, weeks in which Luisa continually crossed herself to ward off the *malocchio*, the evil eye, of the Ungherese and in which the Ungherese, after one violent outburst, paced the grounds eying me malevolently, her horrid little Flash puttering after her. The daughter said nothing, but looked at me sadly, not understanding how I could have done what I did. Mr. Picabia's face became whiter, and seemed ever more ill nourished and flabby. I had never been so aware of the shabby shine of his well-worn suit and of the frayed cuffs of his shirts.

June was approaching and the daytime heat meant that I would close the shutters that opened onto the garden and the view, and concentrate upon the attempted suicide of poor Ethan and Mattie Silver as my opera drew to its tragic close. The rupture with Laura was on the verge of being definitive. I had no word as to my fellowship's renewal and had taken what little money I had left as a down payment on an apartment at Positano, even going so far as to arrange for the piano I had at Capodimonte to be shipped all the way down to the Amalfi coast. The police sent me no word, doubtless thinking it sufficient that I had seen them about. Passing by the police station as I caught the bus downtown in Capodimonte I would sometimes spot them scrutinizing me from the door of their headquarters.

I felt reasonably sure that everyone in the little piazza was look-ing knowingly at me. Luisa seemed not overly concerned and Salvatore's imprecations retreated into the background of my preoccupations.

One morning as I passed by the police station one of the original two policemen I had talked to motioned to me. "Non vi preoccupate, Maestro," he said. "Don't be worried, Maestro." (All Italians are fond of professional titles and the Neapolitans more than most.) "Luisa won't be taken in and there's nothing we can do about Signor Picabia and his wife. You must realize that we have conducted a full and formal investigation, all on the proper and official stamped paper, but we have found ourselves blocked. And you, my dear Maestro, have disturbed many people and have not come out of the whole affair with a particularly *bella figura*." What he meant, of course, was that I had lost face.

It turned out that Luisa's cousin was a *maresciallo* in the carabinieri, which carried with it the immediate implication that she could not be locked up. Signor Picabia was an *avvocato*, and no one but an utter fool would proceed against a man who was a member of the legal profession. This was explained to me as one would explain the simplest moral code to a child, and in-deed I was a child in my understanding of Italian and Neapoli-tan justice. I had, first of all, evinced astonishment that Luisa could be put away before she had been found guilty, which was common procedure under Italian law. Second, I had no concep-tion of the "justice" that reigns within the bands of kinship and its protection and of the safeguards that protect a professional man of the law. I knew nothing of the political jungle that con-stituted city and state.

That justice had been done I finally understood, late one night, sitting out on the terrace as the moon set over my decrepit garden and the fountain dripped in front of the decaying chapel. I could not, in my heart, have intended to increase the burden of misery of the Picabias; Luisa was safe and her eldest son had had the occasion to demonstrate his *virtù*. Who was I to have disturbed the set ways of this place with my foreign concepts of procedure? A place, a nation, that had so recently lived through the bestiality and terror of fascism was hardly the place to expect whatever I had expected to be done. In Naples this was more true than in the rest of the country. Naples had its own idiomatic habits and orders destroyed generations ago when the Piedmontese created the nation state of Italy, imposing their own northern codes upon an ancient kingdom. (The revenge of the South was to send generations of smart lawyers up to Rome where they swamped the ministries and became the virtuosi of the legal codes.) The two police officers at Capodimonte had shown to the foreigner that if he wanted a *perquisizione* he could have one, though it was difficult for them to understand why I had wanted it. They had carried out their part of the bargain, not realizing how ignorant I was of the trappings of their "justice," nor could they fathom the depths of my innocence in acceding to the investigation. In the end everyone had been respected: the foreigner had been given his due, the widow had been protected, and the Picabias left to stew in their own bitter juice. It was, by definition, a comedy and my final day up at the villa provided a finale fit for an opera buffa.

On the day I was to leave for Positano I had arranged to be picked up by yet another cousin of Luisa's, a taxi driver with the pretty name of Giacinto. He would bring me down from Capodimonte to the dock; there I would get the vaporetto across the bay to Meta di Sorrento where there was a bus which would take me up across the ridge and over to the other side, facing the Gulf of Salerno, until finally, after hairpin curves and heart-rending views, I would arrive at the Villa Stella Romana, at the top of Positano, next to the Chiesa Nuova.

My half of the Picabias' villa had been cleaned and scrubbed and all of my possessions packed into two suitcases and one large and battered trunk. Luisa had arrived at eight that morning with both her daughters. At ten Salvatore and his younger brother, Rocco, appeared to help carry the things down to the front courtyard. Mrs. Picabia, who had not spoken to me for over two weeks, glowered at all of us when we ventured out front with my gear; her husband stood sadly by the side, observing the scene. At eleven o'clock the taxi arrived outside the gate. Luisa hurried forth to greet Giacinto and to guide his taxi onto the property. When she arrived at the gate, there stood the Ungherese, her hand on the crossbar which held the gate shut. "No dirty Neapolitan and his stinking taxi are going to drive onto my property," she screamed. There was a tone in her voice which I had never heard before; indeed I had never until that moment paid sufficient attention to her hatred not only of Vesuvius, but of all Neapolitans. "Swine inhabiting a paradise," she spat out, exulting in her foreignness and repeating the taunt thrown so often at Neapolitans by their northern neighbors in the peninsula. The villa, the view, the volcano, the gleaming and famous bay were an Eden that for her, alas, constituted an exile, a misery, a place of bondage to poverty and lost hopes. There was the added canker that Hungary, her native land, was no place to which she could return. She had clawed her way out of desperate poverty with the aid of her nurse's uniform and even if she should be able, by some stroke of fortune, to return to Budapest, it was in the hands of infidels.

Luisa, in her turn, was howling imprecations back in a low guttural strain of dialect, her goiter shaking on her neck like a fleshy gourd. Outside of the gate, through the grillwork, I could make out a gathering crowd of local people, all of them united with Luisa in their detestation of the Ungherese who detested them in return and treated them as members of an inferior race. "*Strega*" (witch) was the least they said, and in that moment they were right: she looked like a witch, clutching her shawl about her scrawny shoulders and peering at them with her yellowish eyes full of malice. Meanwhile, precisely as if it were being staged, in the sheer exuberance of the moment, Salvatore, Rocco, and the two daughters began issuing forth from my portion of the villa bearing in their arms various objects which belonged to the villa: a chair, some plates, a vase, a bedspread. They headed for a small side door in the wall of the estate next to the gate which Mrs. Picabia was guarding. In the midst of the fracas that erupted between Luisa, her children, and the Ungherese as all of these objects from the villa began appearing, a smiling face appeared: it was Franco, the postman.

He was devoted to me, particularly as he wrote songs himself and had found it to be a great pleasure and an honor to climb up to my studio and have the American maestro listen to his productions. He had even listened to some of my music once. He was a dear, only too happy to be of service as he waved in front of my face a telegram which he held in his hand. "Maestro," he called. "Maestro, a telegram from Rome!" I seized it and tore it open. It was from Letizia, my confidante up at the Fulbright office in Rome, and it contained the delicious news that my fellowship had been renewed for a second year. "Work hard," she said, "and have a good time." The finale became a finalissimo, the stage lights went up, and the più allegro burst forth into the sunniest of D majors!

I waved the telegram in Avvocato Picabia's face, exclaiming that now I had money for another year and neither he nor I should worry any longer about anything that had happened. His wife, his dreadful second wife, turned and in her strange English said to me, "No more, no more will I allow you to set foot here and no more will anyone ever speak to me of you again!" Courage counts for little in most marriages, particularly if the woman is unhappy, and Mr. Picabia had never been a courageous man. He could only watch sadly as the scene unfolded: pandemonium both inside and outside the gate, the local people shouting, his wife hysterical, and his tenant, his only sure source of income for the coming year, leaving. It was only later on the boat out on the bay with the profile of the city behind, with Capri on my right and Sorrento's cliff approaching on the left, that the look on his face struck home to me. What had my *perquisizione* accomplished? What would all of his days be like and all of the tomorrows which would succeed them, marooned upon his hilltop, far from Parma, aging, poor, and untalented.

I never returned to Salita dello Scudillo and never again saw either the Picabias or Luisa, though I spent another year in Naples, living on Parco Margherita up the hill from Piazza Amedeo where Laura and her family lived. I never saw Laura that whole year, though I passed by her door almost daily. I would avert my gaze, praying I wouldn't see her or her father and mother, or, most especially, her severe and splendid sister, Paula.

2

EIGHTEEN YEARS LATER, recently divorced from Candida, I returned to Naples, drawn by the ever-present awareness of my own shabbiness of years ago vis-à-vis Laura's family, and wishing to set it right somehow. The ostensible reason for my trip south from Rome was to spend a month in splendid isolation on the heights of Monte Faito, that lofty mountain which towers over the Sorrento peninsula, looking northeastward toward Vesuvius and south to the glitter of the Gulf of Salerno with Positano tucked directly underneath down a dizzying cliff. To the west the view extends along the spiny backbone of the peninsula until the eye jumps across the narrow expanse of blue water to the cliffs of Capri. The top of the mountain still bears remnants of the ancient Italian forest, the *silva italica* which greeted Aeneas as he reached the end of his pilgrimage and which flourishes today only on the heights of the Scylla in Calabria and in the center of the Gargano, the spur of the Italian boot.

In recent years the government had built a motor road up the mountain. It was the kind of road Italian engineers delight in, a complement to the dizzying turns and pierced cliffs of the Amalfi Drive built a century ago. Speculators bought up most of the land and constructed villas, a tramway, and the beginnings of a town up on the heights, drawing heavily on funding from the *cassa per il Mezzogiorno,* the Italian government's slush fund intended to revivify the economy of the South. The endeavor never took off: the tramway suffered a terrifying accident, there were many bankruptcies, and lots of cash went into lots of pockets. These days, Neapolitans would occasionally drive up for Sunday picnics in the woods.

My friend Pepino, a wealthy Roman hotelier, had inherited a property on this speculative height from a maiden aunt, recently deceased; he offered me the house when he heard that I wanted to go south and wished for solitude for my work. The house she had built reflected both her obsessive Catholicism and her maidenly susceptibility to the blandishments of a doubtful lawyer who had taken charge of her estate in her failing years. She thought of him as her *cavaliere*. Vast sums of money had been sunk into an ugly, ill-designed structure. Each night I would walk up an inclined ramp on my way to the bedroom, passing by the Stations of the Cross built into niches in the walls as I ascended the Via Dolorosa to my lonely bed.

I had, in fact, visited Faito eighteen years earlier with Laura. It had been a proper expedition, planned for weeks beforehand. Dr. Venuti's new and commodious Fiat had just recently been delivered to him after months of waiting. It was arranged that the new car, driven by the Venutis' driver, Arturo, would be used for a formal picnic outing, something not commonly done in Naples, hence all the more titillating. There were six of us: Paul and myself, Paula and her fiancé, Elio, Laura and her brother Giacomo. We squeezed into the back, lowering two little jump seats, leaving Arturo in solitary dignity in the front. A large wicker hamper had been loaded into the trunk, the contents of which had been the concern of the daughters of the family for several days. South we went through Portici and onto the autostrada for Pompeii. The road grew narrower as we left Pompeii and wound our way through Castellammare. At Vico Equense the road to Faito began. Everyone teased me because I could not bear to look out as we drove along the edges of cliffs and twisted round the tight hairpin curves. We arrived without incident and proceeded to have our picnic in a grove of ancient trees: *paste rustiche* (pastries filled with sausages and spiced meats), fresh mozzarella, gorgonzola and provolone, focaccia, fruits, and sweet little cakes. We had a bottle of Taurese, a good red wine from Avellino. Afterward we walked in the woods and Laura clutched me behind a mighty oak and pressed her pelvis against my stiffened member. An erotic sylvan scene far from that least sylvan of cities, Naples, though for me it was less a pastoral surrender than a panic lest the others note what was happening.

I took daily walks from the old maid's house, through the grove of ancient oaks where Laura and I had embraced so many years ago, and up and around a dizzying path which was known to my Roman friends as the *giro del mondo* — the "trip around the world." Far below, almost straight down, Positano could be seen. I remembered looking up at Faito and Monte Sant' Angelo the two summers I lived in Positano (1950 and 1951). It is a romantic landscape where nature seems to imitate art, where the brilliance and the fantasy of the crenelated rock formations outdo the ordinary imagination. There is a mountain above Positano which has a hole in it through which the moon shines once a month: it is called Monte Pertuso in the local dialect — Pierced Mountain. Underneath the mountain is a village which bears its name and which in those days had no road connecting it with the outside world, only a footpath. The inhabitants back then were too poor to have mules and carried upon their backs what they needed from Positano down below. At the time of the grape harvest work songs would resound from off their mountain's slope, echoes of a rustic antiquity. Sophisticates down at Positano would invite the old men from Monte Pertuso to a party on the beach, fill them with wine and food, and have them sing their endless story-poems. They accompanied themselves with little drums and would chant in lilting eighteenth-century dialect with rhyming couplets. The stories would hark all the way back to Orlando, range through the Bourbon kings, and climax with that magical moment when from the heights of

Monte Pertuso the men had seen the Allied invasion fleet on its way to the bloody landing at Salerno — that disastrous prelude to the long ordeal of the fight up the spine of Italy.

There was a town still higher and more remote than Monte Pertuso, Santa Maria in Castello, perched on the edge of a precipice. Both of these hamlets were small worlds unto themselves; they had intermarried to such an extent that doe-eyed beauties and monsters emerged with startling frequency from the genetic pool. (Certain of the beauties, rustic Ganymedes, were engulfed in the sexual commerce of the picture-book towns along the Amalfi coast.) Both communes retained ancient feudal connections with Naples and with the diocese of Amalfi. An aging Neapolitan lady, owner of half of Monte Pertuso, would be carried up the footpath on a sedan chair to stay at her mountain properties and twice a year the bishop of Amalfi would make the rounds of his mountain parishes astride a sumpter mule, holding his shepherd's crook, to bless the faithful and exorcise the devils. Three of the inhabitants of Monte Pertuso were known to have the *malocchio* and one was identified as a *lupomannaro* (werewolf). The parish priest up at Monte Pertuso had been exiled to this far end of the world by the ecclesiastical authorities, having been deemed unworthy of a more civilized parish by reason of his ungovernable carnality. He would invite us in to share his stock of sweet wine and would lament his fate and the primitive life he was bound to, far from the delights of Naples and Salerno.

Eighteen years later both towns had roads; commerce with the outside world had begun. Santa Maria even had a trattoria, which was a startling novelty to the residents. I ate there one day and after a substantial lunch of pasta and wild rabbit wandered over to the edge of the precipice and gazed down at Monte Pertuso and Positano thousands of feet below. There were several well-kept fields of vegetables, cultivated to the very edge of the drop. The farmer who tilled these fields came down to talk with me. He spoke of the times when there was no road and

when everyone who came to these remote heights was considered a foreigner, whether he was from Naples, Milan, or America — that far-off promised land which had offered new life to
so many from the South. The old customs of hospitality remained with him and he invited me to his house to share his
midday meal with him and his wife and family. I regretted having eaten so much at the trattoria but went in and drank red
wine while they wondered at my doings and my wanderings
and I wondered at their goodness and their hard work. I was at
the far southern circumference of the world of Naples, and the
metropolis seemed as distant as Boston.

The month in the maiden aunt's house grew long. My daily
walks through the oaks and around the precipices became wea-
risome. I found I could write nothing without a piano and my
composer's vanity was piqued: with my ear and with my training I should not have to depend on the crutch of an instrument.
Each morning I would pass the very oak behind which Laura
and I had embraced and it was as if nothing had happened there
— no cutting memory, no burning eyes. Instead there came a
growing sense, an uneasy urge that I must visit Paula, that I had
to set my conscience at rest after so many years. I became ever
more aware of my cavalier abandonment of Laura and the effect
it must have had on her loyal and benevolent family. My resolve
became fixed upon opening up the past, upon exorcising my
guilt, and Paula, dear straight Paula, was the way to accomplish
that goal. She had to be visited.

When I had stopped overnight in Naples on my way down to
Monte Faito I had looked up the Venutis in the phone book.
There was no listing for them at the old Piazza Amedeo address
but there was one under their name up on the Vomero. I tried
the number. The talkative lady who answered turned out to be
the maiden aunt who had taught school up in the Veneto and
who had been at the Christmas dinner Paul and I had been
invited to so many years ago. Indeed she remembered me and
was sad to report the deaths of both the doctor and his wife.

Paula had been a faithful angel, she recounted, taking tender care of both her parents during their long illnesses. She and Elio would want to see me, she was sure, but, alas, they lived far off, down in the Basilicata. Elio, dear man, was still director of the gas company of Lucania. She gave me their address in Potenza. She made no mention of Paula's brother Giacomo, which struck me as strange, given the good-natured volubility of her account.

I cut my month at Faito short, deciding early one morning to leave for Potenza without further ado. By nine o'clock I was twisting down the mountain road to Vico Equense, grinding the gears in the little *topolino* (a tiny Fiat) I had rented for the month in Naples. After Castellammare I joined the Autostrada del Sole (what a pretentious title!), which was linked to the end of the old Fascist superhighway from Naples to Pompeii, up over the saddle which joins the Sorrento peninsula to the continent, and finally the long coast down to Salerno. The autostrada soars over poor battered Salerno (which has never fully recovered from the famous invasion) and deposits the traveler onto the hot plains to the south of the city. This much of the road I knew, as I had driven down to Sicily by this same route twice. The turnoff came sooner than I had expected, a proper interchange for a brand new superstrada leading to Eboli and Potenza.

Carlo Levi's best-known novel takes for its title a bitter saying of the region: "Christ stopped at Eboli." Many towns in Lucania are too poor to support a priest and the charity of the various dioceses does not extend itself to rectify that lack. It is a godforsaken land that one gazes upon and the brand-new superstrada was an obscene addition to its sere hills and gullies. There were gaps in the progress of the new highway: steep mountain valleys had still to be traversed on old stone bridges, tunnels remained to be dug. There was little traffic. Once Eboli was passed the terrain became steadily higher and more sterile. There were several large towns on the way to Potenza, not villages at all but real towns, and even, as one looked more closely, not so much towns as cities, which loomed enormous in the midst of that spare landscape. Until the postwar emigration of the men north to Germany and the Scandinavian countries the inhabitants had for countless generations eked out an existence from the outlying fields to which they would go each morning, walking miles to some patch of stony earth which they farmed for an absentee landowner. Often they would not know if there was work for the day until they had gathered in the piazza to be bid for by labor contractors. The land was a crazy quilt of varying holdings and the men and women who worked upon it did not live upon it; they huddled together in the enormous town-cities each impaled upon the rocky hillsides of the ancient Basilicata. To enter one of these towns is desolation: a fly-bitten piazza with a dusty bar, the carabinieri headquarters, a few palazzi of a certain age, a disheveled church and, all around, a honeycomb of squalid stone houses with, perhaps, on the outskirts (if their mayor has been able to finesse some funds from the *cassa per il Mezzogiorno*) rows of cement apartments facing out onto the desperate countryside.

The superstrada was completed and glaring with new concrete in the valley just under Potenza. A fair stretch of it was serving as a market and an enormous pig farm stretched along beside it, an establishment again financed by the *cassa*. The road up to the center of the city rose sharply from the valley floor, passing through clusters of ugly *palazzi* built during the fascist period. At the top of the hill I emerged without warning into a piazza packed with booths and people and parked cars. It was market day. A large and handsome young policeman stopped me with a proud gesture and began berating me until the moment when he understood that I was an American looking for the Via del Popolo and the Colucci family. "Ah yes," he said, eager now to please, "Ingegnere Colucci!" He waved pedestrians aside and walked along beside my diminutive *topolino* until we reached the address on Via del Popolo where the Coluccis lived. He had a splendid smile which revealed gleaming white teeth and his name rang with a classical cadence: Marcantonio

Laurenzano. He insisted upon writing it out for me and he begged for my parents' address north of Boston. He was unhappy with his town of Potenza but wary of joining the emigration to Germany and the north, where most of his friends had gone. He cherished the dream of the old "newfound land," America, where so many of his fellow southerners had found work and dignity.

Paula herself came to the door. "Caro Douglas," she said, "benvenuto dopo tanti anni!" — "Welcome after so many years!" She spoke my name without a trace of an accent, as she used to do. Eighteen years had made a difference, however; she was no longer the slim and upright girl whom I had known, but a matron with jowls and gray hair. "Vedi," she said, "Come son' brutta" — "See how ugly I am." She led me into her house: it was a handsome bourgeois apartment — marble floors, polished old-fashioned furniture, large substantial doors closing off unseen rooms. It was not unlike her parents' house in Naples, but smaller.

She had two fine children: a boy of seventeen, Emilio, corpulent and intelligent, and a handsome girl of fourteen, Grazia, who had the upright grace which Paula had in her youth. Her husband, Elio, had changed little. He was a solid and prudent man of middle height who held an important and respectable post. They settled me in the only decent hotel in town, a boxlike construction out over the crest of the hill where the Coluccis had been obliged to stay for several months when they first moved to Potenza, housing consonant with the importance of Elio's position being difficult to find. The clerk at the hotel greeted Elio effusively and with great formality. It could be seen that Ingegnere Colucci was a person of importance in town.

Emilio came over in the evening to bring me to supper. "There's not much to see," he said, as we made our way up to the top of the hill and across the piazza, down the Via Pretoria to Via del Popolo. "The only thing worth looking at is the doorway to San Francesco. Anything else that's old is all tricked up with layers of bad baroque and anyway the poor place was bombed to hell during the war — Who knows why?" he added with a quizzical glance toward me, knowing that I had been a GI. He was an intelligent boy, grown up in his ways, close to his family, but conversant enough with a bigger world than Potenza to be both amused and bored by the early evening *passeggiata* we found ourselves in the midst of. Via Pretoria and the piazza were cleared of traffic for this ritual and the whole town was walking back and forth in a caged circuit, eying each other in an observance that never varied from one year to the next. "Now they are on foot," he said. "In the daytime, 'per fare bella figura' (to make a good impression) they drive their cars the five hundred meters from their house to where they work simply for the conspicuous show of it and the majority of them are helplessly in debt trying to pay for their wretched little Fiats!" It was my turn to glance rather sharply at him, struck by the rancor (however reasonable) of his comments on provincial life.

The evening grew chilly. It was the end of October and Emilio explained to me another of the great drawbacks of life in Potenza. "It is, after the town of Enna in the middle of Sicily, the highest of all the provincial capitals of Italy, with the result that it is as cold as Siberia in the winter and baking hot all summer long." I had bitter memories of the harshness of Italian winters from my two years in the Apennines during the war. "Fucking West Virginia!" my sidekick Joe Isaac used to say. Being from Memphis he hated the mountains.

Dinner at Paula's was just as it should be and was accompanied by a heavy, redolent red wine, surprisingly good. "Volcanic wine from Monte Vulture," explained Elio when he saw how much I appreciated it. "We'll take you to see our volcano tomorrow; it's no Vesuvius but then, Potenza is not Naples."

"Not that Naples is any place I want to live in any longer," said Paula. "It's more corrupt than it's ever been, with the Camorra getting more control of things every day! It might as well be Palermo." There was no nostalgia in Paula's voice, just the same cool judgment, the same moral straightness as eighteen years ago when she as a young woman married her man, kept her contract with him, and never suffered any illusions. Paula nursed both her parents during their long illnesses with equanimity, never complaining, accepting what happened as due to fate. Any bitterness she had was moral and was directed at her brother, Giacomo. He was on his way to becoming a drug addict, she explained, even though he had pulled himself together sufficiently to gain his medical degree. He passed his time with riffraff. "He's the proper match for the way Naples is these days," she continued. "You would not want to live there nowadays, dear Douglas."

During all of the drive from Monte Faito to Potenza, wrestling with the double clutching necessary in the little Fiat, contemplating the increasingly somber landscape and edging down into the deep gullies not yet bridged by the new superstrada, I had been anticipating this moment at the table with Paula, a moment when I could finally ask what indeed her family had felt and thought of me when I had dropped Laura so precipitously. What had been said? My first year in Naples would never reach a conclusion within me until I made open confession, until I could clear my mind of its shame. It was not a pure moral sense that was alive in me; it was rather a twisted concern more intent upon what the whole Venuti family felt than with the fact that I had dropped Laura flat for another woman whom I then proceeded to marry at the end of my second year in Naples.

We opened another bottle of the *aglianico*, as the wine from Monte Vulture was called, and while it loosened my tongue, the knot of my anxiety, which was concentrated upon knowing Paula's opinion of my behavior eighteen years ago, remained obdurate. We talked of the children's schools, of the school my son attended in the States, of the family's trips to Spain and to France, of Paula's desire to move to the North to Turin or Verona. From the tone of her voice she implied that was hardly likely; Elio was fixed in his post as director, with an excellent salary and all of the perquisites that come with such a semi-official post in Italy. I told of my music and of my distant and bizarre life teaching Greek and philosophy in a little college in faraway Maryland. The evening wound down and at a tacit sign from Paula Elio rose and offered to accompany me back to my hotel. My moral quandary had not been made public. I had said nothing.

At nine the next morning Elio, Paula, and the two children appeared in front of the hotel in the family Lancia, a luxurious sedan which appeared all the more so against the general shabbiness of Potenza. The desk clerk treated me even more obsequiously in the presence of the *Signor Direttore*, though it was clear that he was extremely curious as to what the American was doing in Potenza. My policeman of the previous afternoon, Marcantonio Laurenzano, had found out that I was staying in the hotel and had been over to chat with the desk clerk about my arrival in town.

Off we went in the gleaming black Lancia and there on the floor in front of the back seat was a large picnic hamper, which held our lunch. It appeared to be the same hamper that had carried our lunch eighteen years before on our expedition to the top of Monte Faito, as indeed it turned out to be: Paula had inherited many objects from her parents and this splendid hamper with its built-in shelves and cups and drawers for utensils was one of them. It became a focus for me of that erotic afternoon among the oaks, but for Paula it became the occasion for her to laugh at the memory of poor Douglas, his stomach fluttering, as the large old Fiat, chauffeured by Papa's driver, twisted and turned on the precipitous ascent to Faito.

Monte Vulture turned out be a surprise, unexpected in the midst of the grim countryside of Lucania. Elio had prefigured this by serving the red wine from the slopes of the extinct volcano the night before at dinner, but had not prepared me for the twin lakes up in the crater (the Laghi di Monticchio) or the splendid forest ablaze with fall foliage. These turned out to be another remnant of the primeval *silva italica* here, just like the one on the top of Faito. Suddenly I realized that the picnic hamper and the ancient forest were not merely bucolic symbols of an erotic past but present signs of a state of soul that had to be exorcised. In yet another overlay of the distant past, walking around the lake and scuffing the autumn leaves reminded me of New England and our family outings in the Middlesex Fells, that bosky retreat adjoining the suburb north of Boston where I was brought up. Those same woods were also the place, far away from the eyes of home, where first sex was consummated and then made habitual in the frenzy of adolescent awakening.

There was a Seventh Day Adventist hospital on a hill overlooking Spot Pond in the midst of the Fells, while here, above the lakes of Monticchio, stood the remains of two ancient Benedictine abbeys. Just a few miles away, over to the east in the province of Puglia, were the airfields of Foggia, which had been a major goal in the war I had fought in. Distant commanders had deemed it necessary to bomb poor old Potenza, a scraggly little city on a hill, graced with a secondary rail line down in its valley, as a part of their systematic destruction of the ancient city of Foggia and the countryside surrounding it. "All of this whole region was part of Frederick's realm," began Emilio. "He was our only really great man." After we left Monte Vulture he would point out here a tower, there a sarcophagus, there a town gate. "They are all Frederick's doing. He brought twenty thousand Muslims up from Palermo and installed them in the town of Lucera on the very borders of the papal realms and thumbed his nose at Rome and the rest of Europe. 'Stupor Mundi' they called him. For once we were on the map."

What a pleasure it would be if history were a story, if we could make it a whole, give it meaning and slip our own jumbled memories into it. Then Frederick II, the great Hohenstaufen emperor of Italy and Germany, would play a role in our own lives and in our own towns, and in our own wars, as he did in that gigantic fiction of Dante's. What did my war mean to me?

So many died, and here in the midst of Lucania I was intent only upon laying to rest my preoccupation with the family of a girl who had turned out, after all, not to be my type.

A composer's mind is continually seizing on a future not yet present, shoving it into phase and thrusting it back to the past, hoping that the notes which result will make a coherent and passionate whole, with everything safely set down and scored. All of this has to be done by means of an intense concentration upon the present moment. It is a consolation that in music there are no people, no facts, no places, nor is there, in any comprehensible way, any meaning, while in our own stories we are stuck with intractable memories which only the boldest fiction can unite into a whole. When a piece of music is composed, it is complete, all wrapped in a tight cocoon, awaiting its release into the sunlight of performance. For the listener it is a portable memory that can be run through again and again, a vicarious and safe experience, so utterly different from the course of a life, which seems hardly a whole, composed as it is of pathos and shameful bits, of brief joys played out against the backdrop of wars and politics. As age wears us down, the absurdities of daily life contribute to the downward slope. *Tutto declina.*

St. Augustine, once converted in that instantaneous flash of grace which struck him in his suburban villa outside Milan, was sure that his own life was a true story, a whole with a valid beginning, middle, and end. What for us can only be a fictive whole, crafted by our sly and selective recollections, was for him a part of God's creation. A hymn tune was, in his eyes, a mirror of God's time. The mother of his children is all but ignored in his autobiography and a person who might seem to us an obsessive and nagging woman — his mother, Monica — becomes, under God's providential grace, Santa Monica, his beacon and his guide. (Her name always fills me with a secret glee when I pass by that section of Los Angeles which bears her name, and note, on my way to the airport, her statue erect upon Ocean Boulevard.) There is a Manichean twist for us if we consider, according to another belief, our mothers as responsible not only for our entrance into this world but also as the source of our hang-ups and of our griefs. Monica was delighted when her son left the woman who was the mother of his son, Adeodatus, and even more delighted when his official fiancée was abandoned and he adopted celibacy. He was, in both their eyes, reborn and as his mother lay dying in Ostia on their return trip to Africa, the two of them shared an ecstatic vision of Paradise. She little cared anymore for her native land, overcome by the bliss she shared with her son. (To think that my own mother's name was "Grace": Grace Phillips, born in Everett, Massachusetts, in the year of our Lord 1891.)

It all came out that night at dinner. The children had left the table, and the three of us, Paula, Elio, and I, were drinking coffee. "I have to know," I said to Paula, my words lurching forth from their long repression, "I have to know what all of your family felt when I dropped Laura." With no pause whatsoever and with a most winning smile she replied, "Dear Douglas, we were sim-ply delighted. She has a bad character, you know. We were so afraid that you would marry her! The fellow she did marry, a banker up in the Veneto, leads a dog's life. No matter that he's a count. She telephones his office at least three times a day and woe to any woman less than sixty who works for him. She's a monster of jealousy."

Stories have conclusions and the comic epiphany of this one showed me up as blind, as incapable of seeing what had been thrust upon my attention that Christmas day so long ago when Laura's mother, observing me with her clear dark eyes, had la-mented the fact that I had not known Maria, who had such a good character, and who had died so tragically of a heart at-tack as the war was drawing to a close. I saw now what I did not see then. A whole chapter, long festering in my memory, had found its proper conclusion. What I now grasped was that there was no sentimentality in the Venuti family, though they were attached, at times obsessively, to each other. They were not blinded by that closeness — their dark eyes saw each other for what they were with perfect candor. Character was a given — not something to be blamed for, but something to be lived with, a portion assigned like beauty or plainness, poverty or wealth. The evening drew to a close; I kissed Paula on both cheeks, shook Elio's hand, thanked them profusely, and sent my best regards to the children. I left Potenza early the next morning.

As if beginning a new chapter, I chose a circuitous route to return to Monte Faito. I knew that my Roman friends would be up there in a few days and I'd had enough of mountain solitude. As I neared Eboli and the mountains were smoothing out I found a road that cut across the flat land south of Battipaglia and Paestum, reaching the coast at Agropoli. I then turned south, deciding to visit Elea. Twilight was gathering as I rounded a curve in the coast road and read CORSO PARMENIDES emblazoned on a special road marker. The town fathers had fancied up the approach to town, planting eucalyptus trees on both sides of it and christening the approach to their city with the name of its most famous inhabitant. The Australian eucalyptus, a stranger to the Mediterranean, looked out of place in Elea. The little town had no other pretensions: it was the humblest of habitats: one cinema, one small hotel, and a modest promenade above the diminutive curve of its beach.

Autumn being well advanced, there were no other guests at the hotel. The padrone and his family prepared supper for themselves and for me. It was simple and very good: a fresh vegetable soup, fish grilled over fennel, and fruit. I chatted in a rather formal way with the family. They were well aware of the ancient acropolis and of the excavations that were going slowly forward around it; these were the cause of the few steady customers they had each year: archaeologists. The development of the beach held many more possibilities for the future of the hotel and in a few years Elea and its extraordinarily handsome neighbor, Palinuro, just down the coast, would be covered with the tawdry glitter that has now engulfed the whole extent of the Mediterranean littoral from Cadiz to the coast of Asia Minor.

Later that evening I sat on a bench overlooking the beach and gazed out at the sea. A couple was passing to and fro in front of me, deep in conversation. One of them was clearly a student in either *liceo* or university and the other, an older man, talked as if he were the boy's teacher. I seemed to hear the word *essere* (being) repeated several times, ever more emphatically. It was what I had hoped to hear as, guided by imagination, I had deliberately chosen this ancient town, founded by the Phocaeans in the sixth century B.C. after they fled from the Persian onslaught on the Ionian coast. Herodotus tells of their desperate battle with the Etruscans and the Carthaginians off the coast of Corsica where they had hoped to settle. Driven off they had sailed south and settled here at Elea, founding their new town a few miles south of Poseidonia, the ancient Paestum.

But it was not as a place of refuge that I visited Elea. I wanted to visit the city where philosophy began, where Parmenides wrote his poem on Being, and where Zeno invented all of the paradoxes that follow from it. This was the glory of the ancient Mezzogiorno, known to the Romans as Magna Graecia, whence Parmenides and Zeno traveled to Athens and initiated the education of the young Socrates. It was a comfort to sit on my bench by the sea, half hearing and half imagining the talk between the two men. *Being* is so safely out of time that its paradoxes reduced my comic epiphany of the day before in Potenza to a mere point of apprehension.

The next morning I climbed the Acropolis of Elea, where a crumbling medieval tower stood near the rather startlingly large base of an ancient temple. Down below the hill were traces of the ancient port. A learned Roman girl, who was studying archaeology at the university, was lecturing to her parents on the latest findings at Elea. I stood at a discreet distance and learned that the ancient city turned out to be much larger than had been suspected, that the water level had receded, leaving sections of the port high and dry, and that the town had been sacked by the ancient Lucanians. She made no mention of the philosophers. Her interests were strictly archaeological. She investigated what she saw. I looked at what I saw but inwardly I wanted to fix the time and place of Parmenides' town in some ratio to my own time and to my own understanding.

Visiting historical sites, and in particular obscure ones, is a pure work of the imagination. All that remains to be seen are objects in various states of disrepair. I guided my son, then a rambunctious boy of eight, around the Roman Forum once and he yelled at me when I chastised him for clambering up and over a wall, dislodging several stones. "There's nothing to break, Papa; it's all broken already!" Greek ghosts hover over all of southern Italy. They are the ground of a palimpsest upon which Lucanians, Romans, Lombards, Saracens, Byzantines, Angevins, Swabians, Piedmontese, Germans, and Americans have all etched their images. The straight street that cuts through Naples, Spaccanapoli, is the original rational spoke of the Greek city. Naples' Greek name, ΝΕΑΠΟΛΙΣ (Newtown), refers to the fact that its existence is predated by two places still more ancient, Cumae and Ischia. My second year in Naples I became acquainted with the town's philosopher, Benedetto Croce, and with his daughters, who lived in a massive palazzo on Spaccanapoli. The daughters would recount how often intense, dark-eyed young men would show up wanting, with real passion, to study philosophy. So often they would depart dissatisfied, not willing to undergo the disciplined historical studies that the old man, Italy's Hegelian, insisted upon. Naples' own university, founded by the great Frederick in 1254, was secular in its foundation and Naples' greatest philosopher, Vico, brooded rationally over time and its epochs.

The next afternoon, after my visit to the Acropolis, I paid my startlingly modest bill at the little hotel and headed north toward Salerno and Monte Faito, stopping at Paestum on my way. There in front of the honey-colored temple of Poseidon I witnessed the same sight I had seen both other times I had visited Paestum in the past. A wedding party was in full regalia on the steps of the temple: the bride in virginal white, the groom in appropriate black, mothers and fathers, uncles and cousins, a priest in his vestments, and a professional photographer memorializing the occasion. The group was from nearby Battipaglia, that hot little town in the plain, famous for its canned tomatoes and its mozzarella made from the milk of its black *buffali*. Why was the wedding party there, driving all the way out from the church in Battipaglia and with the enormous wedding feast still to come? Why was I there, having just left Potenza, laying to rest the ghost of a past regret, and now headed north after spending the night in Parmenides' town? Was it a double ritual for the bride and the groom, paying obeisance to an ancient holy place after being blessed in a Christian ceremony or was it merely that Paestum was a nice place to have wedding pictures taken, with the most famous building in the neighborhood as a backdrop?

The temples at Paestum feel holy, however inexact that statement sounds. I remember the first time I saw them. It was in August 1951, my first summer in Positano. A group of us had hired an aging wooden motor launch for the trip: Candida, Pete Steffens (a friend from Harvard with whom I had bicycled through France and Spain two summers previously), and two very Swiss ladies. It was a hot and dazzling day on the Gulf of Salerno and it took two and a half hours of chugging before we landed on the beach at Paestum. There was a brief climb up from the beach to a low wall of stone. Then, across an expanse of undistinguished fields and a bit of desultory planting, stood three temples, magically intact under the blazing brightness of the day. Mirages could scarcely be more wondrous to behold. We were dazzled, struck by the sun and what it shone upon, poor Candida most of all, her white skin blotched under a broad-brimmed hat. She was on the verge of fainting and I was dizzy. The ancient edifices emblazoned their images on my retinas surrounded by a nimbus of flame. Stolid Pete stood stock

still and the bony Swiss ladies momentarily stifled their bilin-
gual chatter. Our seeing was in disarray; we could not bear to
stay any longer in the noonday sun and retreated to the only
refuge on the site, a heavenly arbor-shaded trattoria at the south
end of the sacred enclosure. Within was a cool green oasis with
white tablecloths, cool mineral water, and lunch. There were
postcards for sale with comforting black and white images of the
temples, safely framed within their rectangles of cardboard. I
sent one of them off to Paul in Chicago, establishing a link with
the regular passage of time of my past year in Naples.

The temples awaited us after a lengthy lunch, the zero hour
of noon now two hours distant. Shadows slanted in the direction
of the mountains to the east, from the slopes whence the savage
Lucanians had come, in 400 b.c., to sack the Greek city. Our
motorboat awaited us on the beach and we went out into the
setting sun with the enormous massif of the Amalfi coast on our
right, crowned by the heights of Monte Sant' Angelo a Tre Picchi.
Positano was already in shadow when we arrived, cradled
within its bowl of mountains, the lights from its jumble of white
cube houses twinkling, picking out a pattern of horizontals and
crossing diagonals.

"Another day, another dollar!" my father used to say when he
would return home each evening on the commuter train after
another day at the office. His words were meant to camouflage
his faithful care of the family during the grim years of the Depression, to deprecate the faithful, plodding work that he stuck
to, day after day, never varying. My first day at Paestum stands
clear in my mind, the temples seen in the high noon dazzle, a
retinal shock so clearly etched that the memory recalls it over the
long plateau of gray days that make up the ordinary course of
our lives. Passing through Paestum eighteen years later, on my
way back from Elea to my mountain retreat at Faito, this memory was still vivid to me, even though the actual sight of the
temples that day seemed ordinary enough. It was a cloudy day
in late autumn. The honey-colored stone was of a hue like that

on an old-fashioned sepia-colored postcard. What was linked in my mind with the vision of eighteen years ago was the sound of the word *essere,* which I had seemed to overhear the night before down in Parmenides' town, as the student and his teacher walked back and forth by the edge of the sea, discussing philosophy. The darkness above the sea mingled with the sound of the sea and the sibilants of *essere* to become in my memory a meditation upon Being, on what remains, on what does not change. The linkage between what could be seen as a hallucinatory dazzle at high noon, after hours of exposure to the Mediterranean midsummer sun, and the overhearing at evening, eighteen years later, of a word which gained its impact from being uttered in Parmenides' town, the place which gave rise to the dialectical quandary of Being and Becoming — both of these clear memories, Paestum at noon and Elea at night, were present in me simultaneously, the shimmer and the fixity caught in memory's fabric. Their perennial presence arises out of the burning desire for permanence, a desire which makes of mortal life a perpetual rhetorical question. "Is that all there is?" repeats again and again the tough chorus of Miss Peggy Lee's most famous song.

3

*Mantua me genuit, Calabri rapuere, tenet nunc
Parthenope; cecini pascua, rura, duces.*

*(Mantua produced me, Calabria ravished me, Naples keeps
me now. I have sung of pastures, fields, leaders.)*

— VIRGIL'S EPITAPH

MEMORIES CAN BE EXORCISED by story-telling; they can
be laid to rest, like the dead, in a well-cultivated garden. No-
where is this more in evidence than in the stories told, in all
times and in all climes, after a war. Sing it and it moves us; tell
it as a story and it is anesthetized, the memories cut to fit a
pleasing length — beginning, middle, and end laid out for our
delectation. Tears are no longer necessary. Most people that have
written about wars were far removed from the battlefield. It
is not, after all, their intention to write a story about war itself;
rather they use it as a backdrop against which Achilles' wrath
can play or Stendhal's young Fabrice can be exhibited. If the
authors had been there, on the ground, they would have realized that there's nothing that can be set down, that can be fic-
tionalized: boredom, sudden terror, pandemonium, and dirt
don't reduce to sentences and paragraphs. Too many deaths,
a holocaust, leave us numb, speechless. Moral baseness accrues
to those who make copy of such things.

Telling funny stories about the war and about the army, especially if they are full of interesting "characters," is the usual method employed to distance the reality of the events. For both the listener and the person telling the story they are a kind of rhetoric, a source of enjoyment, a method for paving over the road traveled, well-chosen vignettes that stand out in comic relief against the grim tedium of the actuality of the time.

"All right, son," said the doctor who was examining my eyes as I was being inducted into the army in December 1942. "Take off your glasses and begin reading the top of the chart."

"It's generally E," I said with a complicitous giggle.

"Fine," said the doctor. "Now let's try it with your glasses on." Without them, I was acutely myopic, which had prevented me from voluntarily enlisting in the preceding months, but with them on I did rather well, was classified as 1-A and spent the next three years of my life as a combat infantryman. I always kept three pairs of glasses in my backpack and another with the first sergeant and earned a sharpshooter's badge by aiming at the center of the blur.

The truth of the matter is that good eyesight is not that important in modern ground warfare. Men are killed or maimed by machine guns, by mortars and by artillery. They lose their legs and their testicles to land mines. A few snipers with good eyesight are called for, but not many are needed. The mythology of the bright-eyed frontiersman armed with his long rifle haunted the American infantry. We spent countless hours firing, cleaning, and doing precise and snappy drills with our cumbersome M-1 rifles. I can, on demand, be rather humorous concerning the difficulties my left-handedness encountered with the right-handed bolt of the M-1, a piece of machinery which recoils with some force each time the gun is fired. In actual use in the mud and rain of Italy they would often jam. Those of us who could get away with it would junk them and get hold of an Italian Beretta or, even better, one of the light and efficient little automatic rifles the ordinary German infantry squad was most sensibly equipped with.

The Infantry School down at Fort Benning seemed proud of the automatic weapon they equipped us with; it was standard equipment in every rifle company. This was the famous, and, for us, infamous BAR — the Browning automatic rifle. It was awkward to handle, difficult to shoot, easy to jam — a cumbersome burden inflicted upon every rifle squad. No one wanted to be the BAR man. A cagy jocularity descended upon the rifle range on the day we were to qualify with the BAR. No one but a fool would try for a good score. Sympathetic old-army sergeants would make this known to those of us they favored. We squinted at the target, shot to the left of the bull's-eye, to the right of it, above it and below it. One foolish boy from New Hampshire seemed not to understand what so many of us were doing. He riddled the bull's eye, succeeding in curbing the tendency of the BAR to track away in a diagonal from anything aimed at. He was proud of his success and our platoon sergeant assured him he would become our BAR man. Joe Isaac, my bosom pal from outside Memphis, commented, "Now there's a real patsy, and wouldn't you know the motherfucker was a Yankee!"

The clearest foretaste of what the army was going to be like was the experience of wandering about naked from 9:00 in the morning until 3:30 in the afternoon in the cavernous National Guard armory in Melrose, surrounded by a clutch of local boys and men. This event was the physical examination required of all men who were of draft age. I had gotten used to a bit of nudity in the shower room at high school but here in the armory were not only boys but grown-ups who seemed to me to be at least fifty years of age. That day I saw the men of my town naked, and it was no metaphor: they were stripped of their clothing and were to be viewed shambling about all day long in the dusty reaches of the high-ceilinged old building. There was Hal, whom I had known three years ago in high school; there was Joe, who was a clerk in the downtown haberdashery; and, most amazing spectacle of all, there was George Brown, the conductor of the local orchestral association, a cellist with the phy-

sique of Ichabod Crane. I had played the Schumann Introduc-
tion and Allegro with his orchestra the previous winter when he
had taught me to catch the flick of his baton out of the corner of
my eye. He lived with his maiden sister, Effie, a schoolteacher,
and his aging mother, who taught piano; she played double bass
in her son's orchestra along with the janitor from the YMCA. I
could not bring myself to look straight at him more than once:
he was over six feet tall, cadaverous, with a ribcage that stood
out in such relief that each rib seemed a separate unit. He had a
sunken stomach and, framed between his two hipbones, an
enormous prick and pendulous balls. I wondered what he did
with them.

A doctor whom I took to be a psychiatrist or, at the very least,
a psychologist, interviewed me in a little cubicle, tapping my
knees with a mallet and asking several mildly leading questions.
While mouthing what seemed to me appropriate replies I became ever more acutely aware of my nakedness. "Son," said the
doctor, wrapping up the interview, "I was in the First War and it
was a fine experience. I'm sure it will be the same for you. Good
luck." Three weeks later I was formally inducted and shipped
off to Fort Devens for a week of classificatory madness.

At 5:30 A.M. my first day in the army my mother wept as she
saw me clamber aboard the bus that was to take me from Melrose to Fort Devens, Massachusetts. By 8:00 we had been sworn
in; at 8:45 we were stripped once again with all of our civilian
clothes packed in boxes to be shipped home. Naked we lined up
for inoculations and naked we underwent the first short-arm
inspection of our army life. "Milk it down, soldier; lemme see
it," said a weary and jaundiced medical officer. Naked we lined
up at the end of a long warehouse: underwear, shirts, socks,
pants, jackets, raincoat, overcoat, shelter half, and backpack
were thrust upon us. Raucous laughter and occasional sweet
glances from the supply sergeants accompanied this long parade at the end of which we were properly and definitively
government issue: GIs.

What turned out to be the defining moment of my week at the induction center occurred at around 1000 hours on the second day. I was seated in front of a desk confronting a sergeant with four stripes and a T. He wore an eyeshade, interestingly enough not government issue. He peered at me with a shrewd and pointed gaze. "I am a classification sergeant and I will classify you," he informed me. He was from Boston. We chatted together in a way that struck me as being rather sophisticated. (How young I was and how innocent!) He seemed interested in my background, that I was a musician, that I had studied with the famous Mlle Boulanger, and he chuckled when he heard of my three long years as handyman at the piano at the Mary C. Wheeler school in Providence. I felt I was in the same league with him; he was so very different from all the others, who had called me either "son" or "soldier."

"We'll ship you off to an army band," said the classification sergeant.

"Well, really," I said, dumbly sure of my footing with this older and experienced fellow, "I'd rather be in the infantry than tooting around in a band!" There was a momentary flicker in the eyes beneath the eyeshade and, unbeknownst to me, my fate for the next three years was sealed. He then shook my hand, not a very military gesture, and motioned for the next soldier to step up to his judgment seat.

Our departure from Fort Devens ushered in a day of constant discomfort. We were awakened at 0445 hours. "We can't have you missing the train, can we," said a sardonic sergeant. It was a cold morning with rain turning to sleet: December in Massachusetts! An attempt was made to march us to the railroad siding, the difficulty being that we had as yet had no drill. We'd also had no order imposed upon us, not having been assigned to any squads or platoons. We were an inchoate mass, moving through the predawn murk in uneasy files. We were also encumbered by a large bag, stuffed with everything we had been issued and anything else we might have clung to.

After an interminable wait in the drizzle, we were loaded on board a string of decrepit old Boston and Maine Railroad coaches which were to be our home for the next five days. Food would appear at one end of the coaches at 0530, 1215, and 1750 hours: gray sausages, greenish omelets made from powdered eggs, slabs of tepid meat, canned fruit, and watery coffee. At the other end of the car were large metal vats in which we were meant to wash our mess kits. The water was soon fouled; mild dysentery affected a good half of us. There were no sleeping arrangements as such; I was lucky enough to be placed with only two other draftees in a set of facing seats, which allowed one of us at a time to stretch out full length. We had no idea where we were going and, more disturbingly, we had no idea what branch of the service we had been assigned to. We proceeded west across Massachusetts, and slowly farther west across the state of New York. At one point we were at the Canadian border where we stopped for three hours and then proceeded backward to where we had come from, eventually turning west again. At 0230 hours in the midst of Indiana we stopped with a jolt and a clatter. We were ordered out of the cars with all of our equipment and stood for several hours in a cornfield. It was raining. There had been a derailment of one of the forward coaches. With the dawn came a repair train. At 0800 hours we were on our way again, moving fitfully with frequent stops. We must have passed south of Chicago and then north and west into Minnesota. We noted flatcars loaded with iron ore going in the opposite direction. At a point which some of us conjectured must be a bit short of Duluth we stopped dead in an expanse of snowy woods. Again, as at the Canadian border in New York, we reversed direction and proceeded with a bit more alacrity south and somewhat west. On the morning of the fifth day we arrived at our destination.

There were to be so many days in my time in the army that would be worse than these five days in the train: the senseless fatigue of basic training, the sweaty misery of Louisiana maneuvers in midsummer, the endless months of terror and boredom in the mountains of Italy. Those five days in the old Boston and Maine coaches were nevertheless a time in limbo, a time in which we were suspended in never-never land, awaiting our entrance into the fateful portals. We were more naked than we had been that day in the armory, naked in time and space, without knowledge of where we were and where we were going, and of what the end of our voyage might turn out to be. In retrospect it was a mild enough suffering and a proper initiation for what awaited us if the imagination were to stop and grapple with those contemporaneous European trains rolling east to their respective hells.

They were waiting for us when we arrived at 0600 hours. We could make out on one side of the tracks the name BRAGG on a sign tacked onto the wall of a decrepit wooden railroad station. (We learned later that we were in the state of Oklahoma.) On the other side of the tracks was an expanse of plank sidewalk stretching away in perspective, through the morning sleet and fog. We were herded into a fleet of trucks and driven for several miles across a plain that had been stripped of all vegetation, to be deposited in a large expanse of open ground with yellow barracks stretching in lines to the right and to the left of us. On this open expanse a sizable group of soldiers were uttering cadenced grunts as they jabbed at suspended dummies with the bayonets that were affixed to their rifles. A boy with more courage than I could muster asked a sergeant standing nearby where we were and what branch of the service we were in. "You're in the infantry, bud, and this is Camp Gruesome. This welcome was planned personally for you by Major General Sloan."

Things were preordained. They knew who we were. We had already been sorted out, unbeknownst to ourselves, back at Fort Devens. Most of the boys in my railroad car were assigned, as was I, to Company C, First Battalion, 350th Infantry Regiment, 88th Infantry Division, commanded by Major General Sloan. Camp Gruber, Oklahoma, was the name of our post. It was adjacent to the tiny town of Bragg up in the hills above the city of Muskogee. By the end of the war some of my group were still in C Company, some had been wounded and evacuated, a small number had been transferred to other companies, many had died and been carried off in body bags to GI cemeteries. On this damp morning in December we were all of us in place, a very particular future in front of us.

We were given a surprisingly good breakfast with genuine fresh eggs in the Company C mess hall. We then proceeded to one of the yellow barracks, were assigned a cot, and ordered to shower. This was welcome as we stank after our five days on the train. By 0900 hours we were lined up outside. Training began. Rifles were issued. Close-order drill was initiated with our M-1 rifles assuming the role of a new appendage. It struck me right away as being a remarkably stupid exercise; from a certain distance it cannot avoid being comic as you find yourself ritualistically executing "About face," "Present arms," "Left flank," "Right flank" with your heels and toes swiveling puppetlike through a snappy right angle and your long rifle slanting diagonally over your shoulder. There was, however, despite my tendency to giggle, an odd comfort in performing these movements, a comfort arising from an order and discipline so different from the days in limbo which had preceded them. They were an exercise imposed upon the natural anarchy implicit in any group of men who had been randomly thrown together. We were not only in place, we were in order.

Once upon a time men marched into battle in formation, formed a hollow square, shot all of their rifles in unison at an enemy that was lined up facing them in a formation that was the mirror image of their own lineup. It might have been supposed that the slaughter at such a battle as Antietam would have demonstrated the idiocy of such formations. The fields of Flanders exhibited an archaic pigheadedness as the young men of a whole generation of Europeans mowed each other down in a carnage that numbs the imagination. Our little war in the bitter hills of

Italy, however bloody and protracted it may have been, was fought by individuals and squads hiding in holes or behind rocks, always seeking shelter from enemy fire by crouching behind a hill. The killing came from the air as an artillery shell stopped its whooshing noise and began to whistle, signaling its nearer approach, or from mortars being fired on the other side of the hill and crunching in front and then behind, and then, zero at the bone, as the observer on top of the hill corrected his aim, straight upon you. The sudden chatter of a machine gun signaled the end to many a soldier. The obscenity of land mines soon gave everyone the habit of scuffing their feet, hoping to graze the surface without touching the delicate fuse that would trigger an explosion which, if not fatal, would blow off a leg or mutilate the private parts.

Every day began with close-order drill. It was the basic grammar of our soldierly life. It was extended to movements of companies, battalions, and even entire regiments. When FDR appeared to review the division, we were all of us marshaled onto the expanse we called Gopher Prairie — a rough piece of ground, at least a square mile in expanse, surrounded on four sides by the yellow wooden barracks which constituted the body of Camp Gruber. The gopher holes were a particular menace. You could easily step into one, twist your ankle, or fall, disturbing the precision of an entire battalion's maneuver. Another hazard was caused by several inept rustics who never learned to keep their rifles at an acute enough angle. For the soldier directly behind, the result would be a resounding thump on his steel helmet as he was snappily executing a left or a right face.

Despite all of this I was excited on that special day as we approached the reviewing stand and saw our pint-size General Sloan standing rigidly at attention beside the president's chair. As we were passing the reviewing stand and the order "Eyes right" was being given I became aware of what the division band was playing. The music that I heard as we marched past the commander-in-chief was a band arrangement of a song popular in the early forties: "Mr. Five-by-Five." Back at the barracks we conjectured, with a kind of grim satisfaction, that our general's ambition to have his 88th be the first draft division in combat was well on the road to being realized, which would account for the extraordinary appearance of President Roosevelt. It also accounted for the dizzy pace of our training.

The division had been activated the previous summer, but only reached its full strength with our arrival in early December. Our six weeks of basic training had to be jammed into a timetable aimed at preparing the whole division for summer maneuvers in Louisiana. First, each company had to have its own field exercises, then each of the three battalions — all of this to be followed by regimental field exercises which had to be coordinated with the supporting field artillery. Finally, before we departed for the South, the whole kit and caboodle — all three regiments together with the division artillery — had to be put together under the direction of the division operations officers.

A sagacious scholar once remarked to me that the rule in the social sciences seemed to be "If you can't count, count anyway." In the army everything was done by the numbers; things that by their nature could not be planned were planned anyway. We certainly could be taught close-order drill, though it had no relation to combat. We could be taught to shoot rifles, though very few of us ever killed a German with a rifle. We learned to shoot mortars and machine guns, which at least was as it should be. We learned most successfully to take all of our weapons apart and to put them back together again. I am sure that after fifty years I could still disassemble and reassemble a machine gun in the dark, spreading the parts out on a shelter half, feeling for the shapes with my fingers. It was necessary to toughen us with increasingly long marches with full field packs, though in Italy no one needed to be taught to dig a hole when the shells came in. Nevertheless, in our training exercises we were required, every day, out in the field, to scrape a foxhole for ourselves in the stony scrabble of the Oklahoma hills.

We became inured to living with ineptitude when it came to training. Speeches made to us in his high squeaky voice by our little major general made cynics of even some of the near mental retards of Company C. "I know I am right," the general would shriek at us after we had returned exhausted from an all-night exercise. "My methods work. You are all of you my rangers. We'll show them, won't we?" We remained at strict attention, mute. He would then stride up to the regimental operations sergeant (who was not obligated to participate in any of the night training exercises) and repeat his high-pitched rhetorical question. "I'm right, it works, doesn't it, Sergeant?"

Sergeant Costello was an adroit Irishman from New York City, adept at dealing with the banalities of high rank. "Absolutely right, General, and every one of these men will testify to it!" The general would shiver slightly with satisfaction, like a hen settling down on her egg after the exertion of laying it, turn on his heel, and depart.

The general believed in a shipshape post complemented with the strictest of uniform codes. MPs were instructed to pick up any soldier whose buttons (including an interior one on a little flap at the bottom of our overcoats) were not all buttoned. The side of the street that bordered the central rectangle (Gopher Prairie) of the camp was reserved for officers only. On rainy days when both officers and enlisted men wore raincoats, which more often than not carried no insignia, we would walk on the officers' side glaring with delicious pseudoauthority at passersby.

Costumes are such necessary fictions: what personae are crafted by a uniform and what ironies are implicit when a citizen army is massed together under the authority of rank and rhetoric! The morale which developed in the enlisted men of my division had nothing to do with spit and polish; it rose out of a perverse pride in being dirty, in being the lowest of the low: fear and self-preservation were its principal components. In Italy it was thrust upon our attention at every juncture that every other branch of the service was better off and better dressed and that any officer had a better deal and a fancier uniform. If we did get a pass to Naples everything in town was off-limits to us except coffee and doughnuts at the Red Cross. We had no choice but to make whorehouses our professional clubs. Capri and Sorrento were reserved for officers. The whole glorious peninsula from Castellammare to Punta Campanella (which in later years I grew to know and love) had signs proclaiming it to be OFF-LIMITS TO ENLISTED MEN.

It was only when a certain private named Fox was assigned to our company that we realized with a certain chagrin to what extent the infantry was deemed the ultimate Siberia. He appeared one day with the mule train when we were high up in the Apennines north of Florence, dug into the lee of a hill to protect us from artillery fire. I was obligated to share my minuscule dugout with him. Some months earlier Fox had raped and murdered an adolescent girl in Casablanca. Duly court-martialed he had been found guilty and sent out into the desert to the disciplinary stockade known as the Singing School. He was an exemplary inmate, rising after three months to the status of a trusty, having slavishly knuckled under to all of the idiocies of the camp's discipline: always cleanshaven though issued only one razor blade every two weeks; his uniform always perfectly pressed though no iron was available to him. Fox told me how he would fold his uniform neatly under his bedroll and sleep flat on his back on top of it to ensure a neat crease. He noted any aberrant behavior among the other prisoners and turned them in to the camp authorities. After three months of such exemplary daily performance the army put into effect its policy of parole and pardon. (His original sentence had been for forty years.) He was transferred to a combat infantry unit. If, in the judgment of his company commander, he performed adequately for two months he would be granted a pardon and his eventual discharge would be honorable.

Private Fox had sharp features and pointed teeth. Several times in the middle of the night I was awakened by the sound of his voice. He would be twitching in his bedroll and his voice would hiss imprecations far more ominous than the usual "motherfucker" which was such a basic part of the lingua franca of our ordinary army discourse. I would listen with horror to the sexual fantasies that were being played out in his dreams, hugging my bedroll about me and shifting as far away as possible within the cramped confines of the little dugout. A short while before his two months were completed he stepped on a small wooden land mine which blew off his right leg. I received the news of this with a nervous grin and made no comment. I have often been curious as to what final adjustment the army might have made in his parole and pardon after awarding him his Purple Heart medal.

One night in late January, in the midst of our basic training at Camp Gruber, an extraordinary thing happened: discipline collapsed entirely. In the afternoon we had marched far out into the countryside; the temperature was about twenty degrees Fahrenheit. We were ordered to stay put, to remain where we were and to build no fires. We dug the regulation foxholes as best we could in the frozen ground. Other than this there were no exercises or company maneuvers to be performed. By 2300 hours the temperature had fallen to ten degrees. The area we were in was semiarid scrub with here and there a wooden shack left by the farmers who had scrabbled some kind of living from the land before the army had requisitioned the whole region as part of Camp Gruber's maneuver area. Our pathetic little second lieutenant, a weedy brand-new officer from Louisiana who had great difficulty in enunciating words, began repeating at regular intervals that it was part of our training to get used to the cold and that it was for this reason that the general had forbidden us to light any fires. "Now y'all had just better get used to doin' what the general says you gotta do." Our platoon sergeant, Morgan, old army and a Kentuckian, had reminded our little lieutenant just the day before, when we had returned exhausted from a day-long march, that we should be released to the barracks immediately without further ado. "These men are real tired, sir, and don't need no further talk." Morgan was a good man, solid as an oak, firm and patient with all of us raw recruits; the training we received we owed to him. He was respected and feared. On this particular night he said nothing either to us or to the lieutenant.

We huddled together, stomping our feet, warming each other like members of a herd of sheep, looking to Sergeant Morgan for guidance. He remained silent. A short distance away a platoon from B Company tore down one of the shacks and started a fire. We still hesitated, clinging together for warmth, not willing to break the law that bound us. Then came a moment which I can still recollect with near physical vividness. It was as if the whole group was one body through which passed a common shudder. Discipline ceased: we seized whatever material that could be burned, destroyed shacks, threw in branches, twigs, and bushes. Officers did nothing and our platoon sergeants, the backbones of our units, joined with us. We hooted and yelled and warmed ourselves around the fires, full of the joyous onrush of anarchy. At 0430 hours trucks appeared. We mobbed into them and were carried back home to Company C. The mess hall was warm, the gray sausages and green eggs delicious. Stomachs full we stumbled back to barracks and slept. Many of us in that group spent two winters in the Apennines with snow, Germans, death, and artillery all around. There was never, however, a moment like the one in the freezing maneuvers area at Camp Gruber that January night. We knew why we were in Italy. We knew what we were doing: we were fighting and our lives depended on there being order. Nothing was ever said to us by the officers concerning that night in Oklahoma. Reports must have reached the officers in charge of training at division headquarters. "Them officers is chickenshit," said Joe Isaac. "They just take any crap the general dishes out like it was fried chicken and biscuits." Sergeant Morgan looked glum and said nothing.

In the stifling heat of Louisiana maneuvers the next summer we were subjected to another instance of crass stupidity: something called "water discipline," which purported to prepare troops for hot climates. It was enforced, by the numbers, with considerable efficiency. We would be marched for hours, with full equipment, in the 95-to-100-degree temperatures. Only one canteen of water a day per man was allowed. Squad cars with staff officers would drive past, checking with company officers as to the number of men who had collapsed owing to heat prostration. Percentages were noted. When we were recuperating from the summer at Fort Sam Houston (a brief respite before being shipped out to Africa and Italy) I came across an official brochure regarding water discipline. It noted, laconically, that troops in hot climates should be given as much water as possible, the exercises in the summer maneuvers of 1943 having shown this to be necessary.

General Sloan was a stickler for water discipline, and the sin connected with it which particularly nettled him was the consumption of watermelons purchased from the local farmers. He would cruise the maneuvers area in his squad car looking for miscreants. We would always post a guard by the road to warn us of his approach, though the more discreet among us always consumed our melons from behind a screen of bushes. On one particularly hot afternoon the same slow soldier from New Hampshire who had qualified on the BAR sat stolidly by the edge of the road eating a large slice of melon. He remained oblivious of our warning whistle as the general's squad car, emblazoned with its two stars, came racing around a bend, screeching to a stop in front of him. He was hauled into the back seat by the general's aide and transported to regimental headquarters. Arrived there, the general, all the while emitting his usual high-pitched comments, shepherded the boy up a slight incline to where the regimental commander's tent was located, with the full intention of turning him over for disciplinary action to the regimental commander. The scene became memorable when the general, in parting the flaps of Colonel Lynch's tent, revealed that unfortunate field officer in the act of consuming a large piece of watermelon. The New Hampshire rustic was abandoned and the general's squeaky voice could be heard from within the tent, berating poor Colonel Lynch.

Lynch was a decent man, fair and lazy, who drank a fair amount. He was regular army but not West Point and got on well with all of the noncoms. He would be relieved of his command shortly after we went into the line north of the Garigliano at Minturno. His beloved son, Captain Lynch, commander of one of the regiment's line companies, was killed at Monterumici, the last big hill in front of Bologna, just a few weeks before the war ended.

Black humor antisepticizes the army and its multiform activities. In the deadly round of actual war it assumes its role as negativity's proper language. It is a way of coping with the seemingly endless and gratuitous stupidity implicit in the managing and organizing of inchoate groups of men into units that must kill and maim and live under conditions from day to day that try the soul. It signals the presence of a particular brand of self-consciousness, a kind of pride in reverse. We were the lowest of the low in the hierarchy of the army's troops. In our particular theater of operations in Italy the few (so often too few!) infantry divisions were supported by swollen ranks of support troops behind the lines, a vast pyramid with its headquarters in the largest royal palace in Europe, the Neapolitan Bourbons' Reggia at Caserta. We became intensely aware of ourselves as a group; we shared an inner intuition which revealed itself in the tolerance we demonstrated in all of our relations within our squads and platoons. It was not democracy in any political sense; we were not in charge of our lives and our fates. We treated each other as equals and our eccentricities and our special passions raised no barriers. My books and my precious few scores caused no comment. I would often study a Stravinsky score while a crap game was going on next to me, and no eyebrows were raised. It was not like civilian life; we were all on a level.

Before we got to Italy there were very few officers we had any particular respect for. It wasn't so much that most of them were southerners — lots of our company was southern — but rather that they were a special breed of southerner, products of ROTC units at unheard-of southern colleges. They were provincial and slow, often extremely lazy, a whole other class from our old-army sergeants from the South whom we feared and respected and whom we found we could trust when mindless excess was imposed on us from above or when, in Italy, the crunch of artillery signaled a new barrage. The older sergeants knew the limits of what bound us together and they shared the hardships of the recruits they made into soldiers. We all spoke the same language. (Years later I sensed an analogous commonality in so many of the Neapolitans I got to know: they had their own dialect, their own jokes, their own literature which caught the ethos of the dialect — fatalism and acceptance of what's given.) Our southern sergeants were, for the most part, from the back country of Kentucky and Tennessee. Some of them were taciturn, like our massive and immobile Sergeant Morgan; others specialized in vivid turns of phrase. Inspired alliterations would issue from the mouth of our best wordsmith, Sergeant Stump. He would bring new and illuminating twists to the usual worn-out scatological language which from habit or adaptation we had all fallen into. These offered such solace to all of us suffering from some particularly inane performance of our Louisiana platoon leader, pimply little Lieutenant Landry. "It ain't so much he's a mean little motherfucker," said Sergeant Stump. "He just don't know shit from Shinola."

Stump had been a backwoods preacher and, in his own words, had gone bad. "I slipped and I slithered; my faith warn't sufficient." He joined the regular army and was an ornament therein. When we had performed sloppily in our drill he would forestall the lieutenant by blasting us with ten thoroughly enjoyable minutes of obscene critical hyperbole after which, outmaneuvered, the lieutenant had no choice but to dismiss us to the barracks. Stump stayed with C Company all the way until November '44 when he lost an arm in the bloody times in the Apennines between Florence and Bologna. Three second lieutenants had come and gone in that period, two of them dead, one wounded.

We had another pairing of southerners in our company: Sergeant Stokes and our company commander, Captain Cox, both from Georgia. Stokes ruled the company from his orderly room with unmistakable authority. He was tall, over six feet, with a flat face and a nasal cadence. He seldom spoke, but when he did it was to great effect. "Around here, I'm Jesus Christ," he told all of us new ones when we arrived. He lasted until the end of the war, never wavering in his gestures, and never saying one word more than was necessary. In the last year of the war when I had advanced to be operations sergeant of the First Battalion I would observe him plodding calmly in front of his company. He was never wounded and had had four different company commanders by June '45. His performance of his daily tasks never faltered; he ran the company, steadied its nerves, and kept its records. He was meticulous in his morning reports — a difficult job in bad times, when casualties mount and new recruits appear in the middle of the night, only to disappear never to be seen again. On the other hand, Captain Cox, Stokes's immediate boss, was a soft and verbose man, who would, as weak men do, vacillate between cruelty and sentimentality. Once he canceled weekend passes for the entire company because of some piddling infraction. A certain interchange I had with him at that time became famous in the lore of the company.

Several weeks before this action of his I had gone down to Tulsa on a weekend pass. It had been a memorable weekend in the most technical sense of memory as recall and perspective. Spadafora, a chunky little Italian from the North End in Boston, had gone down with me on the long trek from Camp Gruber: army transport down to Muskogee and then on to Tulsa via Greyhound bus. We checked into the best hotel in town, tipped the porter and procured a fifth of bourbon from him. (Oklahoma was a dry state: a comfortable arrangement for both Baptists and bootleggers.) As we were passing through the hotel lobby on our way out to search for food and entertainment I noticed a poster advertising an early-music concert (a much rarer event in those days than now). I paid scant attention to it as Spadafora was in a hurry to get going. We ate a lot at a combination restaurant and club and drank 3.2 beer with our bootleg bourbon as a chaser. At around 10:30 Spadafora made contact with an aging whore and we climbed into a taxi and returned to the hotel. We were drunk and Spadafora, a most potent fellow generally, was not performing to his complete satisfaction. At a certain lull, while the lady we had hired was bent over him, I heard a voice from the next room, a most ladylike voice, cool and English. I then remembered the announcement of the early-music concert posted down in the lobby and recognized the voice as belonging to Dame Diana, a regular visitor each winter at the Wheeler School. Dame Diana played the virginals. It was a moment of surrealist juxtaposition. The interaction on Spadafora's bed was reaching its climax as I finished the whiskey and passed out in a paroxysm of dizzy glee, contemplating the convergence of the lady whore, of Dame Diana, of chunky little Spadafora from the North End, and of tender little Douglas from his Protestant suburb.

The next day I discovered the Philbrook Art Museum. It seemed to my hungover sensibilities not so much a series of picture galleries as a set of rooms engulfed in Steinways. I counted at least five, and finally settled down to play on the largest of them, not asking anyone's permission and without the guards paying any particular attention. I had not had a good piano under my fingers since I had entered the army. I had two big pieces I wanted to unleash that afternoon: Mussorgsky's *Pictures at an Exposition* and Beethoven's Waldstein Sonata. I was rusty but I made a mighty musical noise, attracting a bevy of listeners. I rose to the occasion, playing the coda of the

Beethoven with aplomb and some considerable glitter. There was applause. A florid man with a string tie came up to me and shook my hand. "That was mighty fine, son," he said. "Wouldn't you like to give us a concert here at the Philbrook? Two weeks from now would be just right for us and we certainly would be mighty obliged." I was not averse to more time in Tulsa and it felt good to be performing again. I told the man, however, that I would probably have trouble securing permission for a weekend pass. "Just you be kind enough to let me have the name of your company commander out there at Gruber," he replied. "Perhaps it can be arranged." We left it at that.

A middle-aged couple with Boston accents introduced themselves and the rest of the day passed by sedately enough with dinner at their house. The conversation turned on the cultural history of the Oklahoma Territory. Camp Gruber, I learned, was located in an old place of exile, the end of what the Indians had called the Trail of Tears, the resting place of tribes who had been forced from their verdant lands east of the Mississippi and marched into what was known as Indian Territory, a country where the trees stopped and the high plains began, stretching west until the mesas and the front range of the Rockies crinkled the arid plains.

When I returned from Tulsa I learned that Captain Cox had canceled weekend passes for an entire month. I thought little more of the Philbrook Art Museum. Late Thursday, after an exhausting day spent crawling under live machine gun fire on the range, I was told to report to the orderly room. Sergeant Stokes fixed me with his gimlet eye. "Captain wants to see you. Salute proper when you enter and stand at attention."

In the captain's office I performed the ritual with what I hoped to be proper snap and polish. "At ease, Private Allanbrook," said Captain Cox. "I want to read this letter to you. It's from the First National Bank of Tulsa, office of the president of the bank, and signed by him." He paused to give more effect. "'Dear Captain Cox, I wonder if you would be so kind as to grant a weekend pass to Private Allanbrook. We would very much like to have him give a piano recital here in Tulsa at our museum. On behalf of the directors of the Philbrook we should appreciate your help in this matter. If your schedules out there at Gruber don't allow for liberty on Friday I should be most happy to arrange for my private plane to come and pick him up at the Gruber airstrip.'" There was another pause. Captain Cox beamed at me. "Why, Private Allanbrook," he said, "I used to play the piano myself!"

It was quickly arranged. I had hoped the Friday permission would not be granted, but it was. There would have been great allure in being ferried in a private plane from the midst of my Siberian encampment. First Sergeant Stokes received the news with a sardonic twinkle, writing out the pass without a word. He must have heard what the captain said to me because later in the day my platoon sergeant, Morgan, an old army buddy of Stokes and generally most laconic in his utterances, sidled up to me in the mess hall with his hand on his hip and said, "Why, Private Allanbrook, I used to play the piano myself!" Several times in Italy in the coming year, in the most untoward circumstances, once in the red plush *salotto* of a Neapolitan whorehouse and another time outside a battalion aid station with the wounded lined up on stretchers, a member of Company C would grin at me and repeat the famous words. Captain Cox transferred from the regiment before we went in line by the Garigliano; no doubt he found himself an easier post. C Company was better off without him.

In May I was transferred to the Intelligence and Reconnaissance platoon of Headquarters Company and left Company C forever. It was a move that may well have saved my life since Company C had a staggering casualty rate in dead and wounded by the time the war ended. I still feel a certain shame at having left my old company, at having quit a post at the bottom of the barrel, at not sharing all of the constant terror, boredom, and ignorance which is the lot of a foot soldier in an infantry line company. It all happened quickly enough. I was one of the few who read the bulletin board posted outside the orderly room. One day I saw an announcement to the effect that the I and R platoon of Headquarters Company, 350th Infantry Regiment needed to fill its quota. Candidates had to be privates. It had been a week of forced marches, of endless waiting for orders while squatting in the dust, of digging new foxholes at every stop, of sleeping out in rain and mud. The regiment was exercising its companies and battalions in small-scale maneuvers, preparing for the coming ordeal in Louisiana. Our little lieutenant, a pathetic and childish twenty-two-year-old, was more than ordinarily inept that week. He had difficulty reading maps, would march us the wrong way, and would wake us needlessly at night. He alternated between yelling ineffectually at us and nearly breaking into tears with worry when a superior officer appeared. We contemplated him dumbly, there being no recourse for us. Our Tennessee sergeant, Morgan, retired mutely into himself, knowing there was nothing to be done with such a fool.

I had no difficulty in persuading Joe Isaac and two of the brightest members of my platoon, Manfredi and Vizetius, to try for a transfer. Manfredi was a slim and physically elegant Italian from Utica and Vizetius a squat and ugly Lithuanian from Gary, Indiana. Sergeant Stokes received us with a glacial stare, forwarded our requests to Headquarters Company and gave us our marching orders a week later when the official transfer came through. "You're smart," he said. "Don't fuck up when you get there."

The I and R platoon functioned directly under the regimental intelligence officer, the S-2. Its mission, as outlined in the official manuals, was to probe the enemy lines, to bring back intelligence. It needed to know the whole terrain the regiment was operating in, to pick out ridges and places of concealment where the enemy either was or might be. For this the platoon had access to all of the maps and air-reconnaissance photos available. I turned out to be quick at map reading and was almost immediately put in charge of them at regimental headquarters. I became peculiarly invaluable to the intelligence officer, who was both lazy and nearly illiterate in map reading. He had a long, whitish face and a drawling but querulous voice. A Georgian like Captain Cox but more adroit in the ways of army politics, he was already a staff officer and was promoted to major by the time we got to Italy. He loved the prerogatives of rank — of hobnobbing with field-grade officers, of being a good drinking companion for the colonel. He wore immaculate tailor-made uniforms. He was clever enough to avoid going out in the field except when it was strictly required of him. I was so low in the hierarchy that he could be perfectly candid with me without losing status.

"Allanbrook," he would say, "I sure don't know what I'd do without you. I never get all of those lines on the maps straight. Now you make me a nice clean overlay so I can tell the colonel just where that make-believe red artillery has its hundred and five howitzers." This was said to me less than a month after I had moved over to Headquarters Company. The Regiment was in the midst of field exercises involving all three battalions and their artillery support. We were playing war games with our sister regiments, the 349th or the 351st, acting as the enemy.

Daily life in the I and R platoon was neither so boring nor so physically awful as it had been in C Company. The slough of ignorance in which the ordinary line infantryman lives was much alleviated. You knew what was supposed to be going on. I began spending half of my time at regimental headquarters, occasionally busy and quickly learning to appear to be so, surrounded by maps and recondite intelligence manuals. The regimental sergeant major, the first sergeant of the first sergeants of the regiment, nodded dourly at me when I passed his desk; he accepted me as part of the furnishings. He was a spit-and-polish old soldier of the regular peacetime army, harsh in his discipline and slow in his reflexes except when the colonel or the occasional general would appear; then like a pistol shot his voice would crackle out, "Attenshun!"

My mentor in the rarified heights of regimental HQ was Master Sergeant Costello, the regimental operations sergeant. He had six stripes as did the sergeant major but was a draftee like myself, an Irishman from Queens, adept at the politics of survival and advancement. He polished his shoes, was quick in his reflexes, and knew how to flatter the colonel and our little bantam of a general whenever he would appear on one of his terrifying inspection tours. Costello also had the good fortune of working for one of the few officers that had the unqualified respect of all of us, Major Melcher, the regimental operations officer. He was from the hill country of West Texas, a good and thorough man of conscience and probity. He worried as an operations officer should about every detail, about the logistics of every operation, about its feasibility, about the placement of every mortar and machine gun and about its cost in possible casualties. When we were in the line he was a bulwark against the frequent folly of generals and colonels who would push in on us, ordering an advance while ignoring the awful price in blood that would result. Costello knew his boss to be a good and decent man; he gave him faithful service and enjoyed the perquisites of his job with no qualms whatsoever. He worried about me like a big Irish uncle, teaching me to keep my mouth shut when officers were talking, concerned for my life when I went on patrols with the I and R platoon. In Italy, when I became the operations sergeant of the First Battalion, a much riskier post than at the regiment, he always checked on me, well aware of the dangers of my new job. A week after I arrived there two members of my squad at First Battalion had their legs blown off on a land mine while we were advancing to a new position. Costello heard about it back at regimental HQ and immediately pushed through on the field phone, afraid that I had been one of those maimed. When he heard my voice, uncertain and distant on the shaky field phone, he exploded with relief. "Allanbrook, you little jerk, why in hell did you want to go up there and be a fucking sergeant!" I was touched and told him I had gone up to First Battalion so as to be free to talk all I wanted to even in front of officers, which was certainly much easier to do in a battalion headquarters.

Our platoon sergeant was a bizarre figure given to bouts of sadism, who drove his jeep like a crazed person. He was a Pole — Supinski by name: not a Pole from Chicago but a real Pole from Poland. He was thin-lipped with startlingly white skin marked by smallpox and a scar that traversed his right cheek in a jagged diagonal. The officers treated him as almost an equal; it was bruited about that he had been a captain in the Polish army. His progress from Poland to Panama to being platoon sergeant of the I and R platoon was the subject of considerable speculation among us; none of us knew much of anything about European politics, but spying and chicanery on an international level seemed to be part of his recent past. We knew about Panama because of his boasting of his encounters with nameless officials down in the Canal Zone. One of them must have cleared him of whatever shadows we suspected him of and the men of the I and R were stuck with him. He affected a military tradition older and more ruthless than ours. Whatever reasons the officers may have had for respecting him, we for better reasons detested him.

Supinski had three sergeants under him; one of them, Israel Tarnow, was undeniably comic in his vanity and in his pygmy size. When we would go on patrols in Oklahoma and Louisiana, simulating search-and-destroy missions, we would all pile into our platoon's amphibious jeep, a most ill-designed vehicle. Sergeant Tarnow would stand with his right arm thrust under his jacket, peering ahead, his imagination full of his mission, the searching out and destroying of simulated Germans. Supinski would invariably puncture poor Tarnow's afflatus with a twisted smile accompanied by a sneering remark uttered in his nasal un-English accent. Anti-Semitism was bred into his Polish bones, and he had chosen and promoted Israel so as to have ready at hand a mouse for his feline games.

I had the ill luck of being a member of Israel's squad on several disastrous occasions. Supinski, well knowing the faults of our miserable amphibious jeep (which some of us called our very own duck-billed platypus), would order him onto swampy ground full of stumps, or shallow ponds full of snags, terrains especially inhospitable to the weaknesses of the vehicle. The amphibious jeep had the innards of an ordinary jeep wrapped up in a kind of bathtub made of corrugated iron. There was a little propeller sticking out at the back and a bit of a rudder to steer with. The bottom of the pseudoboat was quite close to the ground so that protuberances such as low tree stumps or flattish rocks would maroon the poor amphibian on dry land, leaving it tilting back and forth like a seesaw or a turtle on a swivel. It would then be necessary to jack up either the front or the back wheels in order to gain some purchase with the ground, a difficult procedure. An even greater hazard were the plugs on the bottom of the tub, which came quite easily unscrewed, allowing water to enter. To make matters worse, Sergeant Tarnow's driver and the mechanic of our platoon, a full-blooded Penobscot from Old Town, Maine, with the extraordinary name of Louis Socka-lexis, would from time to time remove the plugs. Whether this was done from forgetfulness or by design was difficult to know for Sockalexis was a world unto himself, an enigma that the army was incapable of dealing with. (How strange to have learned, fifty years later, of his famous grandfather who bore the same name. He played a brilliant half-season with the Cleveland Spiders baseball team in 1897, hitting .338, but alcoholism proved his undoing.)

No glimmer of this past ever came from our Sockalexis. He was a taciturn man, short and square with a slight cast in his left eye. He regarded his fellow soldiers impassively and never had anything to say to us. When noncoms or commissioned officers spoke to him his face would assume an oafish smile but the expected "Yes, sir" or "No, sir" was never forthcoming. At least once a week he would make a point of not doing what he was ordered to do. To say that he refused to follow an order doesn't catch the nature of his immobility. He would say nothing; he would not move a muscle. There would only be the flicker of a grin in the corner of his mouth. He was never given even one stripe, never made PFC, and was often restricted to barracks. Whenever he could find booze, he would drink and drink and drink. He got away with all this for one very good reason: he was a marvel of a mechanic. He knew all about motors; he would strip them down and reassemble them with real panache. He could fix any part of any jeep. He kept Sergeant Supinski's jeep in perfect order but the amphibious jeep assigned to Sergeant Tarnow was to Sockalexis a mechanical joke, an ill-designed monster not worthy of serious attention. Supinski's sharp eyes were well aware of this. What better malice incarnate than to have Sockalexis the driver on Sergeant Tarnow's missions: a Jew and a full-blooded American Indian! The hackles of his Eastern European soul tingled with anticipation. Incomparable fuck-ups would occur and they did.

Several times on our patrols we had been hung up on tree stumps; once we had been mired all night in a bog. The climax occurred on a day when full regimental exercises were being held and the new amphibious jeeps were to perform under the eye of the division intelligence officer. Supinski ordered Tarnow and his squad to reconnoiter as far as the bank of a smallish pond and, upon receiving a radio signal, to cross the pond, all the while communicating, via radio, any information gathered concerning the enemy: a classic mission of the I and R platoon. It was never ascertained whether Sockalexis had deliberately removed the plugs of the amphibious jeep or had simply forgotten to screw them in tightly enough after his overhaul of the vehicle. The result was that, slowly, in the midst of our course, we sank to the bottom of the pond. Tarnow had posted himself in the front of the jeep in his usual Napoleonic stance, scanning the farther shore for signs of the enemy, all the while keeping in touch with regimental HQ on the radio. All of us on board were bemused while Sockalexis manipulated the rudder and revved up the motor at what seemed appropriate moments. It was not until we were somewhat awash that we became aware of our imminent submersion. It was a shallow little pond, muddy with green algae around the shore. Though it was chilly, we had no choice but to abandon ship and make our way back to Supinski's observation post, floundering chest-high through the water holding our M-1s overhead. It was a moment of sardonic glee for Supinski; the Jew could be blamed! The low rating we would receive from the intelligence officer and the spluttering fury of our own silly S-2, Captain Collier, were of no importance to him when balanced against the anti-Semitic satisfaction he had received. It was all the more titillating to him because of the real cause of the event: a genuine American Indian such as he had read about in James Fenimore Cooper when he was an adolescent in Cracow.

The amphibious jeep never made it to combat; indeed by the time we were on maneuvers in Louisiana that summer it had been relegated to the exclusive use of the division's chaplains, who were never tempted to walk on the waters with its aid. Sockalexis also disappeared from our midst. It was not clear how he was disposed of; he had several times been soddenly drunk and had crashed Captain Collier's jeep on his last binge. Like Supinski, he never made it to Italy. Sergeant Tarnow got himself appointed to OCS at the end of Louisiana maneuvers and we never saw him again.

The army is not a family although you often get very close to people. This closeness is based upon affection and trust and it establishes a remarkably clear boundary between "us" and "them." Supinski, Captain Collier, Sockalexis, General Sloan were a world apart, an unambiguous "they" separated from those of "us" who were bound together by common judgment and friendship. Rank as such did not enter into this bifurcation.

Combat intensified it to a degree nigh unto despair, for there life itself depends upon those who are close. A family may nourish or wound its members though it is rare that it actually, in fact and deed, allows life to cease. Close-knit families consider all those outside the blood relationship as "them" while ruefully admitting to the eccentricities and occasional horrors of Great-aunt Lou or Uncle Harold or the brother they privately enjoy the thought of killing. In the daily commerce of adult life it is a sign of muddy thought and obscure misjudgment to refer to a ficti-tious "they" who can be blamed for the woes of the world. It is a state of mind that reaches toward paranoia and it is a rueful facet of maturity to realize that there is no "they." In the army this is not so; there is a "they" both in the actuality of certain officers who are pigheaded and dangerous, and in the direct and visceral way of having someone next to you who cannot be trusted with your life. The "us" I was acquainted with in the army were remarkably tolerant of many faults, even of coward-ice if it was owned up to and admitted to without chicanery.

There was a young second lieutenant with the First Battalion when I was battalion operations sergeant. He was assigned to a platoon in Company A. One night when there was a fierce fire-fight above us on the slopes, a dark night, cold and rainy, he came down to our dugout, shivering and crying. It was clear that he could no longer be trusted with the command of a platoon. Our colonel, a sensible man, one of "us," gave him a shot of whiskey and assigned him to a post farther to the rear with the battalion supply officer. No more was made of it. Time passed as it does so inexorably in war; men were killed and wounded, posts were reassigned and the second lieutenant was promoted to first lieutenant and made supply officer of the battalion. On another dark night, under another bloody hill, a pathetic and shivering PFC came straggling into headquarters, obviously near a nervous breakdown if not actually in the throes of one. As fate would have it the new supply officer was the only man on duty. "Back up you go," he said with his hand on his pistol. "No cowards in this man's army!" The soldier gulped, left the dugout, and went back up to his company. There was fierce action up on the mountain that night and the private was killed. From that moment on the lieutenant was a branded member of the race of "them." He was always spoken to with the utmost formality, as befitted a moral failure. He liked the army and moved on to a higher echelon before the war ended, planning to stay on as a regular officer in peacetime.

The faithful and the friendly, the real "we" of the I and R platoon, all lasted through Louisiana maneuvers and we all ended up in Italy. All of us suffered combat; some of us died early on, others later. In our last autumn in combat, on Monte Battaglia just south of Imola, I saw one of us being evacuated with a sucking chest wound; a week before the end of the war another blew off his left foot and his testicles stepping on a land mine only a few yards from our dugout. In that bizarre centrifuge which constitutes the memory of old age, it is the dead who are the most alive; they are the ones who remain.

We were a varied group. There were three Slavs among us, though it is only in hindsight that I name them as such, recent history making me more aware of ethnic classifications: Gorbachewski, a fat Pole from Chicago, patient and lovable; Sohanchek, a chunky Ukrainian, a steelworker from Pittsburgh, full of brio and vigor and unceasingly amorous; and Chabek, a compact Czech from Cleveland, clean and elegant in his ways. There was Bianchi, a tall, ugly, and sympathetic Italian with a hooked nose whose family had a grocery store in Rochester, and my perpetual pal from outside Memphis, the Tennessee Syrian, Joe Isaac. He was round and hairy, lazy and completely reliable.

Then there were the two who died first, Jack McCauley and Leonard. Though it was usual in the army to call people by their last names, Jack was always called Jack. Blue-eyed and blond, he was the most unpretentious of men, distinguished by his utter candor. He worked in his father's hardware store in Canton, Ohio. At nineteen, the year after he graduated, he had married his high school sweetheart and had produced two tiny children, whose pictures we all admired. He was a devout churchgoer, a Baptist by upbringing, and always attended the chapel services when we were at Camp Gruber.

Jack had what some of us called, without malice, a second marriage. His constant companion and second self was a dour Presbyterian named Whitmore. Jack was the radio man of the I and R platoon and Whitmore was a radio repair man in the communications section of HQ Company. It was a profound friendship, unblinking and candid, with never a thought in either of their minds, or in any of ours, that anything sexual was involved. Stronger than the memory of poor Jack's death is the picture in my mind of Whitmore's stricken face, not only at the moment when he received the news, but ever after when I would see him at work in the midst of his paraphernalia of wires and tubes and soldering irons. I often imagine him, a solitary bachelor, moving through the long arch of his years, living with the ache of his loss, visiting Jack's children in some bucolic Ohio where the mother would have married a chum of Jack's from their high school class.

As for Leonard, I was the only one who called him that, even though he always called me Allanbrook and never Douglas. The first time he spoke to me, a week or so after I had joined the I and R platoon, it was direct: "Well, Allanbrook, I hear we're both from Mass." I admitted to being from Boston. "It's the other end of the state," he said, "but it's still Mass. I'm from the valley just south of Greenfield. We grow tobacco." He stated this with just the right amount of familial pride. I had seen those farms on a bicycle trip I had taken the summer I was sixteen. As we pedaled along a level road parallel to the Connecticut River, fields covered with muslin caught our attention. "Tobacco," said one of our group, a boy who had relatives in Greenfield. We continued on our youth hostel tour of Massachusetts and Vermont. The cloth-covered fields never crossed my mind until that moment in the barracks of HQ Company, 350th Infantry, Camp Gruber,

Oklahoma, five years later, when Leonard said "We grow to-bacco" and smiled the pleasantest of smiles, crinkling the skin around his eyes. He had a longish face and walked with a kind of low-slung lope. (Joe Isaac called him a Yankee hound dog.) His voice, to my Boston ear, had a country twang. "We grow a special leaf in the Connecticut Valley that's the best thing to wrap a fancy cigar in," he explained to me. "We ship 'em all down to Cuba."

Half a century later, sitting in a pseudo-Victorian bar on Broadway in Saratoga Springs, the group of men I was with, a generation younger than myself, all of them successful, rich, and moderately pretentious, offered me an expensive cigar. Though I had not smoked for over fifteen years I accepted one, lit up, and took a few puffs. It took only a very short time for my memory to be jolted, for me to apprehend the reason for my near invol-untary acceptance of the fancy cigar, for me to make out within the twisted corridors of recollection the western Massachusetts cadence of Leonard's voice. When I write now it is with a clear awareness of those long-distant times with my fellow soldier Leonard, dead so soon after our arrival at Naples. I am simulta-neously aware that at the time we were not intimate. There was not that stringent friendship that bound poor Jack and Whit-more, though there certainly was mutual liking and affection. When we were still up at Camp Gruber we would often discuss together whether he would be able to swing his forthcoming marriage to his hometown girl after the dreaded summer in Louisiana that we all knew was imminent. Why was he so in-tensely present in future years when back then he seemed only to be one among the "us" of the I and R platoon? "How far from then forethought of" says Hopkins in his sonnet on the death of Felix Randal as he contemplates the brawny and active reality of the now dead blacksmith. After a war, when the killing is over, the mind becomes a dwelling full of haunted corridors, alive with loves and regrets, all inexorably wedded to places and sounds, a memorial realer by far than any public tomb. In it reside known soldiers!

My removal from Camp Gruber to the maneuvers area in Louisiana was a miasma of heat, bugs, sweat, and grease. I drew KP for the entire three days of the move and on into the first three days of the maneuvers. I was not made a corporal until we reached Fort Sam Houston at the end of our stay in Louisiana; as a PFC and not a noncom I was subject to such indignities. Supinski had a lot to do with it; I was uppity and due for promotion and it gave him pleasure to torture me before I got out of his control. KP was unabashedly horrid when we were in camp; on the move and on maneuvers it was a nightmare: loading and unloading pans, pots of food slithering around the back of two-and-a-half-ton trucks, setting up and taking down a mess line in the course of a few hours, feeding stations in the middle of the night, sloshing greasy implements in grayish water full of livid soap bubbles while the trucks bumped along an obscure dirt road. I got no sense of the country we were passing through as we left Oklahoma, plunged into Arkansas and the Ozarks at Fort Smith, and on south into Louisiana. The smells of rancid cooking oil and tired coffee, the taste of green powdered eggs and gray sausage, the slipperiness of grease on the fingers, the stiff resistance of sweat-laden woolen uniforms, the sight of trucks' headlights at ten in the night glancing off trees at a bivouac revealing hundreds of men standing in line waiting to be fed: all of these senses in common mingle into a single recollection, all time erased.

Once released from KP I could open my eyes and take in the piny wastes of the army maneuvers area, a vast tract of land between the Texas border and Nacogdoches, where scrub growth on sandy soil is interspersed with swamps. The heat was suffocating, all the more as we were required at all times to wear our regulation woolen uniforms. As a member of the I and R platoon I was able to ride in a jeep much of the time. I would often pass C Company as they trudged along some dusty expanse and would avert my eyes, ashamed, as I rode by. Nine years later when riding with my rich Genoese friend Aldo in his chauffeur-driven car south of Paestum I was caught by that same emotion. We were on a rough stretch of road south of Agropoli and passed a group of peasant women working by the side of the road, breaking rocks into gravel for a new road surface. "Beati voi!" two of them called out as we rolled by stirring up a cloud of dust. "Lucky you!" They were right; I was lucky. Most remarkable was the lack of rancor in their voices, which carried the timelessness of acceptance and, as so often seemed the case when I was living around Naples, mirrored the state of soul of the ordinary soldier bound to his years of servitude.

The enormous war games in Louisiana that summer were designed entirely by and for the hierarchy of staffs that controlled battalions, regiments, divisions, and army corps. They needed the practice, it was said; we were merely the matter they played with. We were divided into two armies, endlessly backing and filling, moving left and right or diagonally, encircling and enveloping, winning and losing according to a strict accounting by observation teams of staff officers. Experiments with water discipline and with the maximum number of miles possible in a day's march were another part of the exercises. I doubt whether the assembled field officers, clustered under their respective generals, learned anything of any particular value that long, hot summer. Nothing in Italy resembled in the slightest any of the maneuvers which we played at in Louisiana. For all the countless thousands not riding around in staff cars, it was a dreary progression of sweltering misery, black as Hades at night to simulate the conditions to be encountered in combat and hot as Hell in the daytime with the pitiless sun of July and August overhead.

The Sabine River is the western boundary of southern Louisiana. Across it lies the state of Texas. Five of us from the I and R platoon were deposited on a grassy knoll overlooking the river toward the end of August. Two more men, one from the 349th and one from the 351st regiments, were added to our group to serve as liaison with their respective regiments. We were positioned at the extreme left flank of our army so that we might spy out any flanking movements of the "red" army, our enemy in the war games. No officer was with us; our instructions were to keep in touch by radio every two hours, all the while keeping a sharp lookout for the enemy. Jack was our radio man and the rest of us — Joe Isaac, Dreschel, Leonard, and I — had very little to do. The two men from our sister regiments had even less responsibility; they were only required to check in with their headquarters once every twelve hours, unless, of course, there was an incursion of the reds. The PFC from the 349th was a blond fellow, faunlike in appearance; later in Italy he became a chaplain's assistant, a post almost always held by youths of delicate bearing. The sergeant from the 351st was large and ruddy, and, as it turned out, of a most sanguine temperament. We had been given adequate supplies, enough for four or five days. What was most unexpected to all of us after the piny barrens and the swampy miasma of the maneuvers area was the pristine clarity of the waters of the Sabine. It flowed languidly past us, bordered by red cedar trees, nuzzling its way around hummocks and sandbanks. Late the first afternoon our riverine idyll began.

We were all down at the edge of the river, dabbling our feet in the water, except for sweet Jack who remained faithfully attached to his radio up on top of the knoll. Our mood was benign; we were far from the world we had become so inured to, far from the heat and the misery of the endless war games, far from Sergeant Supinski and the whole noisome hierarchy of rank which stretched from our flaccid intelligence officer, Captain Collier, all the way up to our bantam rooster of a general. We were on our own. The little blond from the 349th had slipped off upstream and I was half asleep when I heard his voice. "Come on in, boys; or are you too chicken?" He emerged from the river smack in front of us, naked, his white skin catching the yellowish slant of the late afternoon sun, his slim body proportioned like that of Donatello's lissome *David*, which I saw at the end of the war in Florence. "Lick my dick," said the sergeant from the 351st, "if he ain't a caution. I'm goin' in after." He was only the first to strip and to plunge into the waters of that very special river, which sets off East Texas from Louisiana. Its name, the Sabine, seemed so classical to me as I stripped off my clothes and entered its cooling waters, flashing me back to my high school Latin classes. Our Latin teacher had made a great deal of the rape of the Sabine women. I learned two months later in San Antonio, from a Chicano friend, that the name came from *sabines*, the Spanish word for "red cedar," the trees which cast such dappled shadow on our cove.

We spent the next three days bald-assed naked. We had been burdened with clothes ever since we had been inducted into the army. All that tropical summer in Louisiana we trod our dreary paths with woolen uniforms, full field packs, ammunition belts, steel helmets, and our ever-present M-1s. When we shucked off our military skins — uniforms, insignia, rank — and our bodies played in the light and shade of that limpid stream, we were more naked than any civilian ever was. There was Dreschel like a great dray horse, big all over; Joe Isaac, solid and round as a basketball; myself, 125 pounds, with my hair still jet black, skinny and smooth-skinned; and Leonard, low slung like a sleek hound dog, with muscular thighs, sloping shoulders, and a massive and well-proportioned prick. "Your girl's gonna be one happy little wife when a tool like that ruminates around in her," said the irrepressible sergeant from the 351st, to Leonard's only slight discomfiture. He had already told me he was now planning to marry after maneuvers were over, either going back East to Massachusetts on a furlough or having the ceremony at Fort Sam Houston, where we now knew we were scheduled to go in September.

Only sweet Jack, up on top of the knoll, kept his clothes on, ever faithful to his radio, watchful of the enemy, the make-believe reds. From his eyrie he could contemplate the scene below: the shapes and colors of the bodies, the red cedars shading the silvery current, the water distorting the bodies it rippled over. In later years painters' pictures of bathers would recall to me those innocent days we spent together in that unlikely Eden, the Sabine River. We were so young, none of us over twenty-three.

My trip from Louisiana over to Fort Sam Houston in San Antonio was made in the company of Sergeant Supinski. His Slavic eyes had been studying me during the last weeks of the maneuvers. He felt he had punished me sufficiently with the KP I had pulled at the beginning of the summer and that I would now be rewarded. He had a Polish snobbery, carrying it about with him from the hidden years of his life in Europe. He looked down upon fat, good-natured Gorbachewski as a lower-class immigrant Pole and considered Sohanchek, the Ukrainian from Pittsburgh, to be a member of an inferior tribe, a vulgar Americanized peasant. He had taken note of my books and of my musical scores and knew about my piano playing. I was by now the invaluable map reader of regimental HQ, consulted by my superiors in that capacity. My name was unmistakably English. I found him hateful but he felt it a flattery to share with me his sardonic opinions of his platoon, considering me worthy to be classed with whatever elite he felt he was a member of. For three days I rode in his jeep as he propelled it across East and Central Texas at breakneck speeds. He took upon himself, as the sergeant of the Intelligence and Reconnaissance platoon, to be the avant-garde of the regimental move. We would leave well before the convoy of trucks started, often before dawn, spurt ahead twenty or thirty miles to an appropriate beer joint, drink until the regiment appeared in the perspective of the straight highway behind, and then move on to the next lap, ending the day, lightheaded and buoyant, in the area selected for the evening's bivouac. It was a tonic release from the weeks and months of heat and blackouts, from the bugs and the dirt. The unbelievable delays and the terrible and endless heat of the Louisiana summer were over. Supinski's native ruthlessness made a cutting edge that ended what had seemed an endless course of time. His driving made the Texas plain a race course into the immediate future: Fort Sam Houston.

The two months we spent at Fort Sam were the only pleasant stretch of time the regiment was ever to enjoy. We began to get a feel for what the old army must have been like. The colonel felt at home; the sergeant major was in his native element. There were permanent buildings, barracks like well-endowed dormitories, Spanish-style headquarters, separate houses for officers and married noncoms. A pleasant bus ride brought us into a pleasant city, San Antonio, an oasis afloat with good Mexican beer. Duty was light. We were being fattened for the kill and work was kept to a minimum.

These brief months at Fort Sam were broken by two events: my furlough (two weeks back home in Melrose) and Leonard's wedding in the post chapel. It took a long time to get home; the railroads were in the full flush of wartime traffic, the trains crowded with soldiers and soldiers' wives and babies all criss-crossing the country, burdened with delays and sleeplessness and the anxieties of leavetakings and brief homecomings. There never were enough seats and most of us were chivalrous enough to offer our places to some desperate mother with a squalling baby who had just left her husband at El Paso ten hours earlier and still had to make it all the way to Gary, Indiana. Twenty-four hours to St. Louis and another twenty-four to Penn Station in New York, up to Times Square on the subway, across town on the shuttle to Grand Central, and then what seemed, after the endless western odyssey, a mere jaunt on the New Haven up to South Station in Boston, on over to North Station in a taxi, and, at long last, the oh-so-familiar twenty-minute ride on the suburban train out to Melrose.

My father was tongue-tied, unbearably proud of me. I was now what he had so fervently desired to be, back in his war. He had enlisted in the militia in 1916 and had loved it but had not gone to the war: he was myopic and recently married and there was a child on the way, my older sister. How could I explain to him the misery and the humiliation of Camp Gruber and of the Louisiana maneuvers. I now had a corporal's two stripes and I wore a sharpshooter badge on my chest. I saw that I had proved myself to my father; he had always had doubts about my being a musician, about my endless reading of books, about my ability to make a living, and, even more, about my seeming insouciance. I believe he never suspected the worry and insecurity I felt during my three years of teaching at that fancy girls' school down in Providence, earning my fifty dollars a month plus room and board, scrabbling to make a go of it as a musician in those bitter days at the end of the Great Depression. My father and my mother were both air-raid wardens, equipped with helmets and badges, which they shyly but proudly showed to me. They were doing their part and their only son was doing his. Something began to change: there at home in Fellsview Terrace, two blocks above the railroad station, in the luxury of a prolonged hot bath, looking at myself from my family's point of view, I began to be proud of my year in the army.

When it was time for me to leave they drove me into South Station where my mother wept as I boarded the New York train for the first lap of my return trip, her imagination full of pictures of what might be in store for me. More than a year later, around Christmas time in the cold of the Apennines, I received a bizarre package from her. Moldy fruitcakes were gifts which many of us received from home; there was a surfeit of them, few of us liked them very much, and at this particular juncture of our lives there was a special redundancy in seeing them arrive on mule-back, battered and misshapen after the precipitous climb up from Highway 65. My mother, a teetotaler from a most Christian background, had packed a real surprise. Inside my fruitcake she had illegally embedded a bottle of scotch. "This war has wrought wonders back in Fellsview Terrace," I remarked with a giggle to the only officer I was ever close to, Lieutenant Boatner. I was by then the operations sergeant of the First Battalion and he the operations officer. My little sister wrote that my mother, immediately after dispatching the camouflaged package, had begun to worry, her imagination picturing me as wandering drunk into the German lines!

Leonard's wife was a dear, broad of beam and beneficent;

one immediately pictured her as a mother. She had come all the long way down from Greenfield, Massachusetts, to San Antonio, traveling alone, arriving only two days before the wedding. The whole I and R platoon served as attendants and I was both best man and organist. They entered the chapel with *Lohengrin* but I sent them out with the well-known E-major Sonata of Scarlatti, pepping it up with the astringent clarity that the Hammond electric organ could emit when the overtone drawbars were properly adjusted. She had wanted "Oh Promise Me" for the middle of the service and I gave it to them as they knelt together in front of the chaplain, employing the slight wobble of the organ's diapason in combination with the vox humana. We all went downtown for a meal at a Mexican restaurant and drank a lot of good Mexican beer. Leonard was so grateful to me; he kept squeezing my hand and repeating, "Allanbrook, thank you, thank you!" It came to me that though I knew him and liked him his feelings toward me were deeper and more heartfelt than I had realized.

I had found for the two of them a little apartment attached to the rectory of the Episcopal church in San Antonio. It was the second time that year that my former life at the Wheeler School caught up with me. Virginia, a modest and intelligent girl who had taught there with me, had subsequently married an Episcopal priest. Several times I would spend a decorous but alcoholic evening with them, taking the bus into town, leaving behind the world of HQ Company and Sergeant Supinski for the quiet intimacy of Virginia and her civilized husband. Their apartment made a pleasant nest for Leonard and his bride, only too brief as we left Fort Sam within a month of the marriage.

We knew we were headed for a port of embarkation but, as was always the case, we knew no more than that. The Pacific had loomed large in our speculations but our train headed straight east from San Antonio, passing through Fort Worth and on into East Texas. We were provided with actual sleeping cars on this, the second of my army train trips, a far cry from the anonymous and sordid discomfort of that first cross-country trek from Fort Devens to Oklahoma. As a result we were asleep when we crossed the Mississippi and awoke as we approached Jackson. After several days of slow travel through Alabama, Georgia, and the Carolinas we eliminated New York as a possible port of embarkation. Awakening early one morning in the station at Richmond, Virginia, we heard that we were headed for Newport News. On the station platform was a little black boy tap-dancing all alone on that late November morning of 1943, the sun just barely visible through the gray clouds to the east. He grinned and held out his hat for our nickels and dimes. One of our junior officers let us know that we were headed for Africa and that from now on our whereabouts was a military secret and that all of our letters would bear only APO#88 as an address and that it would be his fucking duty to censor all of the company's mail.

The barracks at Newport News were covered in black tarpaper and smoke curled from their chimneys, merging into the foggy drip of a southern winter. They were situated back from the port, their streets angling off into the dim perspective of the pine barrens. Our principal activity for a week was the packing and unpacking of our A bags and our B bags. The B bags were to go in the hold of the ship and we were to carry the A bags aboard. What was to go into each of these bags was being debated by the upper echelons. Orders and counterorders appeared three times that fateful week, our last on native soil. Upon each order all of our goods and chattels would be set out for inspection on our cots in the barracks and on the floor around them. The company officers officiated at the first inspection and subsequent stowing away, but soon tired of the game, leaving it to the sergeants to police the second and third redistributions.

On the day of our embarkation we left the barracks at 0430 hours. We were still saddled with both our A and our B bags, obliged to stagger under their weight onto the trucks which carted us down to a great shed which abutted the pier. New orders awaited us. An officer with a megaphone announced, "The following items which are now in your A bag are to be placed in your B bag, and the following items which are now in your B bag are to be placed in your A bag." Our first sergeant, a calm and beatific old soldier from the regular army, was livid. "I'd like to shove them bags up your ass," he said to the officers in general and to the supply major in particular, who was bellowing at us through his megaphone. We were packed into the shed; there was no room to spread things out. Hundreds of men were plunging their hands into their bags, trying to ascertain by feel the location of the desired item to be transferred. Their arms would then emerge from the bag and attempt to deposit the required object into the other bag. Hopelessness ensued; rage rose in all our breasts as the list droned on, objects being named at a rate of speed that made retrieval and deposit a near impossibility. The reading of the lists came suddenly to a halt. A naval officer was observed talking to our company commander, who threw up his hands. "Close your fucking bags and take them out that door," said our weary first sergeant. Once outdoors we saw for the first time what awaited us: out in the roads were Liberty ships, cutters, lighters, destroyers, escort vessels, a vast flotilla all gathered under the lowering winter light, the outlines of the further vessels obscured as our eyes tried to penetrate the morning's haze. As we contemplated our foggy future a steely chill settled in our innards. Some relief was forthcoming when we were ordered to deposit our B bags in sizable carts, which were being trundled off to a waiting lighter to be ferried out to one of the shadowy vessels far out in the roads. We had now only to take ourselves and our A bags to another lighter, which then proceeded to bear us over the glossy surface to our appointed Liberty ship, our home for the next twenty-five days.

The bunks were five high with the narrowest of passageways between. They surrounded on four sides a large square space in which stood a number of massive metal trash barrels. A steel gangway led up to the deck, where we were encouraged to go during the day; at night we were buttoned up below. Blackout discipline was strict as there was always danger from U-boats as the huge convoy zigzagged across the South Atlantic. I was lucky and agile enough to secure for myself and for my A bag a top bunk. In the metal of the ceiling just above me was a light, which made it possible for me to read up on the heights, something which was difficult if not impossible in the darkness of the lower bunks.

A crap game soon established itself in the square below. It became a nightly spectacle and grew in magnitude and intensity as the voyage progressed. By the time we hit the Azores thousands of dollars would hang on a single throw of the dice. A special crew of professionals specialized in side bets. I was friends with a mortar sergeant from our heavy weapons company, Joe Kovacs from Kansas City, and it was a pleasure watching him win huge amounts of money. He had run a club back home and boasted of his political connections. "As your friend," he told me, "I wouldn't advise you to get within ten feet of that game. You'd be skunked and them punks would find some way to screw you once they seen your honest little puss!" I stayed well on the sidelines. Joe would sometimes play for me and once made $250 out of a ten-dollar bill I gave him. It was a floating world; neither the $10 nor the $250 seemed to matter; it might as well have been Monopoly money for all the importance I gave to the 1:25 ratio between my stake and my winnings. The professional gamblers, such as Joe, took professional pride in their play, but the money was only a cipher; civilian life — families, jobs, mortgages — was a long way away. We were, all of us, in the hold of that small iron ship, detached from our old world, zigzagging across the Atlantic. We were bound for Africa from where, it was perfectly clear, we would go to Italy. That would be our new world. There would be no more buying and selling as there was in our old world, at home. Dollar bills with their comforting motto, "In God We Trust," would become as much play money as were the pretty Banque d'Algérie notes we got in

Oran and the patently specious money the Allied Military Government (AMG) printed up in Italy.

Objects became important; they could be substituted for money, thrown in as side bets. Somewhere between the Azores and our first sight of the Portuguese coast my wristwatch was stolen. That was a loss! It was a handsome and sturdy Giraud-Perregaux and I missed it. It bore my name engraved on the back, and the date my father had given it to me: April 1, 1943, my first birthday in the army. I resented its being a pawn in the nocturnal frenzy of the crap game. My father had paid for it with real money earned from his labors as an assistant credit man for the Texas Oil Company in its downtown office in Shawmut Square, Boston.

Weeks later, inland from Oran, not far from Sidi-bel-Abbès, we were bivouacked at the bottom of an arroyo in semiarid country. KC Joe came up to me one night. "Allanbrook," he said, "I see'd a watch with your name on it at that game up on top. You want we should get it?" I tagged after him up the hill. A fire was burning; it was a chilly night and the fire provided both warmth and illumination for the game. Twenty or more men were involved, not only from HQ Company but lots of unknowns from the various line companies, including six tough-looking men from Joe Kovacs's mortar platoon. The glow from the fire picked out the five-gallon cans full of the red wine we had been buying from the Arabs ever since we landed in Oran. The cold of the December night increased everyone's thirst. Joe walked up to the game, peered at several men who were making side bets, reached down, and straightened up, holding my wristwatch by its strap. He studied the back of the watch while around him all activity ceased. "I'll be damned," he said. "It's written 'Douglas Allanbrook' right here on the back. That's your name, I reckon." He tossed the watch over to me. "I don't figure we got any more business with these folks. They're playin' mighty rough." His pals from the mortar platoon guffawed and we meandered back down the hill.

Memory is akin to fiction: it selects. Its desire is to encompass and to encapsulate. More than eighteen months later, Joe Kovacs and I were still extant, alive and kicking in the city of Modena where the regiment was in charge of a German POW camp. We had survived the war as had the German prisoners. Joe and I, and a former horse-room operator from Jersey City called Mike, set up a nightclub for enlisted men in the basement of an automotive factory just outside town. There I was able to match and even to cap Joe's gesture back (so far back!) in that arroyo in the desert out beyond Sidi-bel-Abbès. These two events are linked in my memory; it leaps over the dreary time, the blood, the mud, the dead, and the bitter Italian mountains. Why look at the Gorgon's head? There's no dividend in spelling out the daily truth of a war as it plods from one dreary day to the next.

All of us there in Modena were survivors and good times were our prerogative. We wanted to drink and get laid; that's how the nightclub came about. The Germans had a warehouse full of loot: Biscuit cognac in amazing abundance, Moët and Chandon champagne, case upon case of excellent burgundies, silk stockings, and frilly lace underwear. Our officers were helping themselves to all of this and drinking themselves silly. I had become aware that the SS division behind our barbed wire included a full-fledged symphony orchestra; their medical battalion did double duty as it was largely composed of professional musicians. Some music-loving SS general had arranged all of this. Putting the orchestra and the liquor and the silk stockings together was my invention: liquor for the boys, silk stockings for the girls, and music for everyone! We would all benefit from the goodies the Germans had so painstakingly gotten together. Joe thought highly of the project and enlisted Jack, the heavy-weapons sergeant from Jersey City. I was to be boss; I was the battalion operations sergeant and eminently respectable. Joe ran the liquor, and Mike the ladies and the games. We got it ready within a week. There was a boy from my old C Company who had been a sign painter and was clever with his brush. (He was among the mere twenty percent of my old line company still alive at the end of that brutal nineteen months.) He covered the walls of the huge factory basement with slashes of blue and white clouds, all sailing over a green ocean replete with mermaids and sharks. At one end a platform was created for the orchestra; at the other end was the entrance and, more important, my office. We sold our Biscuit cognac, our Moët champagne, and our burgundies at ridiculously low prices; we paid the local girls who were our waitresses in silk stockings and perfume. They were delighted; such things had not been seen in years.

On the eve of our opening black marketeers appeared, bartering dreadful local cognac and grappa for cartons of cigarettes or bundles of lire and AMG money. We quickly made a hard and fast rule against such commerce but the practice continued, local men slipping in with the waitresses. Many of them were pimps since few of the girls remained as waitresses for more than two or three nights. On the third night of our operation I saw a clear case of illegal activity: bottles were being bartered at one of the tables up under the orchestra's platform. Our SS symphony had just finished a fervent performance of "Tales from the Vienna Woods" and was launching into a spiffy arrangement of "Tea for Two." (I had tapped the Army Special Services up in Milan for the score and parts.) From my office I could see the misdemeanor clearly. I motioned to my two henchmen to flank me and strode forth onto the dance floor. As I approached the guilty table I gestured to the conductor, an SS sergeant, to stop. He had the habit of obeying orders instantly and "Tea for Two" was strangled in midphrase. A hush ensued. I walked up to the table, picked up the offending bottle of local liquor and smashed it against the wall. I signaled the orchestra to resume, turned on my heel and regained my office with KC Joe on my left and Jersey City Jack on my right. "Well, fuck a two-bit whore," said Joe. "If you ain't quite the dude, Allanbrook. You can come work for me in KC any time you want." I grinned and held up my wristwatch, flashing back nineteen months to the crap game outside Sidi-bel-Abbès. My performance and Joe's admiration bucked me up more than my staff sergeant's stripes and the medals I wore on my chest: the combat infantry badge, the two campaign ribbons, and the Bronze Star.

4

THE TWENTY-FIVE DAYS on the Liberty ship dragged on. We tried the showers out. They were salt water; the more you took the itchier you got. We gave them up. Eating was a trial: not only was the food bad but the requirement was that it be eaten up on deck. The order was meant to be salubrious; the hold was noisome and overcrowded. The difficulty lay in attaining the deck. We had to negotiate a steep iron stairway which led through a hatchway to the upper world. The food, deposited into a metal tray, was generally semiliquid so that we had to firmly grasp and balance the tray against the ship's motion, a difficult exercise in coordination as the sea was often rough. The ascent of the stairway accomplished, we had to exercise great caution or the narrow hatchway would catch us on the back of the head. Three meals a day came and went in this manner.

Our own officers and the Merchant Marines could be observed eating chicken and steaks at proper tables in a wardroom adjacent to our squalid square. A Liberty ship is a small vessel with little opportunity for concealment. Up on deck the authorities attempted to have us do something besides eating and sitting in the sun. I cooperated, reading French conversational phrases and military terms in a loud voice while certain members of the I and R platoon would hoot them back at me. We learned not only to say "bonjour" but, as befitted our military

status, to address French officers as "mon capitaine" and to learn
the French words for machine gun, rifle, and artillery piece. I
taught them to count, to say "vin," and to know that the word
"baiser," given the appropriate circumstances, meant "fuck"
rather than "kiss."

One night in mid-Atlantic, just before dawn, there was an
enormous thump, followed by an echoing boom. All of us,
sealed below decks in our hollow square, piled five high in our
bunks, awoke with a shudder. Ever since Newport News we had
been zigzagging to avoid German submarine attacks. It was a
false alarm: one of the metal trash cans had broken loose from
its moorings and was rolling from side to side across the central
square. The gamblers, startled out of sleep, took advantage of
their wakefulness and began a game that lasted until breakfast
appeared. Supinski snarled at us: "What you do when the Germans aim mortars at you and you know they know where you
are?" The scar on his right cheek flushed red against his sallow
skin as he spoke. We got to know mortars well enough in a few
months. One round would land in front of you, then another in
back of you. You knew very well from having directed mortar
fire yourself that the next one would land precisely between the
first two and that that could very well be "it." Terror, shrinking
terror! You wait for the dull plop over the hill to tell you that the
mortar shell has left on its arched journey. Sometimes there was
no third round and out of relief you sweated just as heavily. You
had not been pinpointed. There turned out, after all, to have
been no observer up there on the crest.

We arrived in Oran the day before Christmas, 1943. On the
right as we entered the roundish harbor was an old Spanish fort,
medieval and properly foreign. Once we disembarked into the
actual city nothing so picturesque was to be seen: the waterfront
might as well have been Hoboken. Toting our bags we piled into
the usual two-and-half-ton trucks and pulled off up the hill
through a series of streets that looked like Worcester, Massachusetts — except for street signs written in French and the presence

of a few Arabs dressed in bathrobes. Old-fashioned streetcars ran down the middle of roads flanked with ugly nineteenth-century apartment houses. The city was quiet as we drove through on that Christmas Eve. We were unceremoniously dumped on a muddy hillside on the edge of town. It abutted onto a ravine on the other side of which was a poorish quarter with a few cafés, a Catholic church, lots of Arabs. It had a more "foreign" atmosphere than downtown.

We were lined up by platoons, each man instructed to make for himself a place on the ground where he could sleep, spreading out in a rectangle a shelter half (part of a waterproof pup tent) and blankets and placing his A bag so as to define the top of the rectangle and to serve as a pillow. Food was provided from the back of mess trucks. Slit trenches were dug at the extremities of the company streets for defecation, while large, square tin cans stood at regular intervals along the streets for urinating. It grew colder as night fell; we heard the bells from the Catholic church. There was a desultory feeling in the encampment and no orders were given regarding anything in particular. The church bells gave some suggestion of Christmas but the sky was starless, sullen and dark. Occasional herds of goats passed by, tended by Arabs: no sheep and no shepherds. The keening of a muezzin floated over the area, coming from some unseen mosque.

As it grew still darker and colder, Arabs appeared with mule-drawn carts. They bore large demijohns of wine, which they bartered for cartons of cigarettes. It was rotgut red. We wandered down the ravine and up the other side to a tawdry café we had spotted. Our only order was that we were to be back in the area by midnight. Some of us ventured into the little Catholic church and watched the priest officiating, while a group of old women quavered out the responses in the "Missa Angelorum." Everyone, even those of us who went to the mass, drank; most returned to the encampment drunk. The exception was, of course, faithful Jack, the radio man, who had remained up on the area playing rummy with his buddy Whitmore, the radio repair sergeant. In bedding down, the most difficult variables to be dealt with were the irregularities, the rocks and roots on the rough ground. Was it feasible to soften the irregularity with items from the A bag? As the hours passed that proved far less important than trying to keep warm. The temperature descended to below freezing. No one undressed. After careful mummylike envelopment in the blankets our GI overcoats were draped and tucked in as an outer layer. The officers and some of the staff sergeants, including Supinski, had lovely eiderdown sleeping bags: yet another tangible, and elemental comfort that distinguished "them" from "us." (Twelve months later in the high Apennines south of Bologna I purloined an eiderdown sleeping bag from an officer of the 42nd Division as we relieved them in the line. What a happy theft! — such warmth and such lightness to carry on the icy mountain tracks.)

We had not foreseen the physiological effects of sleeping on the ground in the cold African night after twenty-five nights in the fetid confines of the Liberty ship. Four and five times a night the bladder had to be emptied. The red Algerian wine added to the burden. Curses rang out all through the night on that hillside outside Oran as men fought against undoing the cocoon of their blankets and overcoats, against leaving their warm nest, against the absolute necessity of relieving their bladders. It was seldom possible to reestablish the warm coziness that had been abandoned just minutes before. Men varied in their actions: some would slither slowly out, leaving the blanket roll intact; others, in a blaspheming fury, would kick off their covers with a howl. Christmas Day dawned. The tall tin cans which lined the streets of our encampment were overflowing; the pale reek of urine was omnipresent in the cold morning air. (Unbeknownst to us on that Christmas of 1943 our future whereabouts was being decided on that same North African coast. Churchill met with Eisenhower, Alexander, and other high Allied leaders outside Tunis, on the site of ancient Carthage. He wanted them to at-

tempt a landing at Anzio, just to the south of Rome, and perse-
vered until they agreed, though none of them were enthusiastic.)

Later that Christmas day the first sergeant gave me orders to
report to the regimental chaplain. "Corporal Allanbrook," he
said, "get your ass over to Chaplain Beaufort and play some of
his Baptist hymns for him. We ain't got no choice; we're all in
this together." The first sergeant was a Catholic, a Cajun from
Louisiana. He had small regard for Protestants and detested
Captain Beaufort, a Baptist minister from South Carolina. Beaufort called himself a "riding parson" and all through Italy would
flash his captain's bars at frightened country people and procure by hook or by crook leather saddles for his happy return
to the back country he came from. Once in the line in Italy the
first sergeant had no choice but to work with the man, as their
duties were complementary: the chaplain's principal task being
to write letters of condolence to the families of men who had
been killed, and the first sergeant's to keep track of morning
reports and casualties and to turn over to the chaplain the appropriate names.

Two pieces of equipment were standard issue for a chaplain
in the field: the first, a portable altar which could quickly change
its orientation from Catholic to Protestant and just as quickly
from Christian to Jewish by the simple device of rotating on its
base and exposing to the worshipers the appropriate icons; the
second, a small portable pump organ. A surprisingly large
group of men had gathered by the edge of the ravine. I pumped
vigorously through the solid Baptist hymns the chaplain had
chosen. He exhorted us to be of good faith in this joyous Christmas season of Christian fellowship. As the service was ending
Arabs came up the hill with more demijohns of Algerian red on
their carts. I noticed a flicker of interest in their eyes as they
glanced at the altar and the organ. Several pimps appeared soon
after, clutching their crotches and naming their price: "Fucky-
fuck — one carton." Those who followed them down the ravine
and over into the Arab streets came back with differing reports.

Forty-year-old Kerrigan, a horny little Irishman with parch-mentlike skin, always writing to his wife Mary in South Boston, found it perfectly satisfactory. "A load's a load," he said. "One whore's as good as another for dippin' it." Others were put off by the lack of regular "houses" and objected to dirt floors with grass mattresses on the floor. "It was so fucking dark in there you couldn't tell if they was twelve or forty. I dunked my lily and got out fast," Sohanchek reported to me when he returned to the area. Chabek, our elegant Czech, told us his was only eleven years old and he liked it all the better because of it. "Nice and tight," he said, holding his curled forefinger against his thumb to show us how small the hole had been. Gorbachewski, fat and usually of a most sanguine temperament, had been put off by it all. "I couldn't get it up with all that stink and all them Arabs." He proceeded to drink heavily of the rotgut for the rest of Christmas day. The mess truck appeared with a Christmas dinner, which we spooned out into our metal mess kits. Officers there were few: in HQ Company only two lieutenants, one of them a shavetail. As the evening chill descended they disap-peared. Down in the city the hotels had all been requisitioned for use as officers' billets, and there were English-American-French officers' clubs, with French cooks and well-stocked bars.

As bedtime approached on this our second night in Africa the straight streets of our encampment melted away. Everyone looked for some spot where his bed could be placed with mini-mum discomfort: an appropriate natural hollow in the ground which could be comfortably filled, or a space where there would be fewer rocks or olive tree roots and into which one could ensconce one's body, curled up like a snug fetus in the warmth of the womb. Some began to pair up; double blankets and two bodies might do the trick. All that remained of our rectilinear bivouac were the lines of pee cans marching up over the crest of the hill. I found a spot between the roots of an ancient olive, so snug that I resisted, even more than the previous night, the ne-cessities of a full bladder. Lurid dreams resulted, all having their immediate source in the tension within the body, though their erotic content arose out of that subterranean pool wherein lie entwined the particular memories and fantasies which constitute the erotic content of our imaginings. Twice after having peed and reestablished myself within my nest I imagined I heard my name being called — "Allanbrook, Allanbrook!" sounding softly and persistently. That night, the night of Christmas day, was colder than Christmas Eve had been but much clearer. I lay in my cocoon and looked up at the African stars, clear and luminous, shining down through the gnarled branches of the ancient olive. Did I hear the voice or was it my imagination manufacturing pictures out of my bodily state? I drifted off to sleep to wake to the jangle of the bugle cutting through the morning air like a bloody rooster.

The next day, officers made their presence felt, bringing with them the customary illusions of efficiency. We were lined up, the contents of our A bags inspected, lectures given to us as to who we were and who the French were and how they were to be treated. There was quite considerable confusion on this subject what with the Free French, the Pétain French, General Darlan, General de Gaulle, and the French Foreign Legion. We were informed that we would move on the following day to an encampment inland, passing through Sidi-bel-Abbès, the headquarters of the French Foreign Legion. Dire warnings issued from the medics concerning the particularly virulent strain of gonorrhea rampant among the Arab whores. Late that afternoon we were actually submitted to close-order drill followed by that ritual dance called bayonet drill. I had gotten rather adept at it way back at Camp Gruber. One sarcastic lieutenant had suggested I enter a ballet company when the war ended. (In Italy we quickly shucked off our bayonets and every other redundant piece of equipment to ease the burden of our packs as we struggled through the Apennines.) At the end of the day we stood retreat. In the gathering gloom the mess truck appeared and Arabs beckoned around the periphery of our encampment offering their wares. The usual group drifted off down the ravine, over to the cafés and the back alleys. Crap games sprang up, but by midnight we were rolled up in our blankets, dreading our third African night and cursing our bladders.

Wrapped up in my blankets after my first pee, ensconced in my hole under the ancient olive, the voice came again: "Allanbrook, Allanbrook!" I closed my ears, plunged into the retreat of my own body. After my second pee, stumbling back again to my cocoon, I heard it again: "Allanbrook, Allanbrook!" I blocked it out and plunged into my bedroll. The voice continued, insistently and, as I suddenly realized, tenderly. With a leap of intuition I knew the voice; I caught the western Massachusetts twang. It was Leonard, plain Leonard, my tobacco farmer pal, whose wedding I had just played for back at Fort Sam Houston. He was cold; he wanted me. Together we would be warm.

We were already friends; we liked each other; there was mutual respect. I admired his forthright pride in his family's tobacco farm and he admired my music and my books, my difference from all the rest of the I and R platoon. He often seemed proud of me. Again that night, the third night spent among the olives on the hillside outside Oran, I looked up at the stars. As on the previous night it was clear, the stars glittering. The difference now was that I knew whose voice it was. It was not sounding in that border region between sleeping and waking, where the fancies of the dream world are slipping away with the advent of full consciousness. I was wide awake! Nine years later, up on the sixth floor of Signorina Conzetti's apartment on Parco Margherita in Naples, I fancied I heard the voice again and I started awake, walked over to the balcony and gazed out over the sleeping city toward Capri, clearly remembering sailing into the bay with Leonard. Forty-nine years later, waking at night in the fitful clutch of encroaching age, I remember the voice and am flooded with regret. Leonard was present in my mind, sealed fast within by my rejection of his call.

Remorse was the fixative; but remorse for what? We were

friends with no seeming inclination to be lovers. Indeed after that third, fateful night outside Oran we remained on the same footing as before. Was his death, the first of so many, the cause? Is past time, squatting in our minds, the cause: a time, ever present in memory, though long past? Was it a later awareness of the insouciance of youth, realized, alas, too late by a tardy self-consciousness? I had rejected affection that night, rejected it for the most abject of reasons: laziness. Ensconced in my bed-roll I had been engulfed in the terrible present fact of my solitary warmth. In retrospect it seems to me now the equivalent of moral sloth — ennui, the ultimate sin of apathy in the face of that which moves us, whether it be friendship or God's grace: the turning inward of oneself upon oneself. A canker resides in the memory wherein lie centered all the times when nothing was done, when retreat and its attendant narcissism were the order of the day, when communion was rejected. Remorse, that reiterated bite within, is born from what was not. All the triumphs where love, licit and illicit, had its day are forgotten; accomplishments and worldly victories vanish and ghosts of what might have been remain to haunt the corridors of the mind. In Leonard's case it may be that my memory is composing a fiction; but what is a fiction but a recounting of what might be, or, in one's own life, what might have been? A love story is a fiction, present in aspiration, in realization an end. Such a story is closer to what is than the dreary chronicle of all of our days, laid out in a row, sounding out like soldiers in a close-order drill — "Present, sir."

On the morning of our fourth day in Africa the trucks appeared. We had packed our bags by 0600 and had been waiting for three hours, not at all unhappy to be leaving our hillside. Down the ravine, up through Oran, and on into the interior. The coastal strip was green, pleasant, with wheat fields and grape vines. As we approached Sidi-bel-Abbès the terrain became drier and one could sense the nearness of the desert, though the town and its immediate environs were well cultivated. There was nothing particularly exotic or even Arabic about the place, which was a bit of a disappointment given the anticipation aroused both by its name and the fact that it was the headquarters of the Foreign Legion. We barreled through the town in our convoy of two-and-a-half-ton trucks, pushing farther south and west into drier and hillier country. At dusk we pulled into a proper encampment: an advance party had laid out an entire regimental area, large pyramidal tents, streets, latrines, a mess tent and a proper HQ tent plunked down in the dead center.

Here we rested in limbo, forgetting our recent sea voyage and not wishing to contemplate our next move; we had heard of the bloody landing at Salerno and were reading daily about the battle for Monte Cassino. There were halfhearted attempts on the part of division operations to initiate training sessions in the field, which didn't amount to much though the official history of the division talks brashly of maneuvers in the Algerian hinterlands in preparation for the heroic show we put up in Italy. The poor infantry! What training can they be given other than being well acquainted with their weapons and toughened for long marches? Patience they will gain from the never-ending inefficiency of the hierarchy of command which bedevils their days. They will learn quickly enough to dig a foxhole for themselves when the rounds come pounding in: animal instinct will drive them to cover and concealment. Until then they should be cosseted and taken care of: warm food and lots of comfort with perhaps a daily march to keep the breath steady.

About seven miles from our encampment was a Foreign Legion fort. A day or so after we had arrived a trim but harried French captain appeared, bearing official greetings to our colonel. I was sent for to act as interpreter. I was still too naive politically to catch the nuances of his speech and carriage. Several weeks later when I had gotten to know soldiers up at his fort I understood him a bit better. The ambiguity of his role was a reflection of the ambiguities that were part of the everyday life of Frenchmen in those days, ambiguities which reached a particular crisis in North Africa. Our French captain had been ordered to cement relations with the nearby Americans. Though he was a follower of Darlan and Pétain his habits of military courtesy and the formal cadence of his French skated over any political friction that might be present; in addition it was most unlikely that the American officers had the slightest sense of what was involved. He was punctilious in his address to our bumbling but good-hearted colonel and bore gifts that were much appreciated: cognac and good red wine. I was delighted to translate his last words to the colonel as he was leaving: "My dear Colonel, I would beg you most sincerely to avail yourself of my commissary, which is well provisioned and which we should like our American allies to enjoy. We should be most happy if your stay in Algeria were made as comfortable as possible given the exigencies of these times of war." His driver, Jean-Pierre, whom I had gotten to talk with outside the colonel's tent just before the captain left, informed me with conspiratorial relish that for American dollars and American cigarettes I could have the whole goddamn fort and good riddance! His eyes glinted with malice as the captain left the colonel's tent though as the officer approached the jeep he gave a most elegant salute.

Two days later, dispatched by the colonel and his staff, I was off to the fort, my wallet stuffed with officers' dollars. In addition I had two hundred dollars from my friends in the I and R platoon and the back of the jeep held several dozen cartons of Lucky Strikes. The invitation to use the fort's commissary had been extended only to the colonel. My role as purchasing agent for the enlisted men had hardly been envisaged and was most probably illicit. Jean-Pierre seemed to indicate that it was an open market, an invitation to commerce. All of us since our arrival in Oran had been drinking the abysmal red wine supplied to us by the Arabs. (A good two thirds of our five-gallon water cans at our encampment were full of the stuff.) If anything better was available, demand would have its way.

Once the road angled away from under the hill where we

were encamped it ran straight as a die across the desert to the Legion fort. Dun-colored bushes flanked the road at regular intervals. As we drew closer, the fort revealed itself as a true fortress: a massive gate, heavy adobe walls, and a central square. A gang of black men, chained two by two, were pounding the earth with slow steady thumps as we entered; they chanted as they thumped. Within their chant I could make out "Américains, Américains." Our entrance became part of their litany. They were wielding flattened disks of pig iron on top of which were affixed oaken poles. It took two of them (chained together) to lift the dead weight, which would then be released to fall with a thud which made the balls of the feet shudder. They were tall and superbly muscled. The African sun shone on their bare chests.

"Blacks, court-martialed blacks from Equatorial Africa. They're being punished," Jean-Pierre explained with a Gallic shrug. I had spotted him immediately when we entered and parked next to the motor pool. It was lucky that I found him so quickly as it was not clear how and where I was to purchase the colonel's liquor and it was even less clear how I was to obtain the loot I was commissioned to procure for my friends. Once he had ushered me into the fort's canteen the two of us warmed up to each other. My high school French tumbled forth in a meaningful enough jumble, and, as is usual on such occasions, he assumed I caught everything he said. He detested the French captain he had chauffeured to our encampment, calling him "un sale fasciste." Jean-Pierre claimed, as far as I could ascertain, to have been in the resistance, though whether that had been back in France or here in Algeria wasn't at all clear. There were many languages to be heard in the canteen, lots of German and Spanish. "Most of the Spaniards," explained Jean-Pierre, "escaped from Franco and when their boats touched Africa they were clapped into the Legion. Poor boys! The Germans," he said rather proudly, "are almost all of them party members." This was the first indication I had that he was a Communist. Europe,

in that moment, was thrust upon my twenty-two-year-old consciousness — Europe and all its political horrors here framed
and accompanied by the incessant African thump from the
courtyard outside where the sun was blazing on the black bodies
of the Equatorial convicts. It was the first time I had seen myself
as an American abroad in a new world of blood, hatred, and
history. "It's not only the captain that's a Fascist," continued
Jean-Pierre. "Half the noncommissioned ranks are from the
same race of pigs; but we have them under our thumbs nowadays, things are changing. Don't you worry!" I realized in looking around the room that my own curiosity was matched by
those I was scrutinizing. "The 'copains' who run this canteen are
all comrades. Buy every goddamned thing you want both for
your colonel and for yourselves. If our captain's supplies are
exhausted, so much the worse for him." He was of course just as
anxious for dollars and cigarettes as he was intent upon flaunting his hatred for the fort's commander.

　After an hour of hard drinking we transacted our business
with the cohorts who were in charge of the liquor. Our jeep was
loaded with one large box full of the colonel's liquor and two
others filled with what I could not help thinking of as bootleg
stuff. Jean-Pierre and his pals found the whole transaction immensely satisfying, all the more so as the French captain could
be discerned staring at us from the door of his office, across from
the motor pool. He was still standing there as we drove out
through the massive gateway of the fort, leaving behind us the
incessant throbs of the prisoners' poundings, a background resembling the Alexandrine regularity of Racine's verse, that in-
exorable formality against which the lusts and hatreds of the
characters of the drama unfold.

　The road back lay straight in front of us. In back of us the
sun cast its lengthening rays in such a way that we were not
aware of the vehicle that had been following us until it passed
in a swirl of dust. It was the French captain hell-bent for leather.
Was our liquor contraband? Was he headed straight for our

camp with the intention of reporting us for insubordination? Panic ensued. We agreed it would be best to cache our two crates under one of the many thorn bushes growing so symmetrically on the flanks of the desert road. We were worried and hot, and not a little drunk. The bush we chose had low-slung branches which offered perfect cover and concealment. Upon reaching our encampment we quickly ascertained that the French captain had not been spotted anywhere in the area. With considerable relief I proceeded to the colonel's tent and delivered his box of liquor to him. He was appreciative, offering me a bottle of cognac, which he accompanied with his good Irish smile. I accepted with a grin, saluting as I turned smartly on my heel and left his tent.

It was night when we set forth to retrace our steps. Joe Isaac and Leonard were insistent upon accompanying George, the driver, and me. We had been drinking. The moon had risen, casting oblique shadows on the ground beside each of the thorn bushes which lined the road on both sides. We were certain that we had deposited our cache under a thorn bush on the right side of the road so that at least one thing was certain: the liquor had to be on the left side as we journeyed back toward the fort. We ventured an opinion that we had been perhaps five miles out from the fort on the ten-mile stretch that separated the fort from our encampment. The thorn bushes stretched surrealistically into the perspective, looking remarkably alike in the moonlight. At about four and a half miles from camp we began shining the jeep's headlights on successive thorn bushes. Leonard and I would gingerly lift the lower branches, peering under so as to catch a glimpse of our boxes. On and on. We passed the halfway mark. At about six and a half miles out Joe Isaac stepped across the road to take a leak against a thorn bush on the right-hand side of the road. There was a loud whoop. "Allanbrook," he shouted in his broad Tennessee drawl, "You don't know your fucking right hand from your motherfucking left hand!" He had found our cache. Discovery dispelled abashment. We cracked open a bottle of Martel and, dazed by our luck, arrived back at camp around three in the morning, drunk.

We had no more close contact with the French army until we went into the line in Italy, just north of the Garigliano. Three times, because of my high school French, I was sent on night reconnaissance patrols to make contact with the French corps on our right flank. Twice, on these patrols, we were scared out of our wits by the Goums, Moroccan irregulars from the Atlas Mountains. They had never got it into their heads that the Italians were not still the enemy and tended to regard all of the terrain they operated in as a territory to be raided and raped. On night patrols they distinguished Americans from Germans and Italians by the dog tags which the Americans wore around their necks. They would approach from behind, reach around to feel for the distinguishing tag, recognize it and then grin, saying "Américain!" They were stealthy as cats at night in their long dun-colored bathrobes. I remember late one afternoon, somewhere between Santa Maria Infante and Roccasecca dei Volsci, a week after the May 11 assault on the Gothic line, watching a Goum bringing back to us, as he had been specifically ordered to do, a German prisoner. They approached at a slow trot; the German, short and fat, had the green pallor of mortality on his mottled face. The Goum, tall, with his burnoose loose about him, was prodding the buttocks of his prisoner with his bayonet. He grinned at us. "Prisonnier," he said, pointing proudly at his prize. They had been running for hours; it was a considerable hike from the mountain down to where we were in the valley. The German vomited and then fainted as we turned him over to the MPs. He recuperated, I'm sure; his lot was more fortunate than that of the other members of his company.

Several days after the escapade with the Foreign Legion's liquor the colonel called me into his tent one morning. He showed me a letter he had received from the French captain up at the fort. "I can puzzle out some sense from the French but not this part," he said. I quickly got it all straight for him. Captain DuVal thought that the colonel might well enjoy something that was only possible in North Africa: a gazelle hunt. He enclosed specific directions: the colonel and his party should proceed to the village of El Arish and contact a certain Arab resident there, a local merchant. This man would provide a guide as it would be necessary to trek forty or fifty kilometers farther south and west toward the Moroccan border to reach the best hunting grounds. The captain then indulged in a bit of whimsy, saying he was sure that the American jeeps with their four-wheel drives would serve as "New World Camels," and he wished the colonel "bonne chasse." "What the hell, Collier," said the colonel to our intelligence officer, Captain (soon-to-be Major) Collier. "We might as well get a little shooting in before we get to Italy." Thus began the colonel's gazelle shoot.

We left two days later, five officers in two jeeps and a small truck with a driver and myself, the interpreter. The truck was loaded with bedrolls, liquor, food, and guns. I was surprised to see BARs as well as M-1s and carbines. Slaughter was intended! We arrived at the hamlet of El Arish a bit after midday. Our maps showed it as a minuscule dot at the southern edge of the road network, though broken lines stretched south into the Sahara — all the way to Timbuktu, I told our vapid intelligence officer. El Arish had a most unpromising aspect, a few fly-bitten alleys lined with adobe structures and a walled compound at one end. I inquired of a lounging Arab the whereabouts of the merchant Captain DuVal had written to, who would find us a guide for our expedition into the desert. He pointed out a cube house with a bit of a courtyard, somewhat larger than its neighbors but just as shabby in appearance as everything else in El Arish. I got out of the jeep and approached the front entrance, uncertain as to whether I should shout out "hello" or find something to knock on. It was only when I was squarely in front of the door that I noticed I was being observed through a small latticework medallion. The door was opened by a young fellow of about my age and height, dressed in an immaculate cream-colored robe.

"Good day," he said in what struck me as a most elegant

French accent. "You must be the Americans that Captain DuVal wrote to my father about. I am most honored to meet you. I shall act as your guide with great pleasure." We shook hands and smiled. "My name is Mohammed," he said. The officers observed him with the kind of wooden curiosity they exhibited toward all foreigners.

"Tell that boy that we're ready when he is," said Captain Collier. It was clear that he, as a southerner, regarded Arabs as a species of light-skinned Negroes.

"You may tell the captain that I am already prepared," said Mohammed. It became clear to me that he understood English perfectly well though he would speak only French to me. He went back into the interior of his cube house and reappeared immediately with a natty-looking pack, not the sort of goatskin bag which might have been expected, given the ambience of El Arish. "I would have offered coffee to you and your officers," he said, "but I sensed that they were in a hurry and I felt a bit at a loss." The young Arab had social antennae.

We headed south and west from El Arish, Mohammed guiding us through a tangle of tracks and trails where only at times could the traces of wheeled vehicles be made out. Several times, at a distance of two or three hundred yards, we passed groups of black tents, oblong in shape with camels tethered nearby. It was a long way from Oran; it might have been the Old Testament — Abraham and Isaac living in the tents. Twice Mohammed stopped to talk with Arabs who seemed to be waiting for him by the side of our path. I understood nothing as they weren't talking French. (I couldn't take my eyes off the camels' way of chewing: their jaws went round about as well as up and down.)

Some sort of business was being conducted as both conversations ended with effusive signs of agreement. Captain Collier became irate at the second stop. "You tell that boy we didn't hire him to pass the time of day talking to his nigger friends!" Mohammed looked at me ironically and said, "You must inform your officer that my father and I are doing this as a courtesy to the French captain and to the Americans who are now allied with the French. We are not doing it for money." I translated this for the officers. "Goddamn your fat Dixie mouth, Collier," blurted out the colonel. "That boy might just understand English and we represent the U.S. of A. here in Africa whether the Arabs are niggers or not; anyway that boy looks pretty white; he's probably a Berber." I was gratified to find the colonel so knowledgeable in North African races. "Just like St. Augustine, sir," I added, knowing him to be an Irish Catholic. Sergeant Costello had always warned us against saying too much to officers. He was right; the colonel fixed me with a fishy glare. "Corporal," he said, "Arabs ain't Christians!"

Though the floor of the desert was solid enough our going was often slowed when we would descend into what I soon learned to call a wadi, a washed-out sort of gully like the arroyos I got to know later in life in New Mexico. At around five o'clock, as we were passing through a wadi, Mohammed pointed out a peculiar protuberance of rocks, about one half mile to the left. "We will make camp up there," he said, "in the ruins of an old French fort. Beyond is the plateau where the gazelles flourish. The fort is a landmark which can be spotted from quite a distance, so that your officers, even if off hunting at a distance of some kilometers, can orient themselves and return to camp easily." I translated this as precisely as possible, aping his elegant diction.

The fort had been abandoned for several generations. Its crumbling walls were a helter-skelter of abutments and angles, with the rudiments of a round tower in the center. The dark came quickly and as the night chill of the desert set in we gathered thorn bushes for a fire. The flames cast flickering shadows on the walls, making a refuge in the midst of the enormity of the desert. I offered Mohammed some of my army C rations: pork and beans. He accepted politely, but ate of them gingerly. I hardly felt I should explain to him that if you were not used to them diarrhea often resulted. The officers began to play poker and to drink the colonel's whiskey. I built a separate fire for myself in a corner behind the tower, spread out my blankets, and lit a little Coleman lantern so as to read a new Stravinsky score that Mlle Boulanger had sent me at Fort Sam. Mohammed came to join me in my little pool of light, carrying with him his knapsack, which I noted had the label *Made in Switzerland* on it. He unearthed a can of pâté, which he spread on some crackers. "Better than your C rations, no?" he said in English with a grin that was only slightly sly.

Just at the moment when I noted once again his Swiss knapsack he spotted my Stravinsky score with its French greeting on the front cover: "A mon très cher Allanbrook, N.B." "So you are a musician," he said. He was bowled over when I told him that I had been studying with Mlle Boulanger up until the moment I was drafted into the army. "My professor at the lycée in Algiers talked of her when we discussed the Paris of the twenties. You are fortunate *(bien heureux)* to have worked with her." He had foreseen my astonishment at his knowing of Mlle Boulanger, intending to make it all clear to me by bringing up the lycée in Algiers. We became suddenly aware of each other in one moment of revelation: the distance between the Arab in his burnoose, inhabitant of the fly-specked hamlet of El Arish and Douglas Allanbrook, corporal of the I and R platoon from Melrose, Massachusetts, became negligible. France was the link, a more bizarre link for me certainly as I recalled my four years of French in Melrose High School, in the last two of which I was the preferred student of Miss Mabel Dodge. She would bend over my desk, encouraging me in my recitations of the *tirades* of Corneille, accompanying her praise with her physical presence and her overpoweringly bad breath.

"You must realize," said Mohammed, "we are a *département* of France, however much the settlers of French blood mistrust us. *Liberté, Egalité, et Fraternité* means that we are all part of the French school system. My father is a most successful merchant with the proper connections, so that after I passed my exams I was able to go to Algiers for my *baccalauréat*." There was a glitter in his eyes as he explained all of this to me in the most elegant French. He forestalled my question of his living in El Arish by going on to explain that his father acted as a go-between in all kinds of selling and buying that went on between the desert folk, the inhabitants of the outer rim of villages, and the large coastal cities such as Oran and Algiers. "Here in El Arish we must not appear greater than our Arab brothers; we have a very comfortable house in Sidi-bel-Abbès and an apartment overlooking the Mediterranean in Oran." I felt myself very suburban in that moment though in his eyes I had the status of a Parisian because of Mlle Boulanger. The differences canceled out: the equilibrium of friendship between equals emerged as we talked on into the night, surrounded by the desert, all the while accompanied by the background noise from the colonel's poker game.

The gazelle hunt was not a hunt, it was a slaughter. At dawn we all stood on the small escarpment outside the walls of the fort, gazing over the vast plateau which stretched south into Africa. With the aid of binoculars groups of grazing animals could be spotted. "*Geizal*," said Mohammed, mouthing carefully the lovely-sounding Arabic name. He led us down from the escarpment onto an ancient track which wound out into the plateau. At about two miles from the fort a small knob stuck up from the desert floor, a kind of geological chimney. We parked the truck and the jeeps behind it. It was only about ten feet high. From the top of it the officers saw their prey: a herd of gazelles, alert and attentive, delicate with ringed and lyre-shaped horns; reddish-brown stripes on their cheeks were matched by the same pattern on their slim flanks.

"Let's get 'em, boys," yelled the colonel as he climbed into his jeep. They had no luck the first time for the herd scattered when the men emerged from behind the knoll. Later in the morning they became more adept at waiting and at stalking. In the afternoon the kill began. They got the feel of the terrain and discovered that the floor of the desert was smooth enough to keep up with the herd, even to outpace it. They also noted that the herd would split up into groups of ten or twelve. The BAR turned out to be the most efficient of gazelle killers, a real "weapon of choice"; a blast from it into one of the small groups of gazelles was sure to score, whereas a rifle demanded a sure gaze and a remarkably steady hand.

The sight of the delicate creatures slung over the hood of the jeeps jarred. "The slaughter of the innocents," I murmured to myself. Soon enough in Italy I would become inured to the sight and smell of death, to body bags grotesquely slung on the backs of mules bumping down the mountain trails; friends would have their feet blown off and their balls mutilated by "bouncing Bettys." Habitual horror does not dim the sight; the soul grows scar tissue; night arrives: another day passes — tenderness is rationed, equilibrium safeguarded. The colonel's gazelle hunt stands sharp against the weeks and months in the line. Its gratuitous nature links it in recollection with another event, spontaneous and likewise gratuitous, which occurred toward the end of the following summer.

We were in Tuscany in late August '44, our headquarters established in a substantial estate on the terrain that slopes down from Volterra toward Empoli. The villa itself was lovingly positioned on a long oblong terrace, elevated about twenty feet above an entrance road. Old carriage sheds now did service as garages under the terrace. Woods stretched away below, growing fairly close to the approach road. The Germans had been slowly withdrawing, pulling back to a main line of defense on the other side of the Arno. The partisans were particularly active in this part of Tuscany and most of the towns and villages had their own local committees. I was well aware that members of the carabinieri were being shot by the partisans so I was both puzzled and relieved when a group of partisan boys brought a carabiniere sergeant to our headquarters at the villa. We had an MP detachment that was bringing German prisoners to the rear and I tried to explain to the sergeant that he would be much

safer going back with our military police than he would be returning to his nearby town. He was green with fright; sweat
poured down his face on both sides of his enormous nose. The
partisan boys were alive with excitement and accomplishment.
While I was motioning to him to go with the MP corporal who
was standing beside me, he caught a glimpse of the German
prisoners who were being brought back to the rear. He panicked,
dashing suddenly to one side of the terrace and down the stairway that led to the open ground between the garages and the
woods. Instantaneous glee seized both the partisans and, to my
horror, the soldiers of my company. Volleys of rifle fire stopped
him short of the edge of the woods, where he fell, riddled with
bullets. It was a gratuitous killing, lethal sport. His wife came up
from town later in the day. She had hoped to retrieve his wedding ring and his gold watch from his body, which was in the
garage under the villa, but they had been stolen from his corpse.

All the many deaths I had witnessed the previous winter,
spring, and summer of our advance up the boot had been infantry deaths. There was no sport involved — only war's necessity, never any exultation, never any glee. It was this difference
which marked the death of the carabiniere sergeant, which
caused it to be stored away in my memory alongside the colonel's gazelle hunt.

Mohammed and I talked far into the desert night as the officers roasted their kill and feasted. I couldn't get him to acknowledge the superiority of Debussy over Ravel. I said, "If only I had
a piano here, I would show you!" We both burst into laughter at
the remark, conversing as we were on the edge of the Sahara,
next to a flickering fire twenty feet away from the carousing
hunters. He introduced me to Baudelaire, reciting poem after
poem, pointing out felicities, and indicating depths that I knew
nothing of. I tried to explain to him that in Miss Mabel Dodge's
advanced French at Melrose High School we had not come further than Tartarin de Tarascon and Louÿs's *Le Pêcheur d'Islande*,
most of our time having been spent on Corneille and Racine.
"But my dear," he said (at that early time of my life it was still

amazing to be called "my dear," though of course it does not adequately translate *mon cher*), "however modern Baudelaire may be he still employs the most classic Alexandrine line." He quoted for me "Le superbe fantôme de l'antique Vénus" from "Voyage à Cythère." "How different," he said, "is that from Phèdre's cry, 'Vénus toute entière à sa proie attachée.'" Our idyll was of brief duration. The next morning we departed, leaving Mohammed off at El Arish, and arriving back at our encampment in the late afternoon. I gave Mohammed my address in Melrose and he gave me his in Oran. He never wrote and I lost his address.

The following week we left Africa. When we arrived down at Oran from our inland encampment we learned that Supinski had broken his legs. "Both of them?" asked Joe Isaac. "Both of them," replied the MP who came to report the accident. "He was driving like a bat out of hell around a curve back out of town about ten miles. The jeep flopped over into a gully and broke his legs real clean just above the knees. He didn't say one word when we lifted him into the ambulance, no groans, no nothing; just stared." We all grinned sheepishly at each other, thinking of his thin lips, his hooded eyes, his pockmarked skin. We could better face what we were to face without that malevolent presence. We finished up our cache of liquor that night and drank to Supinski's happy demise. "That Polish fucker was up to something fishy taking off all by himself and it wasn't pussy he was after." This from Sohanchek who hated the Pole as only a Russian could. Major Collier went to see Supinski in the army hospital before we sailed off for Italy. "I feel I'm a bit responsible, Corporal Allanbrook," Major Collier told me later. "Did you realize that he had been in the Polish Intelligence Service when he was younger? I felt that I should help a man like that and in my function as a staff officer in intelligence I was in a position to do something. I gave him a letter to the CIC (counterintelligence corps) people down at Oran and told him take off early and get down there to talk with them before we shipped out to Naples."

Supinski had played with Major Collier, tantalizing him with tidbits from his doubtful past. We were all to suffer from the infatuation with "intelligence" and "counterintelligence" which he had planted in Collier's lazy but furtive mind. Except for this, however, Supinski's departure from our midst, like Iago's, was marked by silence.

We sailed up to Naples on a British transport. It was a filthy ship with a sequestered stink of bodies and bad food down below. Leonard and I spent most of our time up on deck. We passed by Syracuse and docked for a night at Porto Augusto. We left there before dawn, passing Catania as the sun's rays caught the mass of Etna beyond, snowy at its summit, rising ten thousand feet in splendor above the Strait of Messina.

It was volcanos all the way. We passed Stromboli and Vulcano and reached the Bay of Naples at night, sailing in through Punta della Campanella and Capri and anchoring out in the bay until we received permission to dock in the crowded port the next morning. "Christ, Allanbrook, what's that mountain over there doing?" said Leonard, pointing with his right hand through the starlit night. "This is Naples and that has to be Vesuvius, the world's most famous volcano and we're in luck: it's erupting!" We were even more in luck: there was an air raid going on. In the clear winter night a red glow could be seen emerging from the cone, crossed by the fiery diagonal of the funicular which had caught fire from the molten lava. Tracer bullets from ack-ack guns floated lazily skyward at an acute angle to the funicular's red path. "There must be a war going on," I said to Leonard, "and we're going to see Naples!"

We really did see it in the bright morning sunshine: the bombed jumble of the docks, the clutter of the streets, the disorderly sweep of sea front around to the royal palace, the look up to San Martino, and Vesuvius way off to the right with its plume of smoke. The moment we hit the dock, we were surrounded by swarms of boys. "Hey, Joe, carry your bags — two packs of cigarettes." I handed mine over to an eager *scugnizzo* with brilliant eyes. When we reached the waiting trucks I handed him two packs of Camels. "When you come to Naples I fix you up. Fuckee-fuck, nice clean girls, anything you want." The same entrancing grin and flashing eyes. "You just ask for Giacomo in the Galleria. They know me!" Leonard was a bit shocked but I was taken, sold on the place, seduced by the looks of the people, by the brilliance of their eyes and the quickness of their wits. Urban life teemed in the bombed city despite the desperation and the disease that we were told was rampant in it. This was only my first glimpse but later years never erased my feelings for the place.

The trucks made their way from the port, past San Carlo and the vast expanse of Piazza del Plebiscito, past the Castel del'Ovo, along the Riviera di Chiaia, plunging into the tunnel after Piedigrotta, finally depositing us for the night in a clutch of Fascist army barracks next to Pozzuoli. Only by hindsight can I name the route: that morning it was an unnamed shower of sights and smells. We were bustled off the next morning, bound for the interior, some of us never to see Naples again, others returning on two-day passes to whore and to drink. Six years later I returned to live there for two years.

Our route inland wound through the devastation of Aversa and Capua, ancient cities of the Campania Felix. The eye accustomed itself to the sight of buildings eviscerated by bombs, to glimpses into the guts of domesticity: gas ranges dangling at forty-five-degree angles, beds tottering on the edge of a shattered wall, a bathtub standing naked and alone, exposed to public view — and below a sea of rubble. Standing walls were covered with Mussolini's inane boast — "Conquer, we will conquer" (Vincere, vinceremo). The streets were alive with the desperate commerce of daily life coping with desolation. That was what we saw and what we got used to. This was Italy. "At least it ain't fucking Africa with them Arabs and the French lookin' so pissed off," commented Bianchi, whose father came from a town near Caserta and his mother from Ischia, out in the bay. He was in place; his family's dialect made him a native. Lots of us, even without the language, began feeling at home, just as he did.

There was an encampment prepared for us a few miles from Piedimonte d'Alife. Bianchi went out to reconnoiter; he lost no time; this was his country. That evening he shepherded six of us over to a household he had found in a neighboring village — a mountain village with precipitous streets that were not so much streets as narrow stone pathways flanked by dwellings that appeared more Stone Age than medieval. Goats were tethered in the back of the houses. A minuscule church with an ancient stone cross over the portal presided over a tiny piazza. The household that welcomed us to its hearth had three uncles in America: one in Brooklyn, one in Rochester, New York, and one in Shreveport, Louisiana. We were the liberators from the land of hope, bearing in our hands cigarettes and coffee, goods not seen since before the war. Wine flowed, tough salty bread appeared, roast goat sizzled on a spit in the fireplace. The house was a domestic cave: a somber shelter made of stone with a fire sputtering in the hearth. There were little children, nubile adolescents, a mama and a papa, and an appropriate old crone of a grandmother on a rush seat close to the fire. It was a complete place, real and full of heady smells; it didn't seem strange. When I had to pee I was at a loss for a moment but Bianchi pointed to the back door. Outside was a rocky little patch of ground with goats. It bore a certain resemblance to what back home would have been called a back yard. It was while I was actually peeing that I became aware of a rumble to the north, a disturbance in the night which ebbed and flowed, at times stopping entirely. So that's artillery, I thought. A dog barked and one of the goats shifted its hoofs and bleated.

When I went back in the son of the family grinned and gave me another mug of red wine. "Did you hear the guns?" he asked. "That's Cassino up there. *Tanti morti.* I was a soldier too, but when the Americans landed, I ran." He made a gesture with his arm. "I made for the mountains and finally got back here. But it's taken you so long," he said, "so long to get up here from Salerno and now so long up there!" I nodded, acutely aware that I knew nothing of what the war was really like. Cassino and Anzio were simply names and places on a map. We were all of us ignorant of the real war, of its halting progress up the peninsula, of what was happening on the ground. (We knew even less of the monumental slaughter going on in that very moment in distant Russia.) We would learn a lot in a very short time though we never had any grasp of the campaign's larger movements, of its rationale, if indeed it had one. We did know that Rome was to the north.

Once we were in the line, living our day-to-day existence, bored and dirty with spots of terror to relieve the ennui, we had little curiosity about the longer view of things. We had no strong feelings about the reasons for our being where we were or why we were stuck with what we had to do. After much blood, when we were the first troops to enter Rome, we couldn't understand why we then let the German army slip away north to fight another day. General Clark, hot for glory, came racing in on our footsteps: it was one of the few times we saw him. "All them motherfucking generals act just like horny roosters," was Joe Isaac's comment. "Clark looks like one too," added Sohanchek. "Look at that beak of his."

The regiment did not go up to Cassino but I did. Orders had come down from corps command that a few chosen officers should proceed to Cassino; they would billet with the British who were in line there. They were to observe what went on in this crucial sector, gain some experience as a preparation for the division's entering the line down by the Tyrrhenian Sea, just north of where the Garigliano enters. Colonel Lynch, in a perfectly proper way, chose the executive officers of the three battalions for the mission, not wishing to do without any of his own regimental staff and judging that it would be the battalions and not regimental headquarters that would be doing the dirty work. Major Collier volunteered me. "Corporal Allanbrook," he explained to the colonel, "already is a real fine map reader. We couldn't do without him. He should be the one to go on up there and see how it works right there on the ground. We need some real experience." He and the colonel had been drinking together. Joe Isaac, as usual, put his finger on it. "Allanbrook," he said, "you got your ass in a sling by being so goddamned quick at them maps!"

Four days up there was all new; there wasn't time to get bored. The artillery fire came close enough for terror only once and the very novelty of being in the line had a tonic effect. The British noncoms taught me to distinguish between the gentle *whoosh* of "safe" incoming fire and the impending danger signaled when the whoosh turned into a whistle. The shells came from two directions, some of them from us, others from the Germans. On the second night up there some of our rounds began coming in too low. Blasphemous phone calls back to division fire control did not stop two rounds from screaming down onto a dug-in position up the slope from our battalion HQ.

"Bloody sons of bitches have got their elevations wrong," snarled the sergeant who had been showing me the topographical maps of Cassino and Mount Cairo. Later that evening I saw my first body bag coming down the hill, slithering back and forth on the mule's back as if it were full of some inert liquid. A soldier was carried by on a stretcher, one of his legs swathed in a gory bandage. "A nice one, mates," he said. "Just what the doctor ordered. I didn't lose the bloody leg but it's enough so I won't be back up. Toodle-oo to all you dearies!"

"Both those chaps have been in since El Alamein," the British sergeant explained, "and now they've gotten it from our own fire!" I began to pay particular attention to the wiggly curves of the contour lines on the maps we were using up there, spotting the sharp drops where the lines were close together with the metric numbers jumping suddenly upward. I understood how tricky it was for the artillery to clear a hilltop and to drop its shells just over the crest onto the enemy positions. Why had we received no training in the special problems to be solved in ground warfare fought in mountainous terrain? All of our war games had been played either on the plateau surrounding Camp Gruber or in the piny barrens of southern Louisiana.

British-American friendship was flourishing by the third night of our stay. I had had three good slugs of the dark, dark rum which was standard issue to the British soldier. Our corpulent and gregarious Captain Simpson, proprietor back home in central Tennessee of a successful spread of cattle, was drinking scotch with the brigade officers. He felt very "Allied," as he said. It was the first time in his life he had ever switched from Tennessee bourbon. We were in the bombed-out cellar of a stone farmhouse, moderately well sheltered from mortars and artillery. A tall, thin British major strode over to Captain Simpson; he swished his swagger stick as he spoke. "What say, Captain Simpson, care for a bit of a recce?" Most aware of being an officer and a southerner, a guest of the British army, our captain had no choice. "Sure thing, Major," he said with a note of puzzlement in his tone. How was he to know what a "recce" was. Five minutes later they were out of the cellar and on their way, the slim Englishman with his jaunty cap and stick and portly Captain Simpson with his steel helmet and carbine. The British officers exchanged glances whose meaning I could not decipher. The sergeant I was drinking with commented, "That major is a bloody devil, he is."

Twenty minutes later the major and the captain were in trouble on the slopes above. I had learned by now to distinguish the quick chatter of machine guns and the thud and pop of mortar fire. "Nice little firefight going on upstairs," said the British sergeant. "They'll get a spot of eighty-eights in a minute." And so they did. The shriek of the shells and the crash of their arrival introduced me to the Germans' most effective artillery piece, the 88 antiaircraft gun, which they had adjusted to ground warfare with startling success. "Better than anything we have," said the sergeant. "They're strange buggers; they must know their jig is up, but it makes no difference to them." The major and the captain reappeared in an hour, unscathed, the major still jaunty, the captain sweating and white, his jowls shaking with his heavy breathing.

"Rather a success, I'd say," said the major. "We ascertained that Jerry has repositioned his machine guns and that he has the entire gully up there covered with both mortars and eighty-eights, all nicely zeroed in with the proper coordinates. You would agree it was well worth our while, wouldn't you, Captain?" This last was spoken with a certain calculated effrontery.

Poor Captain Simpson, who had been so frightened that he had peed in his pants (something that I soon learned was very common), had enough presence to reply in his drawl in a manner that testified to his status as a southerner and a gentleman. "I believe, sir, I did learn something and I am certainly indebted to you for the opportunity."

"He's a game bloke," whispered the British sergeant to me. "I'd sooner trust him than that tight-lipped bastard of ours!" Captain Simpson lasted all the way through, making major and then lieutenant colonel, leading one of our battalions with restraint and good sense, which is about all that can be hoped for when there's actual fighting going on. When we returned he regaled our officers with the story of his "recce." I talked some with our good operations officer, Major Melcher, about the rounds that had come in from our own artillery and was delighted to see that, as always, he was well aware of the problem. "We're going to be sure we have a forward observer from the artillery batteries right up with us. They'll pay more attention if their own tail might be blown off."

Two weeks later the entire 88th Division moved into the line, relieving the British, who at quite some cost had pushed a bit north of the Garigliano some months earlier. It was the first of many night moves: jeeps and trucks had only a glimmer for headlights and cigarettes could not be lit. The grinding of motors and gears could not be hushed but every restraint was used.

Leaving Capua behind we crossed the Volturno River on a Bailey bridge, proceeding northwest toward the Garigliano and the sea. There was an occasional mutter of artillery ahead; low clouds parted at times to reveal a sliver of a moon. It was in one of those moments of sporadic moonlight that I glanced at a stone kilometer marking at the edge of the road. "Via Appia," I murmured first to myself. I shook Leonard and said, "The Appian Way."

"Allanbrook," he said, "what the hell is the Appian Way and who cares? We're goin' where we're goin' and it's creepy!"

We all were tense. Unease settled on us like a wet fog on the coast of Maine. This was the end of a road that had begun at Camp Gruber, so long ago. For me the sensation of reading VIA APPIA on the kilometer stone was like gazing through the wrong end of a telescope; my Latin classes with Miss Kershaw back at Melrose High were the locus of the reflecting and shifting light of my memory's gaze. Miss Kershaw had waxed eloquent when she talked of the legions who had marched forth on the Appia, bound for Brindisi and the East, of the terrifying revolt of Spartacus, which had begun at Capua when he broke out of a gladiator's school and which had ended with Crassus crucifying thousands of his followers along the whole length of the Appian Way. Now here I was on that same Appian Way, the genuine article, going north as an infantryman with the artillery muttering ahead of us, pushing through shattered towns and approaching yet another Bailey bridge built alongside the shattered arches of the bridge that the Romans had built.

Our relief of the British was accomplished in quiet confusion. We heard a bit of artillery up beyond Minturno, toward Castelforte, and the crackling of machine-gun fire on the slope down toward Scauri and Gaeta. By dawn the British had left and we were ensconced in their dugouts and caves. They had been fixed in these positions since the offensive had ground to a bloody halt on the whole length of the line from the mouth of the Garigliano to Cassino. Just above us in no man's land was the ancient town of Minturno; on our right was the French Corps, distributed across the roughest of mountain terrain; on our left was the sea with Gaeta and its peninsula enclosing our view.

Regimental headquarters was installed partly in a cave in the hillside and partly in a camouflaged truck drawn up beside the mouth of the cave. Leonard and Joe Isaac found a cozy dugout for the three of us, which we lined with shelter halves and blankets. At 0900 hours that first morning three artillery shells landed in quick succession. No one was hit but, for the first time, our very own bodies were the targets. Carnal knowledge of our own likely demise, not in some distant future, but right now, became a part of our souls' equipment.

The most notable casualty in those first days was the sergeant major of the regiment. It took us a week or more to realize this, as his injury was not physical. He had set up his portable desk at the back of the cave under the hill, issuing forth only to minister to the wants of the colonel, who was to be found either in his dugout or in the camouflaged truck next to the cave's entrance. The sergeant major had been placed in front of us as a paradigm of the old army. He was the first sergeant of the first sergeants, the highest of the noncommissioned officers; at Camp Gruber and at Fort Sam he had been the ruthless center of discipline and spit and polish. His boots gleamed; the crease in his pants was geometrically precise. We draftees knew he was stupid but he was an ornament to headquarters. He could crack out an "attenshun!" upon the entrance of the colonel that curled up your toenails. He had a flat face, dour and pale, with thin lips and piggish eyes. He was perhaps forty years old: the army had been his whole life since he left Arkansas and joined up in the 1920s.

Joe Isaac spotted it first: "That man is really full of shit! He's too scared of them shells to skedaddle out of his cave down the hill to take a crap. He's about to bust!" Full of shit he was. His cowardice became manifest, his fall from grace both abysmal and necessary. The colonel, a regular old-army officer who had risen from the ranks, was abashed when his sergeant major asked to be relieved. In his bones he knew his own days were numbered; he was too old and he drank too much; he was to be replaced a few weeks later by a gung-ho West Pointer. All of us draftees felt exonerated in our opinion of the sergeant major, though this feeling was coupled with the realization that the center and the control in the approaching time of travail would now be "ours," that the old established "they" had not held — that the sergeant major was now in the rear echelon, stripped of his stripes along with his honor.

Our true baptism now began. In that first week, which had been marked by the sergeant major's departure, the I and R platoon began its reconnaissance patrols. I was spared many of them; I had become too valuable to both Major Melcher and Major Collier. We had detailed maps of our sector, which I covered with overlay paper: all of our positions were shown and all of our guesses as to where the German ones were. We had long strips of overlapping air-reconnaissance photos, which we would examine with a stereopticon device, peering into ravines and gullies, trying to envisage in three dimensions what we would stumble through on our night patrols. No casualties ensued from these first patrols of ours; the front was quiescent and didn't respond to our probing. It was in the service area, near the regimental motor pool, that the first blood was spilt. A mechanic stepped on a land mine and lost his leg. We had been warned of mines by the British but had not been prepared for what soon became an ever-present wariness. We had been told about the large, round mines designed to blow up tanks and vehicles, and had been instructed in the use of mine detectors. What we now became aware of was a whole panoply of antipersonnel mines; while some of these were aimed at killing, most of them were designed to maim, to blow off legs and feet, to explode upward so as to mutilate pricks and balls. Many of these "bouncing Bettys" were not detectable by our metal-sniffing detectors. They were of a stunning simplicity: little wooden herring boxes with their lids slightly ajar. They contained only the minimal amount of metal necessary for the trigger mechanism. Across the road from our headquarters was an orange grove, full of ripe fruit. Mines had been carefully planted there by the Germans. "Them motherfuckers," said Joe Isaac. "Forbidden fruit," rejoined Private Wallace, a new addition from the red-clay country of Mississippi. "Sure death." He was a hard-shell Baptist, devout, but of the sweetest and most innocent of dispositions.

We patrolled three sectors: left, right, and center. To the left we sent patrols down past the village of Scauri toward Formia and the sea. It was never quite clear to me what their purpose was; we had orders to "probe the sector." The Germans seemed to have the same instructions. If we heard them or they heard us there would be an instantaneous wariness; nerves atingle, each would listen, trying to fix the position on the ground so that it could be spotted on the overlay maps back at headquarters. After an hour or so we would creep quietly back and so would they. Toward the end of the second week the Germans sent up a couple of flares. We froze in place, all over with goose pimples. Having reported this on our return, Major Collier ordered us to shoot some flares ourselves on the following nights to see what we could see. Our new platoon sergeant, Short, a solid man from Oklahoma who had taken Supinski's place, did this only once out there in never-never land and then refrained from using them. "They'd put mortar fire on us right off the bat. You can spot where a flare comes from easy as shit." Sergeant Short was a tough and quiet man and Major Collier, a natural coward, didn't have the stomach to push him on this matter. Disaster struck in the left-hand sector some weeks later, however, when Major Collier decided we should have a semipermanent listening post down toward Scauri which would consist of a radio man and two other I and R members.

In the middle sector lay the ancient town of Minturno. We were called upon to investigate the place, as lights had been observed flashing from a window in a house high up on the ramparts. The town had been emptied of its inhabitants since before the bloody halt some months earlier. It was a spooky place, medieval on top of Roman, full of dark alleys with a crumbling amphitheater on one edge of town. It lay between the lines, neither side venturing within its walls. Major Collier became excited: a no man's town with flashing lights! He had been talking at Division HQ with a garrulous counterintelligence lieutenant, who had filled his head with the manifold duties an intelligence officer was responsible for. The CIC lieutenant was coming around to our HQ the next day, which thrilled our major. "Corporal Allanbrook," he said. "There must be some Eytie up there flashin' signals to the Krauts. I want for all of you to go up there tonight and find out what's up." The very name "Counterintelligence Corps" struck his ear as having so much more glamour than anything he did as a regimental intelligence officer, a job which up to now had to do with getting along with the colonel and giving all the responsibility for map reading and air photos and perusal of intelligence analyses to Corporal Allanbrook.

We edged our way, Indian file, through Minturno's ancient gate, working our way up to the top of the town, hugging the shadowy sides of the stony streets. The moon shone; no dog barked. The town had been bereft of life for months, since before the bloody halt of the Allied advance. Yet, around a sharp corner, high up overlooking the walls, a light glimmered. This patrol had a fixed objective, and there it was, manifest to our eyes. That it must be an object of curiosity also to the Germans was a thought which increased our caution as we sidled up the street to the house where the light was. A wooden door which gave onto the street hung half open. The room we entered stank of death. Animals had been stabled in it and we made out a dead donkey in one corner, his four legs sticking up, his flesh half consumed. A rude wooden stair led up to the living quarters. A fireplace filled with rubble faced a wooden plank table with some filthy plates and glasses on it. From the floor above came a sound between a singsong and a moan. Sergeant Short, ever a cool and prudent man, put his finger to his lips and motioned for me to follow him up a rickety wooden stair to the left of the fireplace which climbed up through the ceiling to the floor above. From below as I was following him up the stair I heard his Oklahoma voice whisper, "Son of a bitch, if it ain't a witch!" The moaning continued as I clambered up after him. Seated on a splayed rush chair in front of a low table which held a lamp, a pack of cards, and numerous nondescript boxes was a female creature, squat, swathed in squares of burlap. She stank almost as badly as the dead donkey. The low keening stopped as she became aware of us; it was replaced by a quick jabbering which I couldn't make head or tail of.

"What's she sayin', Allanbrook?" asked Short. "You know some Eytie."

"She's not talking Italian," I whispered. "I bet she's a Gypsy and is talking Gypsy."

"Them Gypsies is all witches," Short came back.

Whatever she was she had to be brought back. It wasn't easy. When we put out the lamp she whooped and moaned. I kept whispering "Zitta, zitta!" ("Quiet!") as we bundled her down the stairs. "I swear she understands but she won't let on," I murmured to Short. The other two members of the patrol were bug-eyed when we hit the second floor. Down we went again, past the dead donkey, out into the moonlit alley, trying to stifle her moans, our ears alert for any sounds in the ancient ghost town. When we reached headquarters we were white with fatigue and nearly nauseated with her stink. Major Collier was delighted. "Sergeant Short and Corporal Allanbrook," he said, "I'm goin' to call that CIC lieutenant and let him know that we've got a spy!" The division MPs brought her back to the rear early the next morning and a week later Major Collier received a commendation, praising him for his alertness and efficiency as director of intelligence in our sector of the line. Who the strange creature was and what she was doing up there in Minturno we never did find out, but the sights and smells of that patrol link it in memory with other terrors of the night. As a child I was afraid of the dark. Even in old age I have twinges of this cavelike fear and never enter my front door at night without a steeling of the will.

Later that year we came upon another dark house in the middle of the night in a sector where the Second Battalion had been having severe firefights for several days. It wasn't at all clear to us what the result of the action had been but the colonel insisted upon pushing ahead. "If things are mucked up, I'm the person that's supposed to clear them up," he told us. Major Melcher had urged him not to go so far forward when the line was in such confusion. The colonel had ignored him and when we arrived at the house the colonel pointed it out and said to me, "You go in first, Allanbrook."

In I went, through a portal that was shattered by artillery fire. The smell of dead bodies assailed me, a sweetish stink, akin to the stench of the dead donkey on that night a year before in Minturno, no less pungent but now only too well known as emanating from human flesh; three dead GIs lay on the floor. Remarkably enough there were two clean and uncluttered rooms on the floor above. I issued forth from the house with my report just as we began receiving some incoming rounds out in front of the house. "We got no choice; in we go," said the colonel. "It's not healthy out here." He proceeded to establish his headquarters up on the second floor, twitching his whip erratically as we passed the corpses. We were stuck up there for three days as the artillery fire continued and the open space in front of the house suffered intermittent machine-gun fire and occasional well-placed mortar rounds.

The French Expeditionary Corps held the ground to the right of us, a rough swatch of territory extending through the mountains up toward Cassino. The I and R platoon was expected to make contact with them and my high school French entered the picture once again. "Corporal Allanbrook," Major Collier said, "we need more than contact; we need to talk to those folks if anything happens, and you're the only one we've got who can do that." This meant, in practice, that I and three other members of the I and R platoon would creep out past our right flank all the way to a rocky gulch where, with luck, we would meet with a detachment of French soldiers; we would then utter the password and work our way back. Once or twice I tried out a French phrase, such as "Ça va?" which was received with courtesy and once was answered with a rather elegant "Perfectly well here" in a clipped English accent. Twice, at night, near headquarters, I would freeze, zero at the bone, as I felt a hand around my neck. The hand would reach for my dog tags, and, finding them, would mutter "Américain." I would turn to see a grinning barbarian, dressed in a long robe and sporting a dagger. The Italians, men, women, and children, were inhabitants of the land they were fighting on; they had once been the enemy and the Goums still treated them as such, scourging the countryside. The French, their colonial masters, had them loosely organized in formations called Groupements de Goums and discipline was ruthless; a command disobeyed meant instant execution.

My fear of the dark was enhanced on these patrols not only by the Goums and by the apprehension of encountering German patrols but by the physical encumbrance of a piece of equipment I was ordered to carry: a grenade launcher. This involved clamping a piece of tubing to the barrel of my M-1 and affixing a grenade to it. It had been Major Collier's inspiration that I be the one to be equipped with this device. "You're so blind you couldn't hit the side of a barn, Corporal Allanbrook," he chuckled, "so you might as well carry this piece of ordnance. Just aim it somewhere in front of you and pull the trigger!" A full-size rifle is awkward enough on a night patrol; it is doubly so with the extra length and weight of a piece of tubing with a grenade attached. It was all made more supportable when the rest of the patrol would treat me as a joke: "Allanbrook," said my Memphis pal, Joe Isaac, "if you was a hunter, the Animal Rescue League would give you a medal." We were lucky. We stumbled over that piece of terrain many times on our contact patrols with the French and suffered no mishaps, though when the real fighting began in May, it was revealed that the Germans had all kinds of firepower on the hills immediately adjacent to the route we had been following.

The magnitude of the fighting which began on May 11 and which continued until Rome fell eclipsed, for a while at least, the memory of those first months in the line. A well-functioning psyche covers the memory with scar tissue; when it happens that every day there are dead and wounded, the surprising majority of men become inured to it. They don't break down; they put up with it in an adaptation that is hardly Darwinian, as many of them do not survive. So it was that the disaster which struck the I and R platoon in those early months of patrolling was soon enough eclipsed by the enormity of the general attack north to Rome. There is no history of the 88th Division in Italy which notes the deaths of Leonard and sweet Jack, the radio man, both of them shot in the back of the head by a German patrol on the slope which runs down to Scauri and the blue Tyrrhenian.

That they had been placed down there as a week-long listening post had not only been Major Collier's doing, though he initiated it; it was concurred in by Major Melcher. I myself had noted, peering at my stereopticon air-reconnaissance photos, that there was a slight elevation from which the terrain both north and south could be observed. "I declare," said Major Collier when I pointed this out to him, "you do see right proper when you look at maps." He proudly brought it up with Major Melcher, our operations officer; it was rarely the case that Collier had any concrete duties in his role as intelligence officer of the regiment, so it was all the more important for his amour-propre to suggest a semipermanent observation post be planted out there. It was a move which quite clearly had to do with intelligence, but could well be shared with operations. It would signal to Division HQ, if properly reported, that there was coordinated staffwork being done at a certain regiment's headquarters.

Three members of the I and R platoon were sent out: Leonard, Jack the radio man, and Sergeant Sohanchek, our chunky Ukrainian, a good man, fleshy and sexy as a bull, always with the whores while on a pass and, back with the boys, always trying to get a blow job from the tenderest of the privates or the nearest chaplain's assistant. For three days the radio crackled; Jack would report in every two hours right on schedule. The evening of the third day there was silence. Around 2300 hours I went over to the colonel's truck, which was camouflaged and drawn up against the side of the hill. Major Collier was playing poker with the colonel and the exec. At first he was a bit put off at being interrupted but remembering his position and his authority he said, "Corporal Allanbrook, if you don't hear anything by 0100 we'll do something. You alert Sergeant Short and tell him to get over here." Silence still at 0100 hours. Short, our stolid and dependable platoon sergeant, was then instructed to take one man with him, Corporal Bianchi, and to creep out and reconnoiter the situation. "Ah declare, I'm worried," said the major. He had reason to be.

At first light Short and Bianchi returned, supporting Sohanchek between them. He had a tourniquet around his left thigh. "They got Leonard and Jack, shot 'em in the back of the head. They didn't know what hit 'em. They was dead right away," he said. "I was in a ditch taking a crap when the flare went up. There were three of them. I heaved a grenade at them and they came back at me with a burst of machine pistol and then they beat it. They was as scared as I was." He crawled back a way toward our lines, bleeding, and had passed out before Short and Bianchi found him. His wound turned out to be minor and he was back with us in a few weeks.

These two deaths, Leonard's and Jack's, were the I and R platoon's first definite killings; they were shot dead by distinguishable enemy soldiers. The mass killing which was to descend upon us in May was impersonal. These two deaths were different. In their immediacy they cut deep, so deep that we denied the trauma all the more. We avoided looking at poor

Whitmore, Jack's bosom buddy. He went grimly about his radio repairing, dry-eyed and stricken. He cursed the chaplain when he came around for help in writing to Jack's wife. "That's for me to do, not you, for Christ's sake," he said to him. He had been a pious Presbyterian until then.

I shoved Leonard's death underground, but like a volcano in a dormant phase, he was always there, waiting. It erupted first in an unexpected fashion. Bianchi and I were granted a pass down to Naples. It was pleasant to retrace our steps: back down the Appia, over the Volturno into shattered Capua, down through the fertile Campania with its grape vines bedecking the fruit trees, and finally the descent down the Via Roma, rounding the curves below the palace at Capodimonte to be deposited at last in the vast expanse of the Piazza del Plebiscito. Bianchi headed immediately for the Galleria where all the action was. Squarely in front of it was the signboard of San Carlo, announcing *La Bohème* for that very afternoon. I dragged Bianchi to it; some bit of his father's love of music stuck to him even though he had not come to Naples to go to the opera. It was a ragtag performance with an audience that was half military and half Neapolitan. The singers knew how to turn the phrases and the orchestra knew how to follow. Mimi was fat and Rodolfo shabby. I was sarcastic during the first act but began listening in the second. When Mimi died in the last act and all the friends gathered round to mourn I was suddenly racked with sobs, not for Mimi though she was the occasion, but for good and innocent Leonard, my dead friend, whose voice I could never again answer, just as I had not answered it on that cold night on the hillside outside Oran.

Bianchi eyed me intently as we left San Carlo and went out into the twilight. A desultory blackout was in effect, though it had been some time since German bombers had appeared. As we entered the shadowy Galleria after crossing over from San Carlo he seized me and gave me a bearhug. He was a big man, rangy and ugly in a handsome Italian way, with a hook nose and shrewd eyes. "Buddy boy," he said, "you and I is going to get drunk and laid tonight. You're all stuffed up with them two dead." In the Galleria Bianchi made contact with a man who offered his services for the evening. They talked together in dialect and Bianchi signaled to me that all was hunky-dory. We drank harsh local brandy at a table halfway down the vast Victorian expanse of the Galleria. I looked with curiosity at the fellow who was now in charge of our evening. Perhaps forty-five years of age, of medium height, and chubby, he looked at us benevolently as we drank our brandy. It struck me that he must be a pimp, though it did seem a harsh word for someone who seemed perfectly tractable and decent. Like almost everyone in Naples he was soberly dressed, if a bit shabby. He led us up the Via Roma almost to Piazza Dante where we turned off left into one of the narrow alleys that run uphill under the Vomero. There we ate an excellent meal: *penne con sugo, carne alla pizzaiola* with roasted peppers, salad, even a messy *zuppa inglese* — all new to my New England palate and enhanced by contrast with the army chow we were served whenever the kitchen trucks came close enough to the lines to cook. (The restaurant was, of course, black market and off-limits, as was any establishment of any interest whatsoever. The only legal spots for GIs were the USO clubs. Naples, always resourceful, provided in all ways for the troops' entertainment; money was never a problem; cigarettes and coffee were a currency of the highest illegal tender. No one left for a pass without them. First sergeants crammed our jacket pockets with condoms as we left the company areas, ensuring that sex would cross our minds every time our hands reached into our pockets.)

We drank copious amounts of Lacrima Christi, the gift of Vesuvius's volcanic soil. Our avuncular guide then led us up through several tortuous alleys, finally ushering us into a room which abutted immediately upon the street. The room was furnished with a large bed, flanked on one side by an enormous chest of drawers and on the other by a night table and several cane chairs. There was a garish Madonna above the bed illuminated by a flickering votive candle set in a red glass holder. I glanced uneasily at Bianchi, momentarily confused, my head muddled with the meal and the wine and the brandy that had preceded it all. He grinned at me. "Just wait, buddy boy, just wait," he said. Our host, sensing my discomfiture, pointed at the bed and said, "Voi sarete insieme in quel letto come due fratelli." (You'll be together in that bed just like two brothers.) He then opened a little door I had not noticed and motioned to a girl about the age of seventeen to enter. She smiled modestly at us. Our guide beamed, shook our hands and left.

What I had not expected was that I would not be shy. When the girl, who was dressed only in a kind of shift, had climbed into the bed, I didn't wait for Bianchi but shucked off my boots and uniform and was suddenly on top of her, firmly and tenderly. It was soon over. The girl regarded me placidly; Bianchi beamed at me. "Buddy boy," he said, "It did you a heap of good to get rid of that load!" I turned on my side and fell into a stuporous sleep, waking several times during the night as Bianchi moaned over his orgasms. In the early morning I was awakened by a glimmer of light coming through the curtains in the door that led to the street. The girl reached over and took me in her fist. I was suddenly erect but just as suddenly assaulted by a bout of dry sobs. Leonard's voice calling "Allanbrook, Allanbrook," joined to the sure knowledge of his death, unmanned me. My own regret, which would never fade, violent death, and the expectation of imminent slaughter made a misery of the world, a misery which cleared my head of alcohol and opened my eyes to the grotesqueness of the situation. The girl thought she had failed; Bianchi thought that he had — that I was not cured, and that I never would be.

5

My second year in Naples, my Laura-less year, 1951–52, was preceded by four months in Positano. The landlady there, up at the Chiesa Nuova, in her villa which she had dubbed Stella Romana, was known up and down the coast as Signora Sandwich, no one being able to deal with the Polish difficulties of "Sienkewicz." She felt herself a cut above anyone in town, both because she was "cultural" and Polish, and, more important, because her son, Roman, was a journalist up in Rome. She let it be known that the Communists were eager to have her return to Warsaw but she was not about to go. The main floor of the villa was heavy with Polish bric-a-brac, peasant furniture, dolls in native costume. There was a signed photograph of Paderewski on the mantel. The great joke in town was the time Signora Sandwich had insisted (quite unsuccessfully) that Princess Elizabeth, while touring the Amalfi coast, should stop at the villa for tea. My Polish landlady is not an important part of my history but she is of interest as yet another stranger, another *forestiero* living, as I did, on the outskirts of the Neapolitan world. La Polacca never impinged upon me as had the Ungherese up on Salita dello Scudillo a Capodimonte, and neither of them touched me as did dear Erika, who was my landlady during my second year in Naples. She was Swiss and had been brought up in Naples. She lived perched up on the sixth floor

on Parco Margherita, a steep curving road of bourgeois apartment houses, halfway up to Corso Garibaldi, just a stone's throw
above Piazza Amedeo, where Laura lived. Erika's apartment
was a solitary island, with an elevator that had not functioned
since the first year of the war. Though her situation was the most
desperate of my three landladies, and her plight in Naples the
most heartbreaking, she was the only one of the three who loved
the city, who could speak its dialect. She had sympathies the
Hungarian and the Pole were not capable of.

In the early fifties Positano was already a tourist town,
though before the war it had been known only by a rather special international set. I had first heard of it in the months immediately following the war when the army, after my years as an
infantryman, gave me four and a half cultural months in Florence. The Steiner brothers, German Jews who had weathered
the dark years with the help of loyal Florentine friends, became
good friends of mine. The younger one was a painter and his
older brother was my French professor at the university. They
would talk of their days in that semimythical spot, Positano, in
that semi-mythical interregnum before Hitler had grasped hold
of the continent.

There were a few permanent aliens in town, most notable
among them a crippled German painter, Kurt, who was impov-
erished, bound to his wheelchair. He lived with his tough old
mother. Together they ran a kind of pensione to make ends meet.
From the vantage point of his terrace Kurt's all-seeing eye kept
tabs on the town. There were several upper-class Neapolitans
who had exiled themselves to Positano because of their strait-
ened circumstances: Principessa Carafa and a good friend of
mine, Roberto Scielzo, a stage designer in German opera houses
who had fallen upon bad days. They detested Kurt as a malevolent force in the town, a corrupter of the youth. The townspeople
themselves were not disturbed. The beauty of their boys was a
fact, something to be enjoyed, and if Kurt acted as a go-between
they never dubbed him a *ruffiano*, a pimp, as the princess and

Roberto did. The mothers knew that their boys would marry and pursue perfectly "normal" lives and the opinions of upper-class Neapolitans meant nothing to them. They were a race apart.

Conversation upon Kurt's terrace was enlivening, the company was international, and the wine never ran out. There was an entrancing raffishness about the place, aided and abetted by the poverty of the house and the shrewd voice issuing from the wheelchair. It was a very different place from the establishment set up by a man whom all of us called "il Re dell'Inchiostro," the King of Ink, a rich American, heir to an ink company, who had built a pair of pastel-colored villas on a rocky point that jutted out into the clear waters just east of town. He spent a good deal of money on his pleasures. Kurt would regale us with stories of the ink king's sexual stupidities. (It evidently took a great deal of money to keep the boys over at the pink villas for long.) Despite this occasional commerce Positano never felt like Capri, where the ghost of old Tiberius (or of Tiberius's reputation) hovers above the heights as the foreigner takes a solitary walk up to Anacapri accompanied by the glances and catcalls of the young Capresi. Positano was ruled by the mothers and the commerce that existed, if indeed it was that, had still some innocence attached to it.

Before the war and before polio had crippled Kurt he had been a frequent visitor to the Neapolitan whorehouses, principally as a voyeur. Several establishments had one-way glass installed for such clients as Kurt. The scenes he would describe were often charming. He told of one whore who had just serviced an old client who was nearly a fiasco. It had been a lot of work. She perked up when a fresh young French sailor came in. After the first go-round she left the room for a moment and the sailor, ever ready and alert, tossed his sailor hat with its red pompom onto his upright member, to the unabashed delight of Kurt. It seemed to me at that juncture such a Neapolitan story, well illustrated in Naples' glorious archaeological museum. It stirred up recent memories of Laura up at Capodimonte leading me around the room, her Neapolitan fist firmly clasped about my stiff prick. She would crow triumphantly, "And you thought you were impotent!" and guide me back to bed.

Late one hot afternoon Candida appeared at my door in a carriage, her clear white skin shaded by a broad-rimmed straw hat. She came unannounced and left two weeks later, though later on in the summer she stayed for a longer period. I had met her the previous summer on the beach at Forte dei Marmi; her acting company was playing down the road at Viareggio. A wealthy actor friend, Aldo Trionfo, a member of her company whom I had met the previous winter in Paris, lured me away from my studies in Siena with Maestro Gerlin to spend a weekend with him down on the coast. The evening before I met her on the beach I had seen her playing the part of a rather pacific prostitute in the company's production of Plautus's *Miles Gloriosus*. Within minutes of my laying eyes upon her at the beach the thought of marrying her flooded through my mind. Such calm seemed to flow from her eyes and from her carriage. That winter I went north from Naples and toured with her and the company through Emilia-Romagna: Bologna, Faenza, Forlì, and Ravenna. The company found it rather chic to have an American maestro around and I would play large hunks of my opera to them. They were intrigued that their calm and sphinxlike colleague, who played small parts and who was used by the director as a kind of assistant and advance agent, often going ahead to fix hotel rooms and check on theater arrangements, had found a man. They used to deprecate her full figure, dubbing her Grassattella (Fatty). They mistook her quiet and discretion for worldly wisdom, often making her their confidante in their love affairs, which were many and varied. The truth was that she was of a startling innocence. In later years I would often see certain of the actors from Candida's company in Italian movies and would receive a private delight in thinking of their past lovers and of their varied sexual habits.

The director of the company was a gifted man; he trained his actors well. They were supported by the state and fixed in the far north, in Bolzano, where they were the repertory theater of the city. (Bolzano is the capital of South Tirol and hardly an Italian city; it was the prize awarded to Italy by the Allies after World War I and the Italian government was anxious to establish a cultural presence there.) I visited with Candida and the company the Christmas of my second year in Naples. It was far away from Naples and at an even greater spiritual distance from my previous Christmas down at Piazza Amedeo with Laura's family. Not that Candida was a northerner. Though it seemed at times important to her and to her mother that she had been brought up in Como and Turin, her blood could not have been more southern. Her mother, Delia, was Neapolitan and her father, Alfonso, was from Tolve, a poor stony town fifteen miles east of Potenza.

Having a house in Positano that summer meant lots of company: Pete Steffens arrived from Oxford, Ruth Friedenson, my old solfège teacher, from Paris, and Candida's younger sister from Turin. Nell Tangeman, my mezzo-soprano friend, rented the floor below and had me coach her in the part of Baba the Turk in Stravinsky's opera *The Rake's Progress*, which was being premiered in Venice in September. It was a lotus land of a summer — a special time in a special place, full of the world but distant from anywhere. The sirens' rocks sat out in front of town, inhabited by Léonide Massine, whose motor launch we would observe with great curiosity as it came into town to pick up groceries. None of us were ever invited out to that special place, not even Kurt. The following summer Signora Sandwich was in cultural heaven, her fondest dreams come to fruition. Massine had been commissioned to choreograph a ballet for the Sagra Umbra, a yearly music festival up in Umbria. He rented the terraces of the Villa Stella Romana as his rehearsal place. A touching and simple dancer who was miming the part of Jesus in the ballet became a great friend of Aldo, my rich actor friend from Candida's company. He had rented the house down the hill from Signora Sandwich and lent it to Candida and me as a wedding present. He brought his father's chauffeur with him and for a month and a half we had the luxury of a long black sedan with our own driver. Such were my Positano summers.

What chitchat such places give rise to! They constitute for so many visitors the substance and the fabric of the world of Naples, making of it a never-never land, an adolescent's perennial fulfillment. "It's Venus's flytrap," Kurt used to say in his peculiar but perfectly idiomatic English. All of Italy so easily assumes this role as the foreigner walks its streets, tastes its simple but opulent cooking, looks at its pictures, and is caught by the quick eyes and supple limbs of its inhabitants. It's a country like any other, only too often more vapid and disorganized than the native habitats the visitor has briefly abandoned. "It's nice to know that Switzerland is back up there when we are here in the midst of all of this," said one of the Swiss ladies I got to know that summer as she contemplated the setting sun and her Italian lover.

The second night of my return to Naples from Positano, settled into my room on the sixth floor on Parco Margherita, I awoke to the sound of my landlady, Erika, crying hysterically. She stopped after several minutes and a terrible silence ensued. The following morning no mention was made of it by either of us. As the weeks and months passed I grew to expect these occurrences. I had first seen Erika the year before in the Library of the American Information Service downtown. She was a woman of around fifty years of age with large eyes set in a long face. Her complexion was whitish and unhealthy and she dressed in clothes of an undecipherable age and provenance. I knew the Fulbright fellow who had rented a room in her apartment the previous year. He was a goodhearted man who studied at Croce's historical institute. He was anxious to find her another tenant as he was packing up and leaving for his academic post back in Cleveland, and I was delighted to find the spot after the

Hungarian blow-up at Capodimonte. There was, in addition, a piano which I could compose on.

The apartment was in a well-to-do neighborhood, though not quite so grand as the Via Tasso, which coiled on up above Parco Margherita to the heights of the Vomero. Men in dressing gowns could be seen sipping coffee on the apartment terraces at ten and eleven in the morning, tall skinny men, most of them, with miniature mustaches. "There's lots of barons from Calabria among them," explained Erika with a wan smile. "They wouldn't be caught dead down there in their little towns and are too provincial to venture as far as Rome. Naples is their real home."

Later that year, down at the bottom of the road just above Piazza Amedeo (Laura's address!) Candida introduced me to one of her Neapolitan uncles. He received us at the front door dressed in a silk jacket tied with a sash and escorted us to his study, a paneled octagonal room lined with books. He had been engaged in a literary study of Lord Byron for many years. After a proper bit of conversation we proceeded to the *salotto* for *il thè*. In the middle of the salotto stood a large gold harp. "Both dear Clara and my daughter Elletra play it," he informed us. Elletra, a cold blonde, dismissed her accomplishment with a diffident gesture. Clara, his wife, had always found it rather eccentric of Candida that she had made a profession of her acting. "But then," she explained to me, "Her mother, Delia, my dear husband's sister, always has been a caution; she was scornful of her native city and there she is now, all alone up there in Turin, far from her own!" Uncle Fabio with a certain gentlemanly circumspection turned the conversation toward literature and we discussed certain obscure nineteenth-century playwrights, though he demurred a bit when I ventured to bring up Pirandello. (Candida's company had just put on a very stylish production of *Così è se vi pare*.) On Parco Margherita I began to see another whole facet of the Naples I thought I knew.

The elevator in Erika's building, elegantly enclosed within its wrought iron grillwork, had not functioned since 1941. The full import of this fact and the effect it had upon Erika's life became clear to me only when I had pieced together both the story of her war years and of her Neapolitan childhood. "When I was a youngster here, before the First War," she said, "everything, except for politics, was run by foreigners: the gas works by the Belgians, the streetcars by the French, the boats by the Germans, and, of course, the hotels by the Swiss." She smiled as she said this and I could envisage her clearly in that long-ago era before the First War. There were pictures in the apartment of her and her brother posed with their parents in the gilt dining room of the Albergo Vesuvio, a proper Swiss family, proprietors and managers of Naples' best hotel. "Winter was best," she would often tell me. "The Russians would come by steamer from Odessa and leave their wives and children and governesses with us for months at a time while they went off big-game hunting down in Africa. It was a lovely, well-run hotel, one we were all proud of, something like what the Hassler is in Rome right now. In those days it was so different. You could travel all around Europe without a passport and my father would visit splendid hotels, just like his own, in every part of Europe and even down in Cairo. Of course," she would go on to say, "all that changed with the war. The Italian government requisitioned our hotel for use as a military hospital and we never did get it back. Papa was no good at lawsuits and suing people. Both my mother and my father were so used to Naples that they stayed on; they would never consider going back to Zurich. They had this apartment, which they had owned for years, even though the hotel was lost to them, and money bought them more comfort here than up in Switzerland. We Swiss are a funny race," she said with a resigned gesture. "We live all over the world, but our blood remains firmly Swiss."

Erika went up to Switzerland in 1920, studied and became a librarian in Zurich. She was a shy girl and lived a retired Swiss life, happy enough with her cataloguing in the ordered world of the municipal library. She would come down to Naples two or three times a year to stay with her father and mother, cherishing her visits as she loved the city and could speak Neapolitan fluently. She seldom saw her brother, a businessman in Buenos Aires who returned to Europe only rarely. Neither of them married.

1920 to 1940 seems such a short expanse of time looking back now from the end of this aging century. It passed quickly enough for Erika as I could infer from her accounts of her life. Her parents were both of them becoming a bit sickly in the mid-1930s. She repeatedly urged them to come up to Zurich, if not to live there at least to have proper medical care. They were reluctant to do so; they were used to their cook and their maid, to the splendid view of the bay from their terrace. Their investments dwindled and their life came to be supported more and more by checks from Buenos Aires and portions of Erika's modest salary as a librarian. The bad years approached; the parents' health worsened. The Neapolitan doctors advised against moving them north. "They are so used to our climate, they are old and set in their ways. Why give them any unnecessary shocks?" was what they would say to Erika. She felt she had no choice but to leave Zurich and to return to Naples to care for them. It was by now 1940. The mother had a slow-growing cancer, the father circulatory troubles which gave rise to a series of strokes, minor at first. He had his final and most serious stroke the day the Fascist Grand Council deposed Mussolini, dying just as Patton entered Palermo. The mother was still alive the week the Germans pulled out of Naples, her senses alert though her mind wandered. She suffered horribly and medicines were not available.

There had been four heroic days in Naples; the populace had risen in arms against both the hated *tedeschi* and the Fascists who had worked with them; they drove them out in a frenzy of patriotic zeal. The city awaited the Allies but felt certain that the Germans had mined large portions of the metropolis. Everyone left. The streets were empty and in this most brawling and cacophonous of cities there was silence. Erika and her mother were marooned up on the sixth floor, alone, shipwrecked, the only inhabitants left on Parco Margherita. The mother gave Erika no peace; she peevishly demanded to know why it was so quiet. "I had to make up a story," Erika explained to me. "Naples is never quiet and my mother knew that perfectly well. Her hearing remained acute until the very end. I had to lie. I told her, shouting at her, that she had gone deaf. It was a poor lie — after all, she could hear me perfectly well! I was desperate. She didn't believe me. She became angry and repeated over and over again that she had not brought up her daughter to be a liar. All the time, of course, all the time, every moment, I was waiting for the whole neighborhood to explode into bits and pieces."

The mother hung on for another month in the midst of all the hullabaloo of the American entrance. The bombardments continued, though at a lesser rate as the German air force was hardly the equal of the Allied. The black market burgeoned. The only luck poor Erika had had in all those bad years was that the house had not been damaged in all the pounding that Naples had received from the air. Soon after the elevator stopped, the water and the electricity went. The gas soon after. Money became scarcer and scarcer and counted for little as inflation increased. It ceased being a useful means of exchange even if checks could be gotten from Buenos Aires or Zurich.

When the water first went Erika had depended upon the *portiere* and his brawny son to carry her buckets up the six flights of stairs. They were filled at a faucet up at the top of the street by Corso Garibaldi which functioned throughout the war. "We were lucky in that," she told me. The son fled to relations in the country to avoid being taken by the Germans as forced labor. The porter himself grew more venal along with the times and abandoned Erika to her own devices. Her more fortunate neighbors who had connections in the country and who could ply him with hams and cheeses from their private stock were looked after. Erika, my poor Erika, made herself a yoke from which she suspended two buckets. She would descend the six flights, climb up the steep, bourgeois curve of Parco Margherita to the Corso Garibaldi, fill the buckets at the little faucet (after awaiting her turn), and then retrace her steps. Once a day would most often not suffice, especially when the mother's illness required frequent washings. At times she would stumble on the stairs, necessitating another trip back up to the faucet.

And she had to get food. Naples had become an economy based on the black market. The peasants became capitalists. They had what counted: cheese, vegetables, hams, grain, wine, and oil. They had their day of glory. They were virtuosi in barter and would appear on Parco Margherita in fur coats with gold watches in their pockets. Erika's family had lived in their apartment for nearly forty years — since 1905. It was crammed with objects which could be bartered for food, and, after the gas went, for charcoal. In all of the bargaining which was necessary in such a market Erika was under a severe disadvantage: though she could speak the dialect she was a foreigner both in her looks and in her behavior. She could expect no help in this beleaguered city, and the desperation written upon her face encouraged the black marketeers to sharpen their exchanges. She had no brothers, no cousins, no network of relations either familial or professional to cling to. She was alone, a popeyed virgin, forty-seven years old, with blotched white skin and a terrible burden. The parents, during all the bad years, were too sick to apprehend the state of affairs and even in better times had been too self-centered to pay any particular attention to their librarian daughter. They had ignored all of her appeals to return to Switzerland while it was still possible for them both physically and financially. She, alone, was left to nurture their dying. The mother died on Christmas Eve of 1943, the day I disembarked in Oran with my infantry regiment.

A week after her mother's death Erika's outward life suffered a radical change. She rented her apartment to the U.S. Army's Special Service Unit, the command that was responsible for putting on shows for the troops. The Allied forces were requisitioning apartments all over town but Erika's particular surcease from the daily misery that had been her lot for so long could not have been more unlikely. It was a providential fluke. Her rooms were suddenly full of jazzmen, dancers, clowns, and civilians dressed up as officers running the whole show. Food poured in. Portable gas resuscitated the long-dead kitchen range. GIs climbed the six flights with ten-gallon cans of water. Coffee, Erika's one addiction, reappeared. No less marvelous there was company, and such company; never in her life had she been surrounded with such ebullience, not even as a child in the luxury of the old Albergo Vesuvio, before World War I, so long ago. The piano was in constant use. It was in these months that my regiment went into the line up at the Garigliano River.

Each day during that winter of '51–'52 up in Erika's apartment was marked by at least two pages of full score of my opera *Ethan Frome;* sometimes I would get as much as five pages done. At the conservatory, under Maestro Gerlin's tutelage, I was being guided through Book Two of the *Well-Tempered Clavier* and all of the French and English Suites. Couperin began to fall into place for me as I began, for the first time, to hear him, to sense that he was the greatest of the purely harpsichord masters, wedded to the harpsichord as surely as Chopin and Debussy were to the piano. Erika rarely stirred from the apartment. She rustled through the rooms, dressed in an ancient linen duster, always aware of me but painstakingly circumspect as to my activities. She seemed to live on little triangles of Swiss processed cheese and crackers. She looked ever more sickly and I began bringing home tender little steaks and fruit and fennel to tempt her with. She gradually succumbed to these goodies and a special intimacy grew between us up there on the sixth floor. She was delighted when I began to frequent persons of any distinction in the city, persons about whom she knew many details as she had lived in Naples off and on for so many years: Croce and his family, scientists from the Marine Biology Institute down on the

Riviera di Chiaia, a Scottish family that owned the most reputable department store. Though she had not visited people for years nor been visited by them she smiled the smile of someone who felt herself a part of society. She loved it when I repeated to her Silvia Croce's account of morning in the philosopher's household: "Papa insists we all be up by six-thirty, and as a proper paterfamilias presides over our morning coffee. He then proceeds to his study to work on volume seventy-three of his complete works and we all go back to bed!"

Erika felt it both proper and fitting that the son of Principe d'Avalos, who was earning his piano diploma at the conservatory, should come and listen to me belt out portions of my opera. She enjoyed vicariously my visits to his family's villa out on Posilipo, with its terraces stretching down to the sea, not far beyond the remnant of Sir William Hamilton's seaside "casino," his little Villa Emma, scene of that greatest of ménages à trois: Hamilton, Lady Hamilton, and Admiral Nelson. I often wondered when I visited there if the family that had lived in my Capodimonte villa had been among the illuminati who had been tortured and executed by Cardinal Ruffo and the returning Bourbons. Croce's own *Storia del Regno di Napoli* meditates in great Hegelian loops on that period and his daughters would point out to me with a certain precise glee that my favorite restaurant was located in the Piazza dei Martiri where the cream of the Neapolitan enlightenment had been strung up in 1799. "Of course the Bourbon queen was the sister of Marie Antoinette!" I exclaimed. "Hardly an excuse for the divine Emma, Lord Nelson's light-of-love, who positively enjoyed the agony of her former friends, whatever may have been the political exigencies of the admiral," countered one of the daughters. "Once a bitch, always a bitch," chimed in the other with more asperity than I had thought her capable of.

One moment that in my memory is tinged with perennial regret occurred early that winter. I came out of the door of Erika's apartment and beheld my older friend Edwin Denby puffing up the last flight of stairs. "Let's get a house together, Douglas." With no hesitation I replied, "I can't, I'm ensconced here with Erika Conzetti. I couldn't leave her." He was a man with the subtlest of antennae and understood immediately when he met Erika. Indeed they took to each other; she highly approved of him and they had an immediate rapprochement. I often wonder now, so many years later, at my not insisting he simply move into another of Erika's many bedrooms and share the apartment with both of us for the rest of the year. It would have been a happy trio. Later that winter, when I told him I intended to marry Candida, he said, "You really do act on what you love, my dear." What would it have cost him to ask to stay at Erika's?

Later that same week he took me to see what he called the greatest theater in the world. It was in the most disreputable section of town, near the enormous yellow Stazione Centrale and Castel Capuano. Admission was fifty lire. It was a smallish room with wooden benches. The day we went it was half full of the poorest of the poor: beggars, *scugnizzi* (street urchins), whores and street vendors taking a break. They were all acutely attentive to the goings-on within the proscenium arch of the tiny stage, reciting the lines along with the marionettes, the amazingly large marionettes festooned with cuirasses and shining armor. My ear began catching the cadence of the verse, rhyming couplets in something not too far from alexandrines, recited in a dialect that was certainly Neapolitan but which had a remote ring to it. (I later learned it was from the seventeenth century.) There were tirades, protests of courtly love, sword fights and jousting, Moors and Christians — all played before a rapt audience which knew the score by heart. I remembered accounts of Murat's entrance into Naples as king after Napoleon's victory at Austerlitz. He was the most colorful of the marshals and wore a gleaming white uniform, his horse bedecked with plumes. The enraptured populace hailed him as Rinaldo.

After the performance Edwin and I went to a nearby restaurant and had the padrone poach us a whole fish *in bianco*. He boned it at the table and served it with oil and lemon. We drank a great deal of white wine from Vesuvius and I realized at that moment how much I loved Naples, how I felt embraced by it, how much it felt like home. Edwin lamented that he had not been brought up in the city. "I would never have left," he exclaimed. "What a childhood it would have been!" He talked of his first visits to Naples in the thirties. Then there had been two cycles of marionette plays, the noble *roman de geste* which we had just seen and another cycle, called the *mala vita*, whose characters were all low-life: robbers, whores, and pimps. "Those moral thugs, the Fascists," he said, "in the name of purity banished the low-life cycle from the city and only allowed it to play down at Torre Annunziata. That one went out of business with the war and now this one is going to close in the next couple of weeks. They can't make the rent."

Several days later I was taking an evening stroll near the Piazza dei Martiri with an acquaintance of mine, a scholar at Croce's Historical Institute and a journalist in town. (Erika approved highly of him; he was from a good Neapolitan family and well brought up.) There must have been a strain of cultural boasting in my voice as I talked to him about the marionette theater and of its imminent closure. I demanded to know why such an event was not being lamented in his newspaper. My intention was to challenge him both as an historian and as a journalist, to prod him into taking notice of what was to me a cultural paradigm of Neapolitan life.

He was a man of sweet temperament, well versed in the history of his native city. His reply was all the more startling to me, being couched in terms of reserved passion and polite indignation. "Your view of Naples," he said, "is shared by so many of you sensitive foreigners. I've never been to the Marionette Theater and there'll be no article in my paper. That same populace, those *lazzaroni* who hailed King Murat as Rinaldo, danced with glee just a few years previously when the Bourbons returned in '99; they were the *tirapiedi* who hung on the legs of Elizabetta

Fonseca as she was suspended from the gallows right there in Piazza dei Martiri." He pointed out to me the name of the square we had just turned into. "Their most beloved king was known to them as 'Re Bomba'; he had happily bombed his city of Messina, following the destruction with satisfaction from the deck of his royal gunship. He spoke the same language as his populace, who adored him as their own 'Re Lazzarone.' Don't you realize that you have this whole Neapolitan world upside down? In the only revolution we ever had it was the cultured aristocracy, the educated classes that wanted a republic. The sans-culottes, the *lazzaroni*, were the conservatives; they cheered when their betters were tortured and hung in a public square. This in a city whose university was secular even in the thirteenth century, the city that has provided Italy with all of its philosophers: St. Thomas, Vico, Giannone, Campanella, and my own teacher, Croce. You English and Americans love us so! You relish the *lazzaroni* in the same way that you idolize the rest of Italy because, as you delight in saying, we have never 'suffered' the Enlightenment, which all of you are heirs to. We are supposed to be picturesque, spontaneous, artistic!"

He stopped, aware that I was abashed at what he had said. He had posed a cutting alternative to my views of his city and his country. Not only Naples but all of Italy stood abused in his eyes. Croce in his *Storia del Regno di Napoli* writes of the Neapolitan illuminati who had either fled or been exiled after the Bourbon restoration. When they returned to their native soil after their long years away they were disgusted by what they saw. Abroad and north in the Po Valley they were honored victims of political repression, many of them members of the carbonari, the organization which foreshadowed the Risorgimento.

Of course my friend, the journalist and historian, was well aware of the character of the Risorgimento. It was hardly a popular insurrection but a bizarre wedding of middle- and upper-class romantics guided by the tactics of the continent's shrewdest statesman, Count Cavour. The kingdom of the Two Sicilies (so venerable that it was known as *il regno* — the kingdom) had no place in Cavour's scheme. It was suddenly dumped in his lap by the greatest hero of the nineteenth century, Garibaldi, a naive and utterly honest soldier imbued with the ideals of an imagined Roman republic. The majority of his valiant little band of soldiers who conquered Sicily and Naples for Victor Emmanuel were patriots from the Po Valley, a region which has always been the richest and most advanced region of the peninsula. "The economic miracle" which makes Italy nowadays the fifth industrial power in the world has all its roots in the North and flourishes however bankrupt the Mezzogiorno may be at any particular moment. (The government in Rome has little to do with any of this, though by hook or by crook it always gets its share of the spoils.) The unified state that emerged from the Risorgimento bears all the marks of its antithetical origins, of its stillborn trauma. The poisonous hate and mistrust that existed between Cavour and Garibaldi is engraved upon the psyche of the state. Piedmont and Naples, worlds apart in both geography and custom, were united under a remarkably inept monarch and a parliamentary form of government that resembled not the *virtù* of the imagined Roman republic of Garibaldi but rather the actual habits of the ancient *clientes* dependent on their senatorial bosses. The frustrated hopes of a heroic and united Italy were seized upon by the first of the twentieth century's ruling thugs, Mussolini, and he made his nation ridiculous in the eyes of its best and most intelligent citizens. "Better one day as a lion than a thousand years as a sheep" was emblazoned on the ruins of the bombed cities I walked through as I made my way up the peninsula from Naples to the Alps. Everything one saw and all the people one talked to bore witness to a regime and a war which had reduced Italy to ruins, blighted the lives of two generations of Italians, and sent their sons to die in the snows of Stalingrad.

I had never considered Edwin to have any particular political sagacity, but when I somewhat abashedly raised the matter with him several days later, he had several things to say. "Anyone

with a pair of eyes in their head could have spotted Mussolini for a thug way back in 1921. He could so easily have been
stopped dead in his tracks. Your friend's teacher, Don Benedetto
Croce, the high priest of Italian liberalism, advised people to
vote for Mussolini. He had such faith in the ministerial system
that he urged others to serve as ministers with the new man,
deeming it self-evident that Mussolini would become a prisoner
of the system once accepted within it. He saw his error soon
enough, but it was too late. At least he's a cut above Germany's
leading philosopher, the great Martin Heidegger, who relished
the Nazis." He then turned to me with special attention. "This is
a horror of a century, dear Douglas. Don't expect anything from
the left or the right and the center always vacillates. You love
Naples as it is. Why not? It's never been fucked up by any notion
of progress. The Romans came down here to get away from life
in the capital of the world. Virgil was happy to be buried here,
and as for Tiberius, he has always gotten an undeservedly bad
press." Edwin then smiled sweetly but shrewdly at me. "You
want to be all things to everyone. Well, why not? Your friend
studies history and has to think it means something. He writes
for a particular newspaper and is an old-fashioned liberal, whatever that means nowadays. He loves his city and is ashamed of
it." Edwin was much older than me. I remembered that he had
been in Germany when he was younger, a dancer in Stuttgart,
though he had never talked to me about this period in his life.
We went on up to Erika's where I played large parts of *Ethan
Frome* to him. "It's full of real paragraphs of music," he said.
"And that's meant as a compliment!"

Edwin often had a better ear than I did. We went to San Carlo
to hear Stravinsky conduct the opera orchestra. "Just listen to
that," he exclaimed as they finished up the *Apollon Musagète*.
"Those old professori in the pit know how to breathe. Don't you
think it's more beautiful than the Philharmonic?" He was right.
I was still the student, all taken up with Stravinsky's strictures
that the conductor should simply be a transcriber, that it was all

down there in the written score. "Never mind what Stravinsky writes, that's not important," Edwin told me at intermission. "He's the best of the century, but he wants to be chic and write about aesthetics and unimportant things. That boy that rides on his coattails puts him up to it. Of course, it is true that his vocal music strangles the singers. Remember that poor tenor last fall?"

I had met Edwin up in Venice in the week of the first performances of *The Rake's Progress*. I knew very well what he was talking about as I had coached Nell Tangeman in her part in the opera that summer down in Positano. Stravinsky so often plants the voice part square on the downbeat as if it were a kind of percussion instrument, not giving the poor singer that entrancing lift in the orchestra which liberates the breath and gives rhythm to the phrase, and, most importantly, loosens the singer's diaphragm. Edwin later showed me how Stravinsky's instrumental works found their real marriage in the Balanchine ballets, with the body's movements giving curve and shape to the orchestra's sound.

A whole other side of Erika came out when my friend Jörg and his wife appeared on my doorstep, exhausted after a twenty-four-hour train trip down from Vienna. Erika turned out to know all about Vienna; she even spoke the dialect. I had forgotten about her German roots, her years in Zurich. Her whole professional grown-up life, after all, had been away from Naples, up north in the German-speaking country. This meeting with Jörg in Naples, on the sixth floor at Parco Margherita, linked another European place, Vienna, with Naples. I was growing up away from home. The Old World of Europe was no longer new to me; it was becoming more and more familiar.

I had met Jörg first in June 1949 at Leopoldskron, Max Reinhardt's former estate just outside Salzburg. A group of us, all from Cambridge and all pupils of Mlle Boulanger, came from Paris, not knowing what to expect when we arrived, though we had been told that a seminar in American Studies had been set up the previous year by clever people from Cambridge. That

June proved to be blissfully anarchic: there was no specified program while we were there. All of us musicians played music and a hodgepodge of Europeans of various nationalities and the most varied professions settled in for a prolonged houseparty. My most lasting foreign friendships had their origin there: Giacinta and Vito from Rome, Enrique, a Spanish refugee, and Jörg from Vienna.

The war was still very close in Austria in 1949. The Russians occupied half of the country; refugees drifted across uneasy frontiers. Our director at Leopoldskron, a thin and pleasant blond boy from Harvard, opened the doors of the castle and fed all comers. We slept on cots in vast Baroque bedrooms, ate in the prince-archbishop's dining room, played music at night, and wandered up over the hill into Salzburg during the day. I had no special eye for the rainy town with its vistas of domes and Baroque façades, a failing which was a source of bewilderment to Jörg. He would stand face to face with me in front of the cathedral and give me lectures. He had bright china-blue eyes in the midst of a square and dumpy face and spoke as little English as I German. "Austria is not Germany," he would say as he brought me to see the statue of the boy thumbing his nose at Germany so few kilometers away to the north. It must have been a canker for him that Hitler was an Austrian though I was too polite and too taken up with him at that moment to mention it. I knew nothing of Germany, let alone Austria; France and Italy were my hobbies and my loves. (I had a horror of Germany and Germans from my years in the war, though for a considerable time because of Jörg I did not include Austria in my revulsion.)

When the month at Leopoldskron ended Jörg brought me to Vienna, my intention being then to proceed south to Venice (which I had never seen) and then on to Florence and Siena for my classes with Maestro Gerlin at the Accademia Chigiana. Armed with the special gray card that was necessary for passage through the Russian zone I arrived at the newly reconstructed Westbahnhof with Jörg. He explained to me, in his broken English, that he and his friends called the style of their newly built railway station "Neon-Classik." He was a student of historical architecture and had written his doctoral thesis on certain Venetian houses.

Vienna was in a state of shock from the war: its elegance tawdry, its stores half empty, its streets patrolled by Allied and Russian soldiers. Pieces of buildings often fell onto the sidewalks making walking perilous, especially at night. The hospitality of Jörg's family was touching; they insisted upon feeding me, though it was painfully obvious that food was scarce and hard to come by. Meat was rare and, if available, too expensive, so they gave me dumplings with apricots inside.

Jörg took me to see St. Stephen's and the Baroque palace where the *Rosenkavalier* lived. We went out to Grinzing and drank new wine far into the evening, walking the long road home as the trolley had stopped for the night. I was shown the hill where the Polish king had appeared just in the nick of time to save the city from the besieging Turks, and I touched the Turkish cannonballs on the old ramparts of the town. "Beyond Vienna the steppes of Asia begin," Jörg said. "We were always the last bastion of Europe."

His mother would lament the fact that I had never seen Budapest down in "Ungarn." "Another Paris," she would say. Most of all she would lament the fact that I had no idea of how the city was when they had their Kaiser. I invited her to a performance of *Der Rosenkavalier*, buying the best seats in the house. Off we went on the trolley around the town and down to the Theater an der Wien, where *The Magic Flute* was first performed. The grand State Opera was still a shell, a relic of the Allied bombings. The little house was shabby but acoustically brilliant, all of the voices immediate in that intimate space. The production was sumptuous, the voices splendid, the staging convincing, and the orchestra was the Vienna Philharmonic. It was a Viennese ritual the way a weekly Mass is a celebration or the Fourth of July a patriotic birthday. I was aware of Jörg's mother eyeing me with a certain anxiety; I was a foreigner, a visitor from the New World. Could I possibly savor, let alone appreciate, the most quintessential Viennese experience? "In a few years the fellow playing Baron Ochs will be a marvel," she whispered to me as the singer in question lurched through his drunken waltz. I was bored: the endless spinning out of sugared sequences, the cloying beauty of the high soprano tessitura, the fundamental sentimentality of the piece were all unworthy of this theater where Mozart's marvel had been introduced. She sensed that I did not love the work and though she had become fond of me she considered me a barbarian. Her son's opinion of me, while not unlike his mother's, was shaded by other considerations. He was impressed by my fluency in Italian and French and my obvious talents as a composer and a performer though it remained difficult for him to grant any cultural status to an American.

It was with all of this in mind that I took a special relish in showing off Naples to Jörg and his wife. I showed them Spaccanapoli, the long, straight street that had been the spine of the ancient Greek city, a palimpsest of cultures, one on top of the other: Greek, Roman, Lombard, Angevin, with Aragonese-Spanish façades, Bourbon palaces, and Vanvitelli's monumental stairways. With a special bow to Middle Europe I took them to the Church of the Carmine down by the port to see the tomb of poor unlucky Conradin, the last of the Hohenstaufen emperors. We went out to Pozzuoli to visit the Roman amphitheater and contemplated the temples around what had been the major port of ancient Rome. Finally, I led them down to Positano where I had rented a little house for them just down the hill from Signora Sandwich. It was a pretty place, owned by two maiden ladies of good Neapolitan stock, the Signorine Passalacqua. Jörg and his wife had a fruitful stay, writing to me the next year in America that they had a new baby who was "made" there on top of the hill by the Chiesa Nuova.

Of all the people that came to visit me, it was Candida whom Erika cherished the most. When we announced to her our coming marriage she immediately went to her bedroom and returned with her parents' wedding rings, holding them out to us, nestled on their aging beds of cotton, with an air of modest assurance. We accepted them with what I now realize were inward motions of both gratitude and doubt: gratitude to Erika for her gesture of love and friendship, and a nagging doubt as to what our firm intentions amounted to.

I had fallen in love with Candida within the first ten minutes of seeing her on the beach up at Forte dei Marmi and the thought of marriage had crossed my mind immediately. Just as clear to me, at that moment when Erika brought out her parents' wedding rings, was the realization that this was an irreversible step which would not be taking place if I were not obligated to return to the United States to take up a job. My fellowship was over, my revels ended; my worldly assets negligible, consisting almost entirely of my last checks from the Fulbright commission. I had a job at an obscure little college in Maryland and a boat ticket to New York. In the two years that I had known Candida, the one marvelous asset had been the seeming lack of any problems. She would arrive in a carriage, depart a few weeks later. I would take a train to some pleasant town where her company was playing, tour a bit with all of them, and return back south to Naples.

Her face had a classic calm about it: her eyes were Junoesque, large with gray lights, what the ancients deemed to be "oxlike" though we moderns deprecate them as "cowlike." She had no place, no fixed abode. Her mother, Delia, a giddy young Neapolitan of a family who had been members of the Bourbon court, married at the age of eighteen an army officer, a man older than herself who came from the back country of Lucania. She was snobbish about Naples and only too happy to lead her life in the North, at Como and later in Turin, often left alone when her husband was absent on his duties as a colonel in the Alpini, the crack mountain troops of the Italian army.

Candida was shunted off at a shamefully young age to the strictest of female boarding schools, an establishment which retained all of the provincial severity for which Turin had been famous in the nineteenth century. It was ultra-Catholic, ultraconservative, and reserved for the daughters of army officers and upper-class families. During the war Candida suffered in ways that differed radically from my experiences as an infantryman. She seemed distanced by that time from any ease in forming intimacies and close friendships. Her father died in the first years of the war from a lingering sickness. During all the years of the incessant night bombing of Turin by the RAF Delia persisted in staying on in town. She could always find a capacious apartment near the central railroad station, a favorite target of the night bombers. For over a year they had an apartment on the third floor of a building whose first two floors had been damaged severely in the bombing, leaving as the only access to the third floor a wooden ladder. When evacuation from the center of town was ordered by the authorities Delia would come out of the bombed front door, petite and dressed to the hilt, always topping off the outfit with a stylish hat. She would climb up front and sit in the cab with the driver, leaving the rest of the family to scramble into the back of the truck. At the first opportunity she would drag them all back from the security of the countryside, back to the beleaguered city. During all of this period, Candida and her sister were studying violin and piano at the conservatory and dramatic art at the State Academy. Candida received special tutoring in Latin from a most distinguished lady with the bizarre name of Sottsass. (We came across her name years later in America when we were experimenting with recipes from Alice B. Toklas's cookbook.)

Food became scarce as the war ground on; doubtful substitutes for wheat were found, among them a bread made from rice which would harden into indigestible blocks which often led to ulcers. The black market became both universal and necessary. Neither before, during, or after the war did Delia like to cook. Whenever possible she would go to the finest salumeria in Turin and return home with the best hams, cheeses, pâtés, and other splendid goodies that required no preparation by her. Clothes had always to be of the finest materials, made by the best tailors. Money was scarce but offered no hindrance to Delia: it could always be borrowed at rates which increased to dizzying heights as the years passed and the debts mounted.

It was from all of this that Candida escaped, finding a cherished home away from home in the anonymity of hotels and in the proximity not of family but of professional actors and actresses. She became a sophisticated innocent in a shifting world of passionate players, seemingly knowing but in truth unknown to all, even to herself. I became a center for her, a port to which she could return from her ominously placid peregrinations. It was hardly a port she found, however — rather another refugee fixed temporarily in the foreign world of Naples, perched up on the sixth floor in the apartment of a shipwrecked Swiss maiden.

As the winter of '51–'52 progressed Erika's nightmares began to occur more regularly. Her desperate, whimpering cries would awaken me in the middle of the night. I would sense, the morning after, a special quiet within her. I would run down the six flights, climb up to the Corso to buy some fresh brioches and a morning paper, and then back down the hill and up to the apartment. We would grind the coffee, boil the water in the bottom of the Neapolitan coffee maker, reverse the machine, and quietly read the paper as we waited for the coffee to pass.

The crises at night were the more shocking in that Erika made a fetish of being quiet, generally conversing at a level just above a whisper. She would sit in her room with her ear close to a small radio, listening to Mozart with the volume so low as to be scarcely audible from the other side of the room. "I would not want the neighbors to be disturbed," she would explain to me.

Something now began to happen to me, a phenomenon triggered by the sound of Erika's cries, her poor lonely cries, sounding in the midst of the night. I would awake, hearing a voice calling out my last name in the darkness: "Allanbrook, Allanbrook!" My eyes couldn't have been open when I heard the voice; in that penumbral zone between sleep and waking the exact "where" of attention is most often lacking. For a long time I could not distinguish whose voice it was; whosoever's it was, however, the sound of my name uttered in that darkness across an as yet unspecified chasm of time was for me fraught with feelings compounded out of oceanic waves of regret. It was the voice of someone to whom I was bound; of that at least I was sure. The irretrievable nature of the regret, the memory awake to what is forever gone, to what need not have passed unheeded but which, alas, did — all of this was present to me in those moments, but the place and the person seemed buried, embedded in the detritus of time.

So many things find a response in the intricate jumble of our souls: bells, voices, cries (Erika's midnight laments!), our own body's aches and discomforts, a crick in the neck, a cramped position of a knee, indigestion, and, most rudely, a full bladder. One night, one particular night, I was awakened by an urgent need to urinate and in that very moment of physical awareness I again heard the voice calling "Allanbrook, Allanbrook," simultaneous with Erika's weeping in her bedroom. Returning from the bathroom I stood on the terrace outside my bedroom as Erika's cries weakened and then were silent. The curve of Posilipo on my right was outlined with pinpoints of light, and, far out, beyond the random lights of the fishing boats, Capri's shape could be discerned, standing clear of Punta della Campanella and the Sorrento peninsula. I was seized with a vast undertow of memory, a clear recalling of my first look at Naples aboard the dirty British transport which had brought us up from Oran, past the spectacle of Etna soaring snow-clad above Scylla and Charybdis, past the volcanic islands of Vulcano and Stromboli, and was now arrived in the evening to the Bay of Naples, sailing in between Capri and Punta della Campanella with Vesuvius on my right and Leonard at my side. I was gazing at the same scene; only now it was from Erika's balcony, with Vesuvius on my left and Leonard long dead. It was a mirror image, with the memory and the vision doubling each other, left for right, past for present. The sound of Erika's cries, the clear imagining of Leonard's sounding my own name in the darkness, the memory of so many dead and of so many wounded, my own distended bladder — all these disparate facts brought back to me the enormous presence of the war, my own war, my own dead and my own wounded, all splayed against the unimaginable landscape of horror and desolation which I had been such a minuscule part of.

6

Disconsolate, the two of us, Bianchi and I, made our way down the Via Roma to the vast expanse of Piazza del Plebiscito. Neither of us said a word about our night together with the little teenage whore. Trucks awaited us. We ground our way up the Via Roma, past the royal palace at Capodimonte and on north to our positions in the line. (I didn't see Naples again until seven months after the war ended when I was shipped home in a brand-new aircraft carrier.) When we got back to HQ Company Bianchi and I went to the medics for a prophylactic. Bianchi caught a dose. I was lucky; I didn't.

Preparations began for the May 1944 offensive. An entire new division, the 85th, took up positions in the area where Jack and Leonard had been killed, that stretch down to the sea toward Formia and Gaeta. Our division moved over to the right a bit and the French farther into the wild hills and mountains toward Cassino. Attention was being directed from above upon our staff officers. One sleepy afternoon while I was fussing with the maps and our executive officer, Lieutenant Colonel Balcom, was half asleep in the corner of our dugout, the camouflage netting was whisked aside. In the door stood a slim British officer, mild in aspect with piercing blue eyes. I bellowed "Attention!" to the momentary annoyance of the colonel. My gaze had been fixed upon the various pips and signs of rank on the Britisher's jacket, realizing that he must be at least a lieutenant general and hence the corps commander. It took Colonel Balcom considerably longer to ascertain who and what the officer might be, his face and his posture registering precisely his dawning recognition. "I thought we might just examine the positions of your battalions and in particular the dispositions of your heavy weapons, Colonel," said the British general in a quiet voice. I hastened to hand the situation map to the colonel, who, in his confusion, began looking at it upside down. I was adroit enough to bring over an overlay which showed the 81-mm. mortar positions, placing it over the map in the colonel's hands, meanwhile turning the map right side up. The Britisher had a twinkle in his eyes as the colonel's finger traced a hesitant path on the surface of the overlay.

Poor Colonel Balcom! He was a regular army officer, in his midforties, who had had no expectation that there would actually be a war. It wasn't fair, somehow. He had had a perfectly respectable niche in the army hierarchy in the somnolent years of the thirties. He was a limited man, efficient with motor pools and morning reports. He seemed to us boys old enough to be our father or even our grandfather. Several weeks after this incident he was relieved as executive officer and reassigned to the rear, put in charge of a disciplinary stockade for soldiers who had been court-martialed. Not long after that, our good Irish colonel, the regimental commander, was also relieved of his post. He was well liked, a regular officer grown benevolent in his command; he never interfered with his inferior ranks. He preserved an air of authority and held his liquor rather well. The enlisted men around the headquarters would have been content to have him, harmless, as a commander, and to entrust all the operation of the regiment to our cherished operations officer, Major Melcher.

Replacements came quickly. The new regimental commander, Colonel (later General) Fry was a small man, immensely self-conscious of his role, and intent upon reputation. He was brave, indeed at times foolhardy. A West Pointer who had little respect for officers who were not as "professional" as he, he would flatter noncoms who had a bit of intelligence and give them responsibility at the expense of his staff officers. This endeared him to none of us, the more so as he would often deprecate Major Melcher, who had the good of the men and the order of the regiment at the forefront of his days.

The new executive officer was an ideal exec. He was a tall, saturnine fellow, quick and thorough, who knew how to keep his own counsel, as any executive officer must, but always rose to an emergency. He was physically tough, as was Colonel Fry, and could hold his own on the mountain trails when called upon to do so. His responsibilities generally kept him farther to the rear than the regimental commander. As our way up the peninsula dragged on he acquired certain amenities, unobtrusive but nevertheless considerable. A covered trailer tagged along in the rear with the regiment's more essential impedimenta; it contained a large double bed and a well-stocked bar. Whenever the regiment was not actually engaged, and sometimes even when it was, the colonel would spend the night in his trailer with ladies of whatever province we were in the midst of liberating. He was an active lover and as the war drew to its close he became ever more so. The evening of the day the war ended we cheered the sway of his squeaking trailer, parked in the shadow of the Palazzo del Comune in the heart of the medieval town of Marostica.

Major Collier, to the great relief of the I and R platoon, was shipped off to be executive officer of the Second Battalion. He was replaced temporarily by Captain Matthews, a sarcastic lawyer from Somerville, Massachusetts. He would play at being an equal with me but would pull his rank if he were shown up in any matter, letting me know that he could transfer me back to Company C any time he felt like it. He was dangerous but more interesting than Major Collier and certainly not capable of the same stupidities. Ten days before the May 11 offensive, Master

Sergeant Costello, the regimental operations sergeant and my mentor in the politics of a headquarters, was sent away to Algiers for a special course in operations and intelligence. So many assignments in the army made no sense; Costello was shipped off ten days before the regiment was about to do what an infantry regiment is organized and intended to do: fight a major battle. "Hold the fort and keep your nose clean, Toots," he said. "I'll find a French broad down there and keep the classes to a minimum!" He returned to us two weeks after Rome fell, regaling us with his stories of his French widow and her seaside villa just outside Algiers.

Changes are better understood from a certain distance. We were so young: it shakes the sensibilities to look at photographs of all of us, armed to the teeth with grenades on our belts, rifles on our shoulders, and iron caskets on our heads. We were used to older men as fathers, as school principals, as shop foremen, men whose incompetence might be humorous or even harmful, but whose age and position implied an order, a society, a world in which the pursuits of working and living were carried out, where the daily business was not slaughter but work and nurture. Homer gazes at the killing field which stretched between the walls of Troy and the line of boats down on the shore front and likens the work the young men perform to that of reapers in the field, catching with his simile the awful likeness and the terrifying difference. From Antietam through Passchendaele to Stalingrad, young men in this modern epoch have been mowed down as ciphers, as numbers in a body count, in a mechanical slaughter that goes beyond the grimness of Homer's simile. We were not warriors; we neither killed nor were killed in anything resembling individual combat; it was rare that we were given the distinction of being shot at by individual rifle fire. We were mowed down, to use Homer's agricultural simile, maimed and blown to bits by artillery, by machine guns, by mines, and by mortars. There were extensive "repo-depos" — replacement depots — with spare soldiers to take our place as we fell. So it was that changes in authority, new colonels, new staff officers, new captains, new platoon leaders, seemed only on the surface to have the importance of analogous changes in civil life. Our "business" was endless endurance: boredom punctuated with terror. One of Bill Mauldin's cartoons caught this: two seasoned and seedy GIs are viewing apathetically a mule with a brand-new replacement second lieutenant astride it. The caption has them saying to the mule skinner, "You was suppos'd to bring rations!"

Once real action began there was little for any staff officer to do. As long as ammunition and supplies kept arriving and watch was kept lest our own artillery fall short, the infantry was on its own. Lieutenants and company commanders might buck up the men, but if they didn't, which was not so infrequent, sergeants would step in to the extent that they were needed. The cement that kept the groups together arose out of common necessity and interdependence. If there is not mutual trust no one is safe. "You may survive if you act in such a way as to assist your buddy's survival" is the ethical imperative implicit in the infantry soldier's code. We did hang together, however dulled our faculties were by boredom, apathy, and the anxiety of being blown to bits.

I had been under the illusion in the days preceding the May 11 push that there would emerge a proper grand scheme, that the machine would function according to all our blueprints. I was in charge of the maps and the overlays with all of our positions carefully marked; I had also plotted all of the intelligence we had as to the German positions facing us. I used variously colored pencils for varying types of unit, both enemy and Allied; there were sweeping vectorlike arrows indicating direction of attack and little bars whereupon was written where our units were to be at 1230 hours, the time of the artillery barrages, where units were to be two hours later at 0130 hours, at 0500 hours, etc. It was precise; it was planned; it was all down there on paper. It implied order, just as over and behind it the hierarchy of the powers and the ranks implied a backbone and a central nervous system for the regiment, for the battalions, for the companies as one progressed downward, and, as one ascended, for the division, the corps, the Fifth Army, and the whole Allied Force Headquarters with its center in the gargantuan Versailles which the Bourbons had built at Caserta outside Naples, a palatial stratosphere inhabited by four-star generals and field marshals.

While I was busy with the maps and the HQ staff in that last month before the May offensive Joe Isaac, my Syrian pal from Memphis, made a cushiony haven of our dugout. All on his own he had sneaked up into the no man's land of Minturno and purloined comforters and cushions from the abandoned town. He padded and decorated our earthy refuge, tacking pictures on the walls and making shelves for the scores and books which I had illegally concealed in the regimental intelligence chest. (Beethoven and Stravinsky scores were camouflaged under field manuals and map-reading equipment.) Our new regimental commander, Colonel Fry, was titillated when he discovered me one day retrieving one of the Razumovsky Quartets from its nest. It gave him a chance to establish a cultural bond with an enlisted man, a bond which he considered to be beyond the capabilities of his staff officers. "You know, Allanbrook," he said, "I used to go hear the Budapest do their thing at the Library of Congress."

The sophistication in our dugout went beyond the purlieu of the colonel. Mlle Boulanger had sent me a gift a bit earlier: Gertrude Stein's "Ida." I didn't know what to make of it but one day, quite by accident, Joe picked it up and began reading it out loud. "'And there was Ida and she had a baby, and there she was, Ida-Ida.'" He loved sounding its sentences and would laugh at its cadences and its sweet American mouthings. Virgil Thomson, when I told him years later of Joe Isaac and our recitations in the dugout, nodded and said, "Of course, that's just what Gertrude intended. She's an American writing for Americans." It was a felicitous and timely present, coming from Mlle Boulanger to me and relished in our dugout by my Syrian pal from Memphis in the peculiar interregnum of the weeks before the onslaught of the attack on Rome.

At 2300 hours on May 11 every artillery piece from Cassino to the sea began firing. Tons of steel whooshed overhead. The plan of battle was minutely spelled out; there was a timetable for every company in every battalion and regiment in our division and in every other division in the line. By 0500 hours the arrows and the labels on the maps might as well not have been there: pandemonium was the order of the day. When the barrage had ended independent squads and platoons, subject to terror and uncertainty, moved forward where it was possible to do so, the platoon leader lucky if he could retain control of his squads; the company commander, further removed, trying at least to plot the fire of his mortars and machine guns and to keep in some kind of contact with his platoons; the battalion commander, with still greater responsibility, had correspondingly less that he could actually control. At regimental headquarters the field phones rang, the radios crackled, messengers came and went. The colonel and the intelligence officer, Captain Matthews, were constantly visiting the battalions. There was little they could do, but a frenzy in the air drove them out: control and command had to signify contact and closeness. On the third day of the offensive Captain Matthews was carried back on a stretcher, peppered with shrapnel wounds all over his body, none of them serious, but the aggregate of them sufficient to send him home. Colonel Fry was untouched.

Our regiment, which was in reserve during the first day of the attack, moved into the central sector on Day Two, its goal the village of Santa Maria Infante. We could get no clear picture of the attack as the day progressed, though casualties began piling up almost immediately. We saw our first body bags. On our right the 351st was being bloodied over near Castelforte. There the sergeant who had been with us in our midsummer idyll on the Sabine was blown to bits. ("Shit, man, he was all over the map," a fellow from his company told me later. "The only way we knew it was him was his dog tags lyin' in the midst of the pieces!") Our Medal of Honor recipient, a platoon sergeant in F Company, captured a hill that was sticking up in front of him after his platoon leader was killed. His platoon followed him and Hill 316, a prime objective on our overlay maps, was taken. This did not happen through any order flowing down from regimental HQ; it was accomplished in the sudden fury of one man, galvanized into action by the actuality of where he was and by the makeup of his own temperament.

Artillery came from both sides, sibilant streaks from south to north and north to south. In my four days up at Cassino I had gotten a bit used to reading the degree of danger from the shifts in sound from a whoosh to a whine to a whistle as the rounds came close. It was a sophistication soon acquired by all of us. We envied the effectiveness of the Germans' flat-trajectory 88s which came in with such shattering speed. While all of us were subject to artillery fire I was preserved from the fire of lighter weapons by being at headquarters; it was only when I was out on patrol or accompanying one of the staff forward that I suffered the thud and crunch of the mortars and the quick crackle of a machine gun. For four days, from May 11 to May 15, the medics kept me awake with Benzedrine. With Sergeant Costello away at school in Algiers I was the noncom in charge at HQ, on duty day and night. Someone had to be awake. There had to be, at the very least, the appearance that we were controlling the battle: maps and positions had to be plotted, messages cleared, whereabouts of companies and battalions kept track of. If HQ was not a command post it had to act like one. Not to believe that there was an effective nerve center would have demoralized and rendered futile the whole structure whose foundation was the individual soldier and his squad, even though the infantrymen and their squads and platoons soon learned that they were on their own, that no one higher up was of much help. Their continued existence depended upon each other. The rashness which took Hill 316 and gained Sergeant Shea a Medal of Honor was not planned; it happened. In the ordinary course of combat such an excess of courage might well be the cause of needless slaughter.

Our assistant division commander, a general known as "the Bull," arrived at our HQ only once during these first days of the offensive. He was famous in Italy as having been in charge of a calamitous attack some months earlier at the Rapido River up near Cassino. He bellowed at us, pointing with his finger on the map at various hills we were not taking quickly enough. Major Melcher told him of the casualties we were suffering. He hesitated, glared, and then withdrew. At later times we were not so lucky; he would appear and would insist that the Second Battalion be on Hill X at 1400 hours, that they goddamned well had to be there, and would accompany this with an order. Sensible generals knew their place and seldom ventured far forward. The Bull became our commanding general shortly after this. The last sight any of us had of our pint-size termagant, General Sloan, was of him weeping in his command car as he watched his Blue Devils straggle by him on the Itri-Fondi road. The casualties of the first week had been heavy and the men were exhausted. In all of our days at Camp Gruber and on maneuvers in Louisiana he had been a constant nagging presence. He had pushed and finagled us into becoming the first draft division in combat. Now that we had been bloodied, he wept. The Bull took his place. Fifty years later I read in official army critiques of divisional training that it was General Sloan's competence and energy that forged our sterling record in combat. "There's no trainin' for us," Joe Isaac used to say, "except learnin' to put up with all the shit and not poopin' out on a march! Them generals all think the army's like a nice Cadillac car all tuned up and goin' somewhere and they're the driver, sittin' up front, headin' for New Orleans. There ain't no wheels, just us soldiers and there sure ain't no road to drive on."

My eyeballs were stretched and sore by the third day of my

Benzedrine-induced alertness. The whole attack became one glare of attention, a present moment dragged through days of frenzy, set apart from ordinary time, not measured by the soul's rhythms of sleeping and waking and the earth's steady alternation of night and day. Santa Maria Infante and Castelforte finally fell; the French performed wonders on our right in the wild mountainous terrain stretching toward Cassino. Cassino itself, that tomb of miscalculation, became a killing ground yet again and finally capitulated. The Gothic Line cracked, as was reported in the daily papers and as is written in history books. It was not so clear to us. After the initial five days of steel and blood we packed our things, abandoned Minturno and our dugouts, and plunged into further disarray. As we went north in a kind of rout, I remained in a stupor after my days on Benzedrine. I recall the long narrow valley from Itri up to Fondi choked with vehicles and lines of infantry. We knew that on our left by the Tyrrhenian the 85th Division was pushing north to join the beachhead at Anzio and that the French were on our right. Our sector had few roads and fewer villages. We were vaguely instructed to proceed across the Arunci Mountains to a rendezvous at Roccasecca dei Volsci where we would, if all went well, join up with units coming over from Priverno in the valley below. The colonel decided to plunge into the wilderness and gave orders for two companies of the First Battalion and half of the I and R platoon (as an advance party) to push on ahead willy-nilly, ignoring what might be on our flanks.

We were happy to take off into the mountains, as the valley road where we were dug in had been strafed twice by German planes. The assumption had been that they had no air force left, that we needn't worry about air attacks. But as happened so many times in the last eighteen months of the war, they surprised us. We dived into a roadside ditch, riveted in place by the sight of the bullets kicking up the dust in the middle of the road. A radio jeep was hit and its driver engulfed in blazing gasoline; one of its riders, the First Battalion supply sergeant, was sprawled on the road with bullets tracing holes in a straight line from his buttocks to his skull. Two hours after the air attack we were on our way.

Roccasecca dei Volsci was way up ahead of us; we had no idea whatsoever as to what lay between us and it. The contour lines on our maps showed a high piedmont fringed with mountains, with nary a village, though there were minuscule clusters of black squares indicating some kind of habitation. We received no information from division intelligence as to the whereabouts of the Germans and there was no posting as to the location of any of our own troops, French or American or British. We did feel somewhat secure on our right flank, as the night before we were strafed we had learned where the French were. The radio man we had sent to keep contact with the "groupement des Goums" returned to us, shaken by his ordeal. "Them Arab motherfuckers cleaned out everything, and I mean everything! It don't make no difference if they're Krauts or Eyties. If they was Eyties around, they'd go into the house and fuck the daughters, the mothers, and finish up with grandma. They warn't fussy; they'd brown a boy as soon as his sister. I saw two of them makin' it with a sheep one night. They'd clear the houses of them poor bastards up there and it didn't make no difference when the French officer would shoot a couple of 'em. Nothin' has any effect on 'em." All this came tumbling out of his mouth; he glared around at us, began to speak again but couldn't get the words out as his throat was engorged with sobs. The medics gave him an injection and he seemed okay the next morning; the strafing didn't bother him much.

Later in the campaign, farther north, we had mules when we were off in the mountains. On this surrealist jaunt we carried what we needed ourselves. The full field packs of Camp Gruber and Louisiana were forgotten; bayonets were the first thing to go, and anyone who could get hold of a sleeping bag threw away his shelter half and his blankets. Our food was portable K rations, smallish oblong boxes wrapped in waterproof paper containing concentrated food: dried beef with carrot chips; thick crackers resembling compressed cardboard, rounds of processed cheese, lemonade or coffee powder, and always, thanks to the American tobacco industry, little packs of cigarettes. Constipation was the order of the day with K rations. (C rations, which came in tin cans, were too heavy and bulky to carry on one's back for any period of time, especially in the mountains. They consisted most typically of pork and beans and their effect on the bowels was as extreme as that of K rations; they erred, however, on the side of looseness.) I carried my K rations stuffed inside my shirt and at my side I had a map case crammed with small essentials, in addition to the requisite maps. Over my right shoulder was a bedroll, and on the other shoulder my M-1; around my middle a cartridge belt with several grenades dangling. This was all topped by a steel helmet plunked on top of a plastic helmet liner. When I was tired I felt as if my head were a domed protuberance, a top-heavy tulip perched upon my scrawny stem of a neck.

We walked for days; our crackly radio at times halted our advance, at other times directed us to the right or the left. There was nothing to report; there seemed to be no Germans up on these heights. There were goats, however, lots of them, and goatherders. Both regarded us with veiled expressions, but in no time at all the goatherds were only too happy to fill our mess cups with foaming goat's milk in exchange for our K rations and cigarettes. There was mutual delight in the barter: the goatherds had not seen decent cigarettes for years and they smacked their lips at the bizarre eatables contained in the oblong boxes, while the goat's milk was balm to our guts.

On the morning of the fourth day a little Piper Cub flew over and dropped D rations for us. We were delighted as our K rations were running low; I had just squandered a day's supply on goat's milk and the promise of some goat cheese. These latest rations turned out to be concentrated chocolate bars, rocklike in consistency and, as their wrappers informed us, jammed full of vitamins and life-sustaining grains. They were difficult to eat, the best method being to whittle them with a knife and to eat the shavings. These shavings, melted into a mess cup held over a fire and mixed with some bubbling hot goat's milk, made a delicious drink. Bianchi complemented our chocolate goat's milk beverage with a dish he invented: he melted the process cheese from the K rations and crumbled into it the compacted sawdust biscuits, crowning the confection with wild thyme and rosemary, which he discovered up on our obscure plateau. We gave some to our sarcastic new intelligence officer, Lieutenant McKenna. "Welsh rarebit aux herbes de montagne," I commented for his benefit. "I always thought you were made for country picnics and fêtes champêtres, Allanbrook," he replied with a thin-lipped grin.

Roccasecca dei Volsci awaited us at the end of our trek through this paleolithic plateau, all goats and stone huts. (It was the wild country of the Volsci, ancient foes of the Romans, and of all their towns and roads down in the valleys.) The world of the war began to impinge upon us. As our radio instructed us to proceed to our rendezvous we could hear artillery fire increasingly, both straight north and to the northeast and northwest. "I'm mighty glad we had our little picnic up here," said Bianchi. "We're all here still!" There were jeeps in the tiny square when we got to Roccasecca and in one of them was Major Melcher. It felt like a homecoming.

"We had a picnic," said Lieutenant McKenna to the major. "We didn't," replied Melcher, his face worn and harried. "We lost a lot more, not like the first five days down there at Minturno, but still bad." We drove down the switchbacks into the valley, and turned left toward Priverno, stopping a bit short of it at the Abbey of Fossanova where the colonel had established a temporary headquarters. The splendid Romanesque abbey of the Cistercians seemed more ancient than anything I had seen so far in Italy, ancient in that particular way that medieval structures feel older than Roman ones. It was remarkably intact, bare and unharmed by the war, grand, complemented with a chaste cloister. The body of the abbey itself was being used as a temporary field hospital. Yellow diagonal rays lighted up rows of stretchers on that late afternoon when I entered. I found four men from C Company who had done basic training with me at Camp Gruber. Three of them were cocky, boasting that they had just enough to send them home. A fourth one cried when I talked to him; he'd lost his right arm. Young as I was, I was struck by how young they were: boys, not men.

St. Thomas Aquinas died at Fossanova as he was walking back to Naples from Paris, but he was a famous man, strong as an ox, and he had written all those books. His ancestral home was just back over our rocky plateau toward Cassino, the town of Aquino. All of us, German or Allied, were a passing phenomenon, a blight or a blessing, soon to be forgotten. In recent years I have visited Fossanova several times, staying at a nearby castle, swimming in the river down in the valley with my son and the children of my Italian hosts. From my bedroom window in the castle I looked down across the valley and high up on the other side to Roccasecca dei Volsci. The provincial government has built a swimming pool for the townspeople, way up there on the heights.

"Rome, Rome, who gets Rome?" Lieutenant McKenna was half chanting in his sardonic way. The officers around headquarters didn't like him; he didn't play regulation ball. He spoke too many truths too quickly. We enlisted men were wary of him. It pleased him to play at being one of us until it grew uncomfortable; then he would withdraw with some stinging remark. He never was given a promotion and ended the war still a lieutenant. While we were at Fossanova he had on his own authority commandeered a jeep and driven over to the Corps HQ where he had a friend. What his sharp eyes found there was what future historians of the drive to Rome bear witness to: the burning desire of General Mark Clark to be first into the city. The British felt that they deserved the prize and the French, after their scaling of the heights to the left of Cassino, were also itching to lead the way into the Italian capital. The direction of the breakthrough from the Anzio beachhead was countermanded. General Alexander, the Allied Commander, was outfoxed by Clark. All of the top brass knew the Normandy landing was imminent and those of them who were for glory wanted to be in the headlines with the fall of Rome before Eisenhower landed on the continent. As a result of this unworthy scramble the German Tenth and Fourteenth Armies were not cut off; they escaped to the north and the fighting in Italy went on for another year. If the goal was the defeat of the enemy's troops, the taking of Rome was a military failure. Breaking the German defenses in the high Apennines south of the Po Valley proved as bloody a job as the campaign north from Naples to Rome. It had to be accomplished with a bare minimum of divisions, as the landing in southern France had drained the forces in Italy of many of their resources.

Enlisted men expect everything to be fucked up. It is a conceit founded on their experience from the day they are inducted. We had no vision of the whole war: we knew nothing of the enormity of what was passing in Russia; we had no notion of what was happening inside Germany. In our own theater of operations we had no sense as to why we were slogging up the spiny center of the Italian peninsula. "Sufficient unto the day the evil thereof" was sufficient for us. Lieutenant McKenna, reporting in his smart-ass fashion that none of the brass knew what the fuck they were doing, turned us further into ourselves. His remarks annoyed his fellow officers, who, simply by being officers, felt they had a stake in the good order of the hierarchy and the hierarchy's military wisdom. This tactical disorder in the advance toward Rome saved a lot of our lives, however. While fierce fighting raged at Valmontone and Mount Artemisio and the British Eighth Army slowly advanced up the Liri Valley, our division was constantly shifted about and finally rushed through the center to be among the very first troops into Rome.

We entered at Porta San Giovanni and stumbled across the city half the night, ending up by the Tiber at about two in the morning, exhausted. Some Germans were still around as we began our trek, so there was some sniping and a few casualties. We would also run into groups of Allied troops confused as to who was supposed to be where. We posted a guard to watch a bridge which crossed the Tiber and plunged down on the sidewalk and slept. There was a light haze in the air as dawn broke; I rubbed my eyes, experiencing difficulty in realizing where I was. Straight across the bridge was the sepia print which had always hung above the oaken, glass-fronted bookcase in the living room of my childhood home on Allen Place in Melrose: the Castel Sant' Angelo, that classical cylinder shaped like a municipal gas tank, bathed in the first light of the Roman dawn.

We left the city late that very afternoon, hurrying north up the Via Cassia toward Viterbo. The streets in Rome had begun filling up in the morning and by noon the Piazza del Popolo was full of Romans. History shone in their faces. General Clark lost his way in the city, but finally found the road to the Campidoglio, Michelangelo's incomparable civic center, where he expected a hero's welcome. When notables were finally rounded up and a proper platoon of reporters were on hand he pronounced the fall of Rome to be a great triumph for the Fifth Army. He made no mention of the gravity of the Eternal City's liberation, of its release from fascism and the German yoke, and of the price that all of the Allied forces — British, French, Polish, and American — had paid. He had gotten there first!

Though at first we had hurried north, our pace soon slackened and then ceased altogether. The German Tenth and Fourteenth Armies joined up above Orte toward Orvieto, slipping out of our grasp to fight for another year, and we did nothing in particular to stop them. Later when we passed by Civitavecchia, the port of Rome, preparations were already underway for the invasion of southern France. Few infantry divisions were to be left to us and as we proceeded north, the fighting — which in the month after the fall of Rome was minimal — intensified. The remaining weeks of June were passed in a landscape remote from the grandeur and importance of Rome, a never-never land bounded on the north by the Tuscan Mountains and on the south by the Roman Campania, the Roman volcanic country with sulfurous outcrops. Viterbo, the crumbling walled city of the popes built out of the porous volcanic tufa, was already half in ruins before the Allies found reason to reduce it further with their bombing raids. Its Romanesque palaces and churches retained their air of severity and elegant plainness so striking after the effulgence of Rome's baroque.

North of Viterbo, in an expanse of territory that stretches up to Lake Bolsena, we found ourselves in the lost and ancient town of Tuscania, its eleventh-century basilicas rampant upon the irregular bluffs to the south of the city. We reconnoitered the center of town with the I and R platoon, not knowing whether there were any Germans still lurking in the town and fearful of the mines and booby traps which they were increasingly in the habit of leaving behind when they departed. All around the balustrade of the central square were the heavy stone sarcophagi of the Etruscans, which were topped with benevolent and heavyset husbands and wives, stretched out forever on their coffins, smiling from their Etruscan distance. "Look, Allanbrook," said Lieutenant McKenna, "Look at all the mom-and-pop sculptures!" We ate ancient food in a rustic pergola we discovered, swapping cigarettes for partridge and rabbit cooked in a pot with a black sauce. After we ate, the padrone brought forth some *noce* for us — straight alcohol in which walnuts had been soaked for several years: potent and delicious.

"The Germans left a week ago, Signore," the padrone said to me. "And the fascisti that didn't leave with them won't cause you any trouble. We have a new mayor." He grinned at me knowingly. I was the only one who caught the sense of his Italian and had already noted the hammer and sickle on his coat collar. It took me some time before I realized what was happening in the towns and in the countryside as the regiment moved steadily north into Tuscany. The name *partigiano* — partisan — didn't surface into full consciousness for me until we were up near Volterra. There I was thrust into the present reality of civil war when I was recruited to make contact with a resistance group in the countryside. Down in Tuscania we drank with the padrone to the death of fascism without realizing that the leading citizens and administrators of the town, all Fascists, had fled to the North or were already dead or hidden in some obscure cellar.

We zigzagged north fairly slowly almost without casualties. Sometimes we would simply camp for a few days with no particular directions coming down from headquarters. There was a lovely insouciance about drills and reveille. More and more land mines appeared as we entered southern Tuscany. We would scuff our feet lightly as we walked, testing the loose soil with the balls of our feet, not pressing down until our senses gave us a go-ahead. We also began encountering booby traps, not only in ordinary spots such as doors or under floorboards but in increasingly ingenious places: henhouses, well covers, ploughs, and even in piano lids. They quite clearly were aimed at the civilian population as well as at us.

There was a stretch south of Volterra where the Germans put up an unexpected resistance from certain hilltops. They complemented their defense with a particularly heavy sowing of small mines in the valleys under their hilltop positions. One day several companies of the Second Battalion froze as they ran into the fringes of one of these valley mine fields. It was then that Colonel Fry earned himself the title of "Fearless Fosdick," the name of a well-known comic-strip hero. He strode out in front of E Company, swishing his swagger stick, instructing them to follow him. He stepped on nary a mine though several members of E Company who followed after him were not so lucky. The field was passed and the Germans on the hill above retreated after a small firefight.

It is difficult for me to put my finger upon what is considered

to be an officer's principal excellence, leadership. If Fearless Fosdick had that day stepped on a mine and suffered the loss of a
lower leg as did three members of E Company would it have
been an example of leadership? E Company did move across the
field and the Germans did retreat from the hill. Was this the
result of Colonel Fry's action or of his luck in escaping injury?
Would E Company, unaided, have gotten over its temporary
paralysis and advanced all the same, albeit by a more circuitous
route? Major Melcher, increasingly at odds with Colonel Fry,
would have waited awhile until the support artillery had moved
within range, would then have shelled the German positions
and tried, by flanking movements, to avoid the perilous valley
altogether. He was a prudent manager, not a "leader"; but all of
us, in a pickle, would have chosen to follow him and not our
fearless colonel, who went on to become a general and later, after
the Korean War, to write a book called *The Infantry Soldier.*

When we came close to Volterra Joe Isaac pointed up at it and
in his querulous southern way asked, "Why, Allanbrook, would
anyone want to live way up there with them gullies cutting
down behind and out here in front nothin' but dry fields that
ain't worth a shit?"

"It's a famous place, it's been here forever, Joe," I said. "Look
at the walls; the artillery's just popping off them like we were
shooting bee-bee guns. They're Etruscan."

The Germans had no intention of making a Cassino out of
Volterra; they put up a certain resistance for several days and
then slowly backed off, fighting a lengthy delaying action on the
long slopes leading down to the Arno between Pontedera and
Empoli. "We just got a habit of shellin'," Joe commented. "We
ain't got anything better to do after we haul them guns all over
creation." The cyclopean walls of the city were not even dented
and if certain shells landed in town, they caused only civilian
distress as any group of soldiers would have been secure in the
cellars of the stone houses.

When we first entered this most remote of Tuscan cities we

were greeted by what seemed to be an official delegation: men of a certain age, many of them with the face and hands of working men. There were also groups of youngsters carrying British Bren guns, many of them my age or younger. They were, as it soon turned out, organized, or at least semiorganized *partigiani*.

I got to know some of the older men in the three days we spent up in that strange and austere city. My Italian was, by this time, fluent enough, even if somewhat garbled. Their language was certainly easier to understand than the dialects farther south. Both in their speech and in their habits they were leaner and tougher men than any I had encountered. One of them, Adone by name, proudly asserted his Communist party membership while his great friend Sirio proclaimed himself a true pre-Fascist socialist and he spat as he pronounced "Fascist." In later years, when I was living in Siena, I came to understand the meaning of such classical names as theirs. Many Tuscan working people had long been anticlerical, socialist, and anarchist. They would not christen their children with saints' names but chose rather the glorious names of Roman and Greek heroes. The Risorgimento which gave rise to the nation state of Italy had as its red-shirted hero Garibaldi, who was proud to call himself a "dictator," borrowing that term from its noble use in the Roman republic when a "dictator" was given temporary power as a protector of the republic. When Adone and Sirio were born in the early years of the century Italy was only forty or fifty years old and its radicalism and anticlericalism were part of what was and is a shaky political structure. Mussolini, whose profession was journalism, rode the socialist current, played it for all it was worth. He bluffed his way into power and ruled as a propagandist and thug for twenty long years. As the war passed over the country, old liberal ministers with anti-Fascist credentials were setting up a government in Rome while Mussolini and his Fascists were being propped up in the North by the German High Command (the so-called *Repubblica di Salò*). Here I was in the town of Volterra, talking to Sirio and Adone, keeping my eye on bunches of youngsters walking around with portable automatic weapons and vastly ignorant of the politics of the town and the country we were supposedly liberating. I learned quite a bit in a short time, though at first I was only struck with how different it all seemed from Naples and Rome.

The *partigiani* had good intelligence concerning the Germans' slow and stiffening resistance as they retreated down to the Arno. They were not only fighting the Germans, however; they were even more passionately intent upon clearing the slates in their own towns and villages. The civic fabric was split down the middle. Many of the most important Fascists, but not all, fled north with the Germans: the mayors, the *gerarchi* — the official party thugs — the party secretaries, etc. In the months of the Allied advance they had become increasingly savage and frightened. They aided the Germans in sequestering men and boys to be shipped north as forced labor; they tortured suspects; they turned in Jews. Attacks by the resistance groups were followed by reprisals, which the Germans were well schooled in and which the local Fascists soon got a taste for: hanging would be accomplished with piano wire, rather than rope; an important victim would be left suspended with a meathook through his jaw.

There was a vast gray area which was tarred by the Fascist brush: old employees of the city hall, men who, if they had not been in the party, would have had no job. There were in addition the town police and the carabinieri, traditional national police. Anyone connected in any way with schools or universities had little choice but to join. An entire generation had been brought up in the Fascist schools, where at every age there was an appropriate uniform and title. Little girls were enrolled as *Figlie della Lupa* — "Daughters of the Wolf" — with uniforms and insignia meant to recall the noted she-wolf who had nourished the founders of Rome, Romulus and Remus. A fussy mother would have her girl's uniforms tailored by the best tailor in town. A friend of mine who was a member of a kind of Fascist ROTC when he was in high school in Genoa was enrolled in a cavalry squadron. He told with glee of the dire emergency barely avoided on the occasion of a visit by Il Duce to Genoa, a visit in which Mussolini intended to review the squadron. Considerable amounts of money had been siphoned away from the amounts assigned to equip the squadron. As a result, rather than eight troops ready to parade there was only one sparse and properly equipped company of boys and horses. "We rode by Il Duce at a proper rate of speed, chins up, fists in the air, with the band playing 'La Giovinezza,'" recounted my friend. "After we passed the reviewing stand we turned sharp left and rode like hell around the block reappearing as the Second Troop and then the Third Troop, etc. Everyone was happy: Il Duce, the public, the officers who had pocketed the cash, and all of us students who had such fun being cynical at the expense of grown-ups. What could be more titillating than to cheat the buffoon who ran the whole national farce!"

A generation raised this way could not be other than cynical: after Spain and Ethiopia, Albania and Greece and North Africa demonstrated the venal inefficacy of the regime. When Mussolini became a plucked chicken in the Germans' coop, when boys and men were hustled off in gang roundups and shipped north, violence arose, an existential reflex of the psyche, an aching need for action and blood after twenty years of cynicism and passivity. This was aimed courageously at the Germans but when they left, the target was more ominously against the place where everyone had been brought up — the functionaries of the town, the rich who had prospered, and often those who had had no choice but to remain associated with the regime if body and soul were to be kept together.

The British had been dropping arms for several months in Tuscany and had established regular liaisons with various partisan groups. We knew nothing of this until the week we were in and around Volterra when we received vague memos from division headquarters: we were not to give the locals any arms; we were only a combat infantry division with no civil authority, so we were not to assume any of the prerogatives of the Allied Military Government which would soon be in place when things quieted down; in any case, a civil government was coming into existence with the fall of Rome. Nevertheless we should cooperate with the partisan groups; they could be of help.

My French now being replaced by Italian, I was the person in the I and R platoon to act as go-between and interpreter. This was not difficult as members of the resistance began urging us to perform various tasks for them and giving us intelligence of German positions out in front of us. Many were my own age, eager boys flush with excitement and new freedom. I had already begun to talk with Adone and Sirio when I was up in Volterra: they were different from the young ones, disciplined both by age and party membership. With this background off we went, Lieutenant McKenna, Joe Isaac, two others from the I and R platoon, and I — babes in the woods of civil strife — to see what was to be seen and to learn what was to be learned in the small towns on the slope going down to the Arno. It was in the second of these towns that our reconnaissance squad visited that I first saw (and only later understood) what was happening.

The Germans had left a few days earlier, and the road seemed clear. We went in one of the I and R jeeps, taking the usual chances with road mines. There was not a soul about as we approached the town gate, no one in the fields, no one in the houses on the outskirts. We stopped. "Something fishy, Allanbrook," said Joe Isaac. "Let's take it easy," added McKenna in a voice that for once was free of sarcasm. We parked the jeep just outside the walls. It didn't seem probable that there was any real danger for us; we knew the Germans had left and we were fairly certain as to where they had pulled back. The Third Battalion had had some scattered firefights with them a few miles to the northeast of town. Nevertheless we approached the town gate, a medieval affair with the Medici crest on its arch, as a well-trained reconnaissance squad should, cautiously. As we passed under the arch and entered we became aware of a confused hullabaloo coming from a couple of blocks away in what turned out to be the piazza of the town.

What we saw in that piazza and, more intensely, what we felt, is set more firmly in my mind by one of those doublevisions which telescope time and place and fix them in one particular region of the soul's landscape. It occurred years later when I went to visit the Pueblo of Santo Domingo in New Mexico in order to witness one of their dances. We had descended from Santa Fe down over the ancient lava flow, the *abajo grande,* and drove into the parking lot outside the pueblo. I began to be aware of a familiar strangeness, not so much sensed as recollected, not so much recollected as felt. Pickup trucks filled the parking space. It was quiet and no one was about. I had been to dances previously, both here at Santo Domingo and at nearby Cochiti: they had been public affairs, replete with a carnival atmosphere, though the dances themselves, always held in the central plaza, were authentic, ritualistic and endless, teetering between boredom and hypnosis. This time there was no carnival, no souvenir stalls, no tourists. We had been told that it was to be a ceremonial dance for the men of the pueblo who had died in Vietnam, fallen warriors. We heard the drums, distantly, as soon as we had parked the car. As we traversed the empty dirt alleys and approached the plaza the sound of men chanting became clearer and clearer. Indians ringed the plaza; peering over their shoulders we saw the dancing: men with greased, green bodies, women in dark garments waving pine boughs. I was tapped on the shoulder; I turned quickly about. "We don't want nobody here today," the Indian said flatly. "This isn't for you; it's for us!" We turned and left, fled the plaza and the pueblo, filled with sudden fear. We were aliens there; we didn't belong. It wasn't our brothers who were dead.

What we saw when we entered the piazza of that Italian town, down below Volterra, on that summer day of 1944, was not a ritual, though it would not have happened without previous blood. We were not part of it; it was another war than ours, though it would not have occurred without ours. Facing each other, but randomly strung out, was a double line of men, most of them young, some adolescent, which stretched from the ancient town hall, twisted around the piazza, and then continued on into the principal street of the town. Men, older on the whole than those comprising the double line of the gauntlet, some of them quite elderly, were being shoved one by one out of the elaborate door of the town hall, compelled to walk, or stagger, or run, as the younger men, wielding whips, canes, and clubs pummeled them, aiming particularly at the lower back where injuries to the kidneys are most easily effected. Several men fell flat; one skinny little fellow who looked like Mickey Mouse had dribbles of blood issuing from one side of his mouth. Shrieks, hollers, and catcalls issued from the mouths of those with the whips. Bystanders varied in their response. One man pointed to them and, for my benefit, shrieked, "Fascisti, tutti Fascisti!" Another near to me said quietly, "You Americans have no business here; how can you understand what's happening? They're not really Fascists at all, merely functionaries in the city hall." No carabinieri were to be seen anywhere. The locals were uneasy at our being there; our presence hung heavy in the air. Joe Isaac for once had nothing to say. Lieutenant McKenna said, "We got no business here. Let's go," and we left.

An outsider should steer clear of a civil war. Both the dance at Santo Domingo and the awful gauntlet at that town square are stuck together in my recollection because they were both places where I had no business being, places which brooked no interference and where an outsider's sympathy or compassionate meddling could do nothing. A stranger's mere curiosity is an insult. He can only note what is happening and pass on, wiser perhaps. The civil war in Italy became more and more evident as we moved north, a minor eddy in the enormous worldwide current, having its own local passions and its own justifications which the greater conflict only exacerbated and brought to the fore. We couldn't control it and we seldom understood it. It was difficult enough to justify both our own casualties and those on the other side.

As summer dragged on into fall the face of the regiment changed. More and more of the men were replacements from the Repo-Depo. With so few divisions left in the theater we were seldom relieved, though there might be a bit of a respite when we were shifted from one sector to another. The Germans put up no protracted resistance on the south side of the Arno; Florence escaped relatively unscathed except for the usual bombings by the Allied air forces on the outskirts and in the railroad yards. Our planes did lots of damage upriver at Arezzo and downriver at Pisa. Siena, over the hills east of Volterra, emerged phoenix-like from the war, clean as a whistle with its green and white striped cathedral crowning the red brick and tile of the rest of the town. North of the Arno the Germans were digging in on the first crests of the Apennines. Our air photos showed heavy emplacements at the Futa Pass. Beyond that point stretched the high Apennines, a wild country that is the watershed of both the Tiber and the Arno. It is an immense barrier sealing off the Po Valley from Tuscany; it was toward this barrier that we were now to be committed. Seventy-five percent of our regiment would be wounded or dead before we broke out into the flat billiard table of the Po Valley and raced past Bologna on our way to the foothills of the Alps and the war's end.

No plan was revealed to us as fall rolled around. A Brazilian division appeared and *Stars and Stripes* photographed General Clark and a Brazilian general saluting each other: hemispheric solidarity it was called. We were now somewhat more aware of the enormity of the Russian and Allied advances north of the Alps. "Rome was it; we're shit now!" was Joe Isaac's correct estimate of our situation. At some points in the line north of the Arno there was no enemy contact at all; later in the fall the 92nd Division, black soldiers and white officers, was plugged into a quiet sector between Lucca and Montecatini. Other stretches of the line were dangerous when poked at; there would be sudden firefights and mortars, and increasingly the Germans would let loose with what we called "screaming meemies," large-caliber mortar shells which came in with a noise like a rusty streetcar rounding a curve. They carried an enormous charge of explosive but threw little shrapnel. Highway 65, the main road north from Florence to Bologna, and the only decent blacktop, was going to be a major battleground; we all feared the Futa Pass where 65 reached its first crest. Patrols further east and north toward Firenzuola began to run into real trouble. The division quartermaster began collecting mules; a battalion of mountain artillery, trained in Colorado, made its appearance. The clear and beautiful weather of late Italian summer and early fall lulled us into a limbo of boredom. We didn't want to look north. The thought of winter in the high Apennines with only one good blacktop road to move supplies on worried the good conscience of our operations officer, but, as usual, he kept his own counsel. Lieutenant McKenna spotted the same truth as Joe Isaac but spelled it out more explicitly. "Allanbrook," he said, "there was no goddamn reason except for the pizzazz of taking Rome for us to go any farther north than the Foggia airfields. Germany is done for; Berlin will fall by spring or before. What the hell are we doing and if we're supposed to do it why don't we have more divisions?"

I did get to see Rome again when the regiment went to a rest area in the pine woods between Pisa and Livorno. Passes were issued and four of us from the I and R went back down for a few days. The trucks dumped us off at the Foro Italico, that large and hideous Fascist campus on the other side of the Tiber, under Monte Mario. The Army Rest Center was established in the place, with Red Cross hostesses offering coffee and doughnuts. We abandoned it without a second thought and headed downtown where we found an enormous hotel room, all done up in red draperies, right in the middle of town across from Santa Maria Maggiore. Cigarettes and coffee bought us all the goodies we wanted and the room filled with wine and cognac. It was evening when we settled in. After a black market meal we were replete but too tired to look for ladies and morning found all four of us disposed upon one enormous canopied bed.

The next morning I discovered Curcio's, the big music store on the Corso, and sat down at a piano and began playing the "Waldstein" Sonata. My fingers were stiff but I could still turn the phrases and gauge the climaxes. A crowd gathered, which spurred me on. I succeeded in skidding over the famous octaves in the coda of the Rondo with some panache. Some of the group cried "bravo"; my playing was musical but they were more taken by the spectacle of a GI playing a big, famous work. A girl with a madonnalike face and large liquid eyes spoke to me immediately after I finished. Her name was Miriam. We went to the opera that night and I walked her all the long way home to where she lived on the Via Guido Reni, a fair distance out the Via Flaminia from Piazza del Popolo. There were catcalls from lurking GIs as we made our way across the dusky reaches of the Villa Borghese Gardens. That Miriam was a Jewish name only struck me much later. Her family was too cordial to me; how could I have understood what Rome had been to them before the Allies had arrived? I felt uneasy; she liked me too much. Later, just after I returned home from the war, her mother wrote to say that she had married an American GI and moved to St. Louis, where she was not happy. "It's a pity, caro Douglas," she said in her letter. "She should have married an artist."

What did please me particularly in those four days was an elderly waiter in a café near Piazza Barberini. He was always courteous as he served me coffee and brioches on a silver tray, and later, when he found out I was a musician, he would address me as "Maestro." He was dignified, without the easy turn of phrase and insinuating quickness so common in Naples. My imagination felt it as a window into what a large European city might be and I could see myself living in Rome or Paris in some sweet future. The regiment seemed so far away, so distant, in those half-hours I spent in that café.

As we reported back to the Army Rest Center at the Foro Italico and were loaded into our trucks for the North, all of us infantrymen talked of the enormous and disproportionate number of rear-echelon troops there were in Rome: hordes from the quartermaster corps, the signal corps, from army headquarters, battalions of arcane specialists — all of them enjoying Italy, all safe and sound out of harm's way in the rear, all of them experiencing with no special pain the fun of being abroad. They would go home and tell their families, their neighbors, and their future children about the Italian campaign. It struck us with special force as there were so few infantry troops in the last eleven months of our war with which to launch a major attack on the ever resilient Germans, now stubbornly digging in on the mountain line between Florence and Bologna. When we did get to the rear, which was seldom, our uniforms were shabby and our privileges far more restricted than those of the rear-echelon troops. They were not acquainted with the snag-line of death. We were. We became prouder, bitterer, and drank as much as we could whenever we could.

Major Melcher began worrying out loud as August passed into September. "Why are we waiting so long; if we are to attack in those mountains, for God's sake let's do it while the weather is decent. The terrain will be treacherous, rain and mud with snow and ice once winter sets in." He feared it would be as bad or worse than the fight from Minturno north to Rome and he was soon proven right. When I examined the air reconnaissance photos I was puzzled by the clarity with which the German defense up at the Futa Pass revealed themselves. It was as if they wanted us to notice the gun emplacements. Later Major Melcher and I decided that may have been the case. There was, to be sure, a fierce fight on that first crest north of Florence. We were in reserve, and felt relieved at first when the Germans began slowly retreating north. We thought the worst might be over. Not so.

We waited. No clear reports came back to us. It rained and rained. We could hear our own artillery and the shallower sound of the German 88s coming in. Ambulances came back loaded; replacements were moved up. Orders to move came suddenly: we were to go straight up Highway 65 to replace the regiments at the Futa Pass. This order was remanded twelve hours later and, in some confusion, we were shifted to a hazy area to the west of the highway. This was in its turn countermanded and we were ordered into a sector to the northeast. It turned out that the fortifications at the Futa (so obvious on our reconnaissance photos) had collapsed sooner than expected, though heavy casualties had been inflicted. The German strategy was now to draw us slowly toward the last heights overlooking the Po Valley, obligating us to attack their defenses with our lines of supply increasingly extended. Fall weather and rain made rivers of mud out of what roads there were. Long ridges like fingers extended north and east, tantalizing the Fifth Army's commander, General Clark. He would constantly order us far forward on one of these exposed ridges, and journalists would then report how many miles we had advanced from Florence and how the distance to Bologna was growing ever shorter. On the last of these ridges, just short of the Po Valley, the Germans counterattacked and nearly drove us off Monte Battaglia. We were stopped short and remained stuck in place for the whole, long winter. Our casualties were enormous, nearly seventy percent. The long weeks leading up to the climax on Monte Battaglia were a time of increasing confusion: the Germans were difficult to find; they retreated slowly, sideslipping to attack from a flank, or infiltrating the lines to confound further our sense of disorder. Everyone was on foot; no jeeps could make it over the assorted cart trails and sheep runs which traversed the area. Our mules, their sweaty flanks a solid presence in the dark, were surer of foot than we were in the mountain mud.

One night we set up shop in a squat little house with a courtyard and a pigpen adjoining, arriving there about midnight. "All

right Allanbrook," said the colonel, "you're the intelligence corporal. See if the house is nice and clear for us." (I was afraid of
the dark as a child and still am. At least when I was a child my
mother would keep singing "Annie Laurie" downstairs in the
kitchen when I had to go upstairs to the bathroom, traversing
the long dark upstairs corridor. In my old age I whistle to myself.) I grinned at the colonel, looking straight into his close-set
gray eyes and pushed the wooden door of the house open, traversed the one big room gingerly, scuffing my feet and feeling
for tripwires by the fireplace. I climbed the wooden ladder
and poked my head up into the loft. No mines, no boobytraps.
"Clear, and I trust it will meet with your satisfaction, sir," I reported back to him. It was his turn to grin now, though behind
him I could see the good honest face of Major Melcher with a
more than usually concerned look on it. Lieutenant McKenna
grabbed my arm when we were all inside. "West Point jerk," he
murmured in my ear. He saw how scared I had been. I was
touched.

September and on into October were the worst times we were
to have. Those weeks and months we lived as if entombed under
a heavy lid; psychic scar tissue formed a protective cover. Black
ennui was interlarded with sour humor as one day after another
proceeded on its same dreary path. In these months we learned
with more precision who could be counted on. This had little to
do with rank; it had to do with moral character. At moments of
crisis the person who could be trusted to take charge would take
charge: rank would be superseded; corporals would take over
from sergeants, and sergeants from lieutenants. When the emergency slackened, rank would reassume its customary role.

The queen of the medics, George, was a man who had everyone's trust. "He gives aid and succor," commented Lieutenant
McKenna, pursing his lips. He would go out in the worst of
a barrage to bring in the wounded, often staying under the
barrage to staunch a particularly bad wound if he found someone losing vast quantities of blood. He was a round, solid little

man with nerves of steel. In quieter times he offered sexual comfort to many. "I just lay back and think of Memphis," said Joe Isaac, "and let him blow me right off to kingdom come!" We were a democratic platoon. Our Oklahoma sergeant said it best: "We don't need no shit; we're all stuck here together, equal-like."

7

I T WASN'T UNTIL first light the morning after it had happened that we learned of the disaster at First Battalion. The regiment was in such flux that telephone lines had not been laid; radio contact was sporadic up in the mountains and dangerous: the Germans often listened in on us. The adjutant of the battalion, a mousy little lieutenant from Arkansas with watery blue eyes and a wispy blond mustache, stumbled in, dizzy with fatigue, to inform us of the capture of the entire headquarters staff. He had been off with a mule train on the trail a few hundred yards away and had not been taken. "They got 'em all," he blurted out to the colonel. "Jesus Christ, sir, they got 'em all!"

"And why aren't you back there in charge," snapped the colonel. "You're a staff officer. You left that battalion with no one in charge." He turned to Major Melcher. "Find Major Jones in the Second Battalion and tell him he's the new CO of First Battalion. I'm leaving you in charge here while I go down there and see what's up." With that he was gone, taking three of the I and R platoon with him.

Major Melcher was shaken; it seemed to him foolhardy of the regimental commander to rush off to the First Battalion while the regiment itself was in the grips of enormous confusion. We didn't know where the enemy was and were having difficulty in orienting ourselves between one mountain ridge and another. It was only too clear Fifth Army would continue to shove us farther north and east onto the exposed heights which overhung the Po Valley. This time the major's prudence was mistaken: the colonel succeeded in locating all of the battalion's company commanders; he put the new battalion commander in place, shifted his officers around, and appointed an entire new HQ staff. He was back with us in twelve hours, jaunty and proud. He had restored order and confidence.

Several days after the First Battalion's disaster we began to have a clearer sense of where we were and of what it was possible to do. We probed with patrols both to our flanks and forward. The major exercised great caution, being acutely aware of our supply difficulties and of our lack of artillery support. The Germans seemed to be biding their time, but even so our probes were often met with astonishing vigor and casualties increased. Evacuation of the wounded down rocky mule tracks and across muddy gullies was difficult. The battalion aid stations began to be overburdened. The weather was foul. Even when a few roads in our sector were finally cleared for trucks and ambulances the wounded had to be carried for miles down from the hills on stretchers. Mules were of no use with the wounded, though the dead could be slung in body bags over those patient beasts. "You see, Allanbrook," remarked Lieutenant McKenna several times to me during this period, "how much more efficacious it is to wound rather than to kill. You have to take care of the wounded whereas the dead don't need your help."

We kept creeping forward these two weeks with the German artillery, especially the 88s, zeroing in on us with increasing accuracy and mobility. "They've got the roads for it, goddammit," the major would say. Their fire was more irregular, occurring at unpredictable intervals in contrast to their habitual ways of sending in a barrage at 1730 hours every evening. "I don't know what they're up to," muttered the major, mainly to himself for the colonel paid him scant attention. "I suspect they're trying to suck us up forward and then blast us, make us stick our necks out way ahead of our flanks."

"And wouldn't you know that that was just what General

Clark is going to order us to do," added Lieutenant McKenna, always getting his two cents worth in. "Then the Fifth Army can make all the headlines back in the States, boasting that now we are only ten miles from the Po Valley."

There was a smallish hill a half mile or so ahead of us, with a saddle sitting under the little round bump which marked its summit. A patrol from the Second Battalion had gone to the top of the hill a day before and had drawn a bit of fire; not much however, but it had been precisely zeroed in. They had pulled back down. The colonel was tantalized. "I want to seize that high ground; we'll be able to see almost into the valley and maybe we can really ascertain what the Krauts intend to do." Without consulting Major Melcher, he ordered a platoon from E Company to go up and to secure the round-topped hill. They crept up without incident and were in place at dawn. The colonel shook the major awake and told him the news. "They're on the hill; they have perfect observation. We're going to move a whole company up onto that saddle now; it'll act as a pivot for the whole regiment to get off its ass and to move forward."

Melcher blanched. "Colonel, sir," he said. "We haven't got any artillery to support them. We may be able to lob in a few 4.2 white phosphorus rounds but that's about it." Both of us, Major Melcher and I, remembered that the previous day the Germans had had the place neatly zeroed in. "They want to get us into an exposed place and then clobber us," said the major.

"Infantry is meant to take ground, not sit," replied the colonel. "You get on the phone and tell E Company to take that saddle." The major did as he was told. E Company reached the saddle by midmorning. The colonel then ordered the 4.2 mortars to fire covering fire over the saddle. From a half mile away it seemed to us to be ineffectual, serving mainly to pinpoint where we intended to go. At noon the sound of German fire began, both 88s and regular artillery. The crackle of machine guns opened up from a hidden emplacement which the platoon on the round top had not spotted on the previous day. We could see men straggling down off the saddle. "Tell F Company to get up there and hold that position," said the colonel. "Infantry's mission is to take ground and to hold it and I'm going to see that we do!" The major turned white, his hand trembled, and the phone fell to the dirt floor of the stone farmhouse we were in. The colonel looked at him with disgust, picked up the phone and gave the order: "You enlisted men man the phones; you're the ones I trust!"

E and F Companies pulled back from the saddle as night fell. The German artillery fire had been intense; the platoon on the round top had been overrun by the Germans and the companies on the saddle subjected to withering crossfire. There were numerous dead and more wounded. It was one of the times when George the medic distinguished himself. "Lordy, Lordy, what a mess," he kept repeating that night, after two trips up to the saddle and back under heavy and incessant fire. For three days the major sat in the corner of the room on the floor, silent. By the morning of the fourth day the regiment as a whole had advanced to both sides of the saddle and taken the round-top hill with no more than the expected number of casualties. The major came out of his funk but the colonel had won his battle with him. He retained Major Melcher as his operations officer, holding a whip hand over him because of those days of breakdown. We all continued to revere the major, and the colonel continued his courtship of us sergeants and corporals in regimental headquarters. We had our revenge. Sergeant Bongiovi, a consummate male gossip and the colonel's secretary, read to us excerpts from the colonel's letters home and from his entries into his war diary. His prose did not quite ring true. Like many small men, he had a bold insouciance that flourished alongside his rank and which found its exemplar in Napoleon.

A short while later began the bloodiest battle our regiment was to suffer. It bore a certain resemblance to the affair with E and F Companies which had broken the major's heart. This time, as Lieutenant McKenna had foreseen, orders came down from Fifth Army to press forward to the northeast and to seize Monte

Battaglia, the last height before the Po Valley, our promised land. We were now far in advance of the British on our right and the American division on our left. After several bad firefights, Major Melcher was worried when we had made our way to the top of our mountain without any resistance. "They want us up there," he said. "They've got us in a trap. We'll be clobbered with everything they've got and we haven't any artillery worth a good damn." He was a chastened man, however; the colonel kept him in his place and the major found himself incapable of opposing him. He could only fuss and delay and try to ensure a steady flow of supplies and good deployment of our heavy mortars and 50-caliber machine guns.

The Germans counterattacked soon enough and continued to do so day after day in what became for our regiment the fiercest fighting of the whole campaign. It was bloodier and more protracted than the famous kickoff for Rome way back there at Minturno the previous May. There was the added desperation that our attack soon became a defense. We were not to advance beyond that point until the war ended, seven months later.

The counterattacks grew fiercer. The enemy employed the most extraordinary weapons, not only batteries of exotic multi-tube mortars but several times they charged up the slopes of Monte Battaglia wielding flamethrowers. It was our regiment's epic and the colonel was in charge of it, exposing himself constantly and suffering no more than a slight wound in one arm. We had our HQ a half mile back of the mountain in a rudimentary stone house. The casualties streamed past us. Chunky Sohanchek, our Pittsburgh Ukrainian, went by on a stretcher, his face ashen, with a sucking wound in his chest. An old drill sergeant of mine from Camp Gruber went past. He grinned at me, flapping his left arm to indicate that it at least was still intact though his right one was blasted to bits.

Increasing casualties in those disastrous fall days called for increasing replacements. The Italian repo-depos emptied; replacements would appear who had been in the States a week before or who had been abruptly shipped down from France. They were rushed into the line in this worst of times with, only too often, no opportunity of knowing who their sergeants were, let alone their officers. First sergeants would submit morning reports on men missing whom they had never seen; others had never been entered on their rolls but had been found dead in one of the company's foxholes. They died as a dog tag number, not as a member of any squad or platoon or company. This nearly happened to my cousin David.

He appeared suddenly in one of the quieter moments of those awful weeks, gray-faced from dysentery. He was assigned to B Company, a company which had lost up to forty percent of its men the previous week. I brought him to the medics, who gave him a week's reprieve in the rear to clear up his gut. Through the network of noncoms who by now, after a year in the line, ran almost everything, I had him reassigned to the regimental anti-tank company, a safe enough assignment. There were no tanks in the high Apennines so the company was assigned to various tasks a bit to the rear. As a result of a foulup in the paperwork — most understandable as B Company and the rest of the First Battalion were caught up in the nasty fights on the ridges leading up to Monte Battaglia — he was reported missing in action. I was happy soon afterward to be able to write to my aunt back in Boston that he was alive and kicking and assigned to the antitank company. It gave me a certain relish to be the savior of a member of the family, though it plays on my memory against the terrible number of casualties among so many of my old friends in Company C whom I had known ever since Camp Gruber.

The intensity slackened. We were relieved on Monte Battaglia by a division from the British Eighth Army, who felt that we had been bloody fools to have stuck our necks out so far so soon. We pulled off down to a valley which had a road open to the rear. There was intermittent shelling, which made what happened the next day all the more surprising. Around noon on that second day down in the valley we were gathered in yet another of those thick-walled Apennine houses in which we had established our regimental HQs. We heard a loud "Attenshun!" from outside and in strode General Clark, Fifth Army commander. "Well, men," he said, "we've come fifty of the sixty-five miles to Bologna and we're going to finish the job." There was silence. Master Sergeant Costello, our perpetual New York Irishman, snapped out "Yes, sir!" The general then stretched out his hand. "My name's Clark," he said. Costello shook it. There was more silence. The general walked over to Colonel Fry, pulled a Silver Star medal from his pocket and pinned it to the colonel's jacket. Then rather casually he went to the field telephone, cranked it up and said into it: "This is General Clark. Get me Fifth Army." In an astonishingly brief interval he got through. "Put a general on," he said to whomever had answered. There was a momentary pause. "This is General Clark," he went on. "I've just awarded Colonel Fry the Silver Star. Print the orders!" He flashed a smile at us, turned quickly and left. A copy of *Stars and Stripes* appeared up from Florence the next day, reporting on the triumphal advance of the Fifth Army to the last height before the Po Valley.

Later that week, a few miles down the road and out of artillery range, the quartermaster corps set up a mobile bath unit. You entered one end of a long tent, stripped, leaving all of your filthy clothes in a heap — then showers, very hot with lots of GI soap; finally, at the other end of the enclosure, an entire set of clean, new clothes. Joe Isaac and I gave each other haircuts. A beer ration was issued. We were new men, purified. Venus was served by a platoon of prostitutes that had materialized in a meadow behind the bath unit. Since the fall of Rome their intelligence as to the precise location of troops who had pulled back from the lines was faultless. They would position themselves just out of artillery range and lines of troops would be seen snaking up the meadow seeking relief. The first sergeant doled out condoms; the medics, prophylactic kits. Short-arm inspections took place with more frequency.

Shortly after the battle at Monte Battaglia the second great change of my career in the 350th Infantry Regiment took place: I was called back to the First Battalion to be their operations sergeant. My rank jumped from two stripes to four and I became the enlisted boss of the battalion HQ. Costello, the regimental operations sergeant and my mentor in staff politics, was worried. "You'll have four stripes, Allanbrook," he said, "but your ass is that much closer to the line." I knew that but I wanted the stripes. When I got up to the First Battalion the old noncoms from C Company received me as one of them. "You're smart, Allanbrook," said my old platoon sergeant. "You'll go on back to regiment with six stripes when that slot opens up."

So many of them still inhabited the old world of the regular army. At Fort Sam Houston I had caught a glimpse of that world: spick and span streets, raked walks and flower beds, smart saluting and crisp uniforms. I began to imagine myself with six stripes, a master sergeant, equal in rank to all of the regiment's first sergeants, just below the regimental sergeant major. I would inhabit a world in place, a masculine slot for me and for every man around me with the ultimate responsibility resting on the shoulders of the creatures above, the officers of the regular army. Women would be at a safe distance, downtown, in "San Antone."

A month or so later when he was visiting the First Battalion Colonel Fry greeted me with a remark that was closer to the truth of my life as a soldier than anything I could imagine as a regimental operations sergeant in some peaceful regular army post. "Well, Allanbrook," he said, "you're moving up in this man's army but I doubt we'll ever make a soldier out of you." Even though Sergeant Costello had, with his Irish political good sense, always adjured me to keep my mouth shut and my opinions to myself in front of officers, I had the gall to answer, "Yes, sir, and I take that as a compliment, sir." The colonel looked at me quizzically. He was a bit of a cultural snob as I noted when I met him in the Uffizi in Florence that fall in the company of a Red Cross nurse. There was an exhibition of French Impressionists and he said, "Well, Allanbrook, I suppose one is meant to look at all of this stuff." I proceeded to hold forth on the virtues of color and light and brush strokes much to the amusement of the colonel's lady friend. He was one of those West Point officers who were aware of other worlds, of other careers. He enjoyed the sharp edge of our relationship.

Even now, so many years later, I am somewhat abashed at the recollection of my regular army ambitions; I realize that inside I am still proud to have been a staff sergeant and would not have minded one little bit being a six-striper. The thought of becoming an officer, however, struck me — and most other noncoms — as grotesque. After a year in combat experienced noncoms viewed with an acid eye the ambitions and the prerogatives of the official hierarchy placed over them. A prudent officer would, at the very least, acknowledge the division of responsibilities. A brand-new second lieutenant with no experience of this, arriving at a line company platoon with a seasoned sergeant in charge, had a hard row to hoe; he could easily get stuck in a moral quagmire. At higher levels the situation could be downright peculiar.

Later that winter we received, fresh from the States, a brand-new lieutenant colonel. He was a replacement for our battalion CO, a well-liked man who had been rather badly wounded after the entire headquarters staff had been captured in the weeks before Monte Battaglia. The executive officer had taken over at the time; he was a gruff but decent man who'd been with the regiment since Camp Gruber. The general opinion was that he should have been promoted to the command of the battalion. This state of affairs placed considerable demands on the tact of our fresh, brand-new lieutenant colonel.

His first day at battalion headquarters was a chastening one. We were high up on the saddle of a small mountain in yet another stone house. Behind the house the mountain rose abruptly and in front of the house stretched a muddy expanse of farmyard with a barn containing a pigsty and granary facing the house at a distance of perhaps a hundred yards. The trail which led up to our HQ arrived at the back of the barn. We had pulled into the position at night and were chagrined the next day to discover that the Germans had the open expanse between the house and the barn well covered with their heavy machine guns. The front in those weeks was fairly quiet, neither side interested in a major engagement, though there were plenty of probes and patrols and occasional surprises. We had been up there for four days. The mule trains which moved up at night would leave everything behind the barn, not trusting the animals to traverse the open farmyard. We would creep over under cover of darkness and pick up our supplies. This particular night had been nasty: rain had turned to sleet and ice and the mule train with our supplies and the new colonel arrived only as the sun was coming up. The supply train crew had warned the colonel of the danger and a sudden crackle of machine-gun fire corroborated their report. We signaled across the farmyard for him to stay where he was and so he did, from dawn until dusk, crowded into a smelly Apennine pigsty, nibbling on his K rations. When it was properly dark he streaked across the farmyard, wearing his pack and carrying his bedroll. He had no superior officer to report to, of course: he was the boss.

His command was a motley crew, dirty and unwashed. We had a minuscule fire in the fireplace on which we would heat our K-ration coffee. Maps were spread out on a plank table. Everyone knew what to do. Shortly after he arrived he observed the operations officer and me creep out to check on the positioning of our 81-mm. mortars. There was another room, dark and smelly, where the battalion exec had had his bedroll. This room was turned over to the new colonel and the exec moved in with all of us in the big room.

Colonel Sparrow turned out to be a decent fellow, a fresh-faced midwesterner from Indiana, quite young for his rank. He never caused any trouble and lasted until the war was over, though he never became an integral part of our faithful but war-weary society.

My operations officer, Lieutenant Boatner, was another kettle of fish. He was young and came to us fresh from West Point, several weeks after our ordeal on Monte Battaglia. He was a career officer and the son and grandson of career officers. He had a bigger world behind him than any of the other staff officers, his father having been posted as military attaché to both Ankara and Paris when the lieutenant was a boy. He divided responsibilities: when he slept I ran things and when I slept he ran things. In any real emergency he took over. He was well aware that I had been in the regiment since Camp Gruber and had been in the line since Minturno and the push for Rome and that he was a new arrival. He was a witty man, sardonic at times, but could be a great comfort.

One bad night sticks out in my memory. We were exhausted: it was snowing and we had been walking for over five hours on a mountain trail which was covered with ice. Even the mules, so sure-footed in the mountains, had trouble. One of them slipped over the edge, plunging to the bottom of the dark ravine on our right. We hugged the left and said nothing. I was weak from two days of diarrhea and began to slither and slip every fifth or sixth step, experiencing a kind of despair that saw no end to the night's travail. "Allanbrook," piped up Lieutenant Boatner in a jaunty voice, "if you're going to fall, do it more gracefully. You're no more made to be a clown than you were born to be a soldier." He kept me going that night.

Later that winter, on another snowy night, he and I were out checking on certain positions in the line companies. We had finished with A and B Companies and were on our way to C Company which was dug in on the right side of our battalion sector. It was a quiet night, rather clear; we had been talking about, of all things, tradition — he speaking gracefully about West Point and its continuity, and I pushing him rather quizzically to spell out what in heaven's name he was talking about. At a certain moment we both stopped. We looked about us. The snow we were walking upon was virgin, untrodden: C Company had to be behind us. We grinned at each other out there in never-never land, turned and beat it back to C Company's hill-side dugouts. "Where the fuck have you two been?" said the C Company commander.

"Just a bit of a look-see," Lieutenant Boatner replied. "You might position your machine guns to cover that piece out there in front of you, Captain. I'm planning to have the heavy weapons company cover the gully beyond with their 81s. As far as I can see, anyone could walk right through." He smiled pleasantly at C Company's commander and we left.

Returning to our HQ I couldn't resist saying, "It's mighty handy when tradition is supported by quick wits."

"Allanbrook," he said, "we covered our mistake, we're safe and we made a valuable reconnaissance just as good operations people should." We had been lucky; the next night a German patrol probed the area we had been in, was spotted by Company C's machine guns and retreated down the gully harassed by the 81-mm. mortars from D Company. Many, many years later I inquired about Lieutenant Boatner from the retired lieutenant general who lived next door. I was curious as to his subsequent career. "He's a colonel," the general told me, "now retired. He was too bright to make general."

Boatner and I often talked together not only about military traditions but increasingly about a soldier's duties and a soldier's honor. This was the result of a phenomenon that came to puzzle us more and more. The two of us would often interrogate German prisoners as to the precise locations of their units, where their machine guns and mortars were, where their dugouts were located, where their HQs were. The surprising thing was that, with the exception of soldiers from certain SS regiments, they would tell us exactly and without hesitation what we wanted to know, being well aware that we would immediately zero in mortar and artillery fire on their comrades. They were not frightened — they knew we never tortured prisoners — but for them, more importantly than anything else, the war was over. Duty and honor, which should have preserved their silence and guarded the safety of their fellow soldiers in arms, were inoperative. An hour before, they had been part of a war machine that remained lethal and resilient, even though in these last months it was clear to everyone that the jig was up, that Germany had lost. The men they had been with in the midst of long travail and daily peril ceased to exist for them. We were eager for their information but despised them for giving it. When the war did end, the Germans were the most cooperative of prisoners, submitting precise morning reports and full of helpful suggestions on ways to facilitate the details of their surrender.

Few of us had given much thought to the Germans during our first year in the line. We thought of Hitler as a kind of caricature; we had heard of Nazism, we read about the bombings and had seen with our own eyes the destruction wrought by the air forces on both sides of the conflict. We knew little, if anything, at this juncture, of the death camps or of the "Final Solution." We were happy that the Russians were clobbering them and that our armies were driving across the map to close with the Red Army on Berlin. I realized I had to think more about Germans and began a series of conversations with Lieutenant Boatner after one very special hour we had spent with three prisoners who had pointed out precisely a spot on a hill across the valley where their machine guns and mortars were located. With knowing precision they followed with their fingers the contour lines on my maps, enabling me to fix the coordinates of their unit's HQ.

The prisoners went happily away to the rear with our MPs, their war over and their company about to be heavily shelled on the very spot they had so truthfully and accurately indicated. With a certain deliberate casuistry I argued to Lieutenant Boatner that they were right in their behavior: they had fought month after faithful month; they knew Germany was losing; they knew we would treat them humanely. Then my casuistry stopped and my imagination boggled: I could not conceive of our First Battalion HQ, captured so recently by the Germans, or my old I and R platoon — of giving information so readily and so cheerfully, information which would inflict terrible harm upon my friends and my fellow soldiers. Such feelings and such convictions as I had (and Lieutenant Boatner shared them) were deeper than patriotism, deeper than politics. They seemed to me to have little to do with the United States or with Germany. Were we naive, we Americans, or was this not the case? Could a regime destroy honor between men whose continued existence depended upon each other's trust? Was such honor independent of the dangers of the moment? Was Germany different? It is well-nigh impossible for me a half century later to erase from my mind those prisoners taken by us those wintery months in the Apennines. Whenever I meet a German I recollect those moments and only with an effort of will can I view him as I view other men. The recording of this so many years later is an encoding of my own consciousness, a phenomenon that bears with it indelibly a judgment and the inevitable condemnation that ensues upon that judgment.

We were in the snow on those mountains for much of December, January, and February. We never got used to it, any more than we got used to mud, though we did become inured to both. One snowy night does stick in the craw of my memory, however: it was so American! Without warning we were moved west to a sector in the mountains north of Lucca and Montecatini. Our orders were to relieve the Negro division which was holding that part of the line. They were known as the "Black Buffaloes," their shoulder insignia being a buffalo. The army segregated blacks from whites as was the custom in civilian America. In this division the separation was further exacerbated: the enlisted men were black and the officers white — not only were they white, most of them were southern whites.

The morning of the day we were to relieve the Black Buffaloes, a sergeant from the particular battalion we were relieving came down to report to us, bringing with him overlays of their positions. Our executive officer, a Texan, was on duty in our temporary HQ. The sergeant, tall, very black, and impassive, entered and saluted. There was a momentary silence. The major looked up and said, "What is it, boy, speak up." I was embarrassed; my officer, Lieutenant Boatner, knew it was not proper address in anyone's army; the other officers in the HQ chuckled as they observed the sergeant. He was used to such treatment; all of his own officers were southern. He delivered the materials to us and left, his mask unruffled.

It was snowy and bitterly cold that night; the trails were icy. As we made our way up to the battalion HQ we were relieving, lines of black soldiers were streaming down the trail, their equipment piled upon their rifles which they were employing as sledges, dragging them behind them in the snow. There was no order. It was like a retreat after a battle but there had been no battle; the sector of the line they had occupied had been quiet as a tomb for a month. It felt to me like that anarchic night two winters ago at Camp Gruber when the whole regiment, half frozen, broke discipline, ignoring orders and cursing the stupidity of the officers in charge. There was the same lawlessness in the air.

We effected the relief by first light as files of disorganized black soldiers continued their dismal retreat down to the valley. The white officers thought to cover up the disgrace by not speaking of it, a very southern habit. Most of our officers and even some of our enlisted men took it as a proof that segregation was proper, an American tradition sanctioned by a moral difference in the races. Lieutenant McKenna, who had been moved to the First Battalion as an intelligence officer, noted with his usual acerbity, "If the Germans had attacked this sector it would have been more than a disgrace, it would have been a fucking rout! They could have retaken Lucca just like that. Then the southerners would really have made their case." The Germans had remained quiet, however, and no disgrace ensued to the Fifth Army. Later that month some of us got passes down to Montecatini Terme, a Tuscan spa in the Arno Valley between Lucca and Pistoia. There I would take long, hot mineral baths in the marble opulence of the bath establishment, lying back in the pool, gazing up at the frescoed ceiling replete with cupids and the full effulgence of nineteenth-century baroque. Sporting in the warm waters were naked soldiers, both black and white. There were no officers present; they were segregated in their own establishment. It was as if once out of their sight, race was out of mind. Black Buffaloes and Blue Devils (as the army now called my division), we sported together, momentarily cleansed of the filth of the front. Fifty years later the army is worried once again, concerned about men naked together in barracks, showers, and baths.

My third Christmas in the army came and went, cold and chilly as had been the other two. The first, way back at Camp Gruber when they would wake us up at dawn for close order drill followed by bayonet practice, now seemed centuries ago. The second one was on that chilly hillside just outside Oran. The third Christmas there was snow. We were snug in a fortresslike stone farmhouse with walls thick enough to shield us from the artillery barrage that came in promptly each evening at 1730 hours: German efficiency. The mule train had brought us a beer ration; some of us had illegal whiskey. The line companies reported no particular action. We hazarded a bit of a fire in the massive fireplace, gathered around it, drank to everyone's health and grinned at each other. It was a peaceful evening, a respite after the special horror we had suffered earlier in the week.

Following upon a shift forward in the line by the entire battalion, a small group of us from headquarters had edged our way up through a wooded valley to what seemed to be a sheltered spot. A Company had reported the area to be as clear as could be expected. At a turn in the track, with a ravine below and the slope of the mountain above, stood a substantial two-story house: stalls and a granary downstairs and habitable rooms upstairs. A massive wooden door stood slightly ajar. We gingerly pushed it open and were assaulted with the stench of dead bodies. Lieutenant Boatner had barely said, "Let's get out of here, Allanbrook," when two artillery shells came in, exploding twenty yards from the door. They were followed by a burst of machine-gun fire. We were stuck. There were three dead GIs in the corner of the first-floor stable. The smell drove us upstairs though we were better sheltered from the artillery down below. By the time we had gotten back to our colonel by radio and told him to stay put A Company had gotten in touch with us, apologizing for the spot not being as clear as they had thought it was. It took them two days to clear the machine-gun nest on the hill above our charnel house. We smoked continually, one cigarette after another, hoping to anesthetize the stink. That night as I tried to sleep I remembered my first encounter with the smell of human corpses: it was soon after our breakthrough by Minturno and there the smell was mingled with the sweetness of orange blossoms. Dead bodies in the midst of a grove of oranges. Sight mingled with smell: a grove of oranges with shiny green leaves and white blossoms, perfumed air mixed with the sweet stink of death. A long time it was from that May to this December!

After Christmas time dragged on in a daily routine: checking the line companies, tramping out in the snow and the mud, awaiting the usual evening barrage. We seemed fixed for all eternity in the last line of mountains overlooking Bologna with the Po Valley lying just beyond our reach, a promised land which we could see and which we could shell with our guns but which we seemed fated never to enter. The army sent up tanks equipped with fancy multibarreled mortars. It was pleasant to have them to play with after being barraged so often by the bewildering variety of screaming meemies and large-barreled mortars which the Germans in these last months of the war continued to employ. We had never worked with tanks and it was a novelty when they appeared, trundling up Highway 65 from Florence. One of them sheltered itself in the lee of a hill near us. On top of it was a beehive of pipes. I got to know the tank sergeant and it amused him to watch me play with the keyboard of buttons which controlled the missiles: 5-1-3-4-5, 5-3-4-2-1, my five-finger exercises launching barrages of missiles which scaled over our last range of hills on into the suburbs of ancient Bologna.

All that winter *Stars and Stripes* would report every day that the Allied armies were driving east and the Russians were rolling west. We were the forgotten front. We had the mission of taking Bologna but we didn't have the troops and nothing was done about it. The few divisions that remained to us were never relieved. We depended ever more on the repo-depos as we continued to have casualties from artillery, from mortars, from patrolling activity, from the ever-present mine fields, from dysentery, from hepatitis, from mononucleosis, from gonorrhea, from syphilis, from foot infections, from spongy lungs exacerbated by the cigarettes that were lavished upon us. Cynicism and ennui were the order of the day; there was no prospect that pleased. Once Bologna fell and the war in Europe ended we would be shipped to Japan. There was more heavy drinking and less sex when passes were issued. Groups of infantrymen would throng the red plush anterooms of the whorehouses, drinking bad cognac, often as not indifferent to the doubtful pleasures of going off for a mechanical quickie with one of the girls. We were surly with the MPs and sullenly indifferent to the throngs of cheery and well-shaven rear-echelon troops who outnumbered us in such shocking proportions. We would often opt for a couple of days at the baths in Montecatini rather than face the endless slow train ride back to Rome, soaking in the hot mineral waters for hours after an evening spent drinking into dizziness.

For something to be plucked from the sludge of time, to be recollected and set apart, there has to be a vividness arising out of the senses coupled with a particular intuition that fixes the attention. It can't be something that occurs in the ordinary train of life. Nearness to death is one thing in an old man, another in a young man. An old man views death ironically; it is close and inevitable. One by one his friends disappear; with extinction near the days are cherished, one by one, and while ambition may still be present its brassy call has lost its edge. Deaths from long ago are more immediate to him than those of the thinning ranks of his contemporaries.

I read in the 1994 morning papers of forty thousand corpses drifting into Lake Victoria, slaughtered in the butchery going on in Rwanda. They have no memorial. No poet will intone a sonnet over their bones as Milton did for the victims of the massacre in Piedmont: "Avenge, O Lord, thy slaughtered saints." One death remembered may have been my road to selfhood but others clamor for recognition. My life and my war and my dead won't stay back in Italy, buried in the neat rows of the Allied military cemetery just south of Florence near the old road to Siena. Deaths in a war, after all, are different; something was being fought for and the ranks of those who fell can't end up as part of a body count.

One death, in those last months of the war, sticks in the craw of my memory like a still frame from an antique Keystone comedy, a moment of attention fixed motionless. We were in a stone farmhouse not unlike the charnel house we had been stuck in the week before Christmas. There was a lower floor, half dug into the hillside, and a single large room above. We were a small detachment from battalion headquarters: Lieutenant Boatner, a couple of enlisted men from my squad, and I. Also among us was a corporal from A Company who had come over from his company with messages for us. He was blue-eyed and freckled and had a tender but tough look about him, teetering as he was between boyhood and manliness. He was standing in the middle of the room when it happened; the rest of us were nearer to the thick walls of the house. Without any forewarning whoosh and whistle, an artillery shell came through the roof, plunging straight through the floor to the room below where it exploded. Down went the corporal, down through the hole, head first. I gave a whoop of laughter; his nose dive had the quick clarity of a perfect stunt shot. Horror followed within seconds and his broken body was soon enough stuffed into a bag and trundled off down the mountain on a mule.

The end, when it came, came suddenly. We spent the last month before the Germans' collapse in the bombed-out shell of a hamlet which straddled Highway 65. On the crest of a sizable hill to the northwest, Monterumici, were the Germans; our line companies were dug in around the bottom of the hill and from the shattered little town we were in we had a grandstand view of the scene. To the left of the hill the valley flattened and broadened, the stream running down it twisting in loops with sandy banks as it approached the plain of Emilia. Over the hill a bit to our northeast was Bologna. (Many times since I have peered out at the scene as the train whizzes by on its quick traversal of the Florence–Bologna section of the Rome–Milan express.) A great variety of *Nebelwerfers*, newfangled versions of the older screaming meemies, continued to pepper us, one at a time or in clusters. Some had high-pitched screams, others sirenlike glissandi; some emitted a mixture of simultaneously shifting pitches like a hysterical pipe organ; some simply moaned. All of them carried a tremendous load of explosive which would impact with a shattering effect upon the eardrums of anyone nearby. We had something new ourselves: proximity-fuse artillery shells. They would explode not upon impact, but a bit aboveground, scattering shrapnel much more lethally for those dug in their holes. "It has taken the army ordnance an inordinate amount of time to get those babies up to us," commented Lieutenant Boatner. "When I was at the Point three years ago we were told all about them in our lecture on the employment of supporting artillery."

We took a certain kind of pleasure in shooting them at the hill in front of us, pinning the Germans down and forcing them to cover their holes with thick emplacements of earth and wood. Both sides now had tanks positioned behind the crest of their respective hills. The Germans, in addition, had mobile 88s, which they would shift back and forth on the roads that were so available to them. This made the approach to our hamlet a tricky maneuver, all the more so as we never knew when to expect incoming shells. So often in the past and in other sectors the Germans would shell us regularly at the same hour. Five-thirty in the afternoon would roll around and if there was no incoming fire there would be a vague unease among us. "It's like missing your daily shit," Joe Isaac said. "You get used to it, regularlike." In this last month there was no such regularity. Jeeps and even 2½-ton trucks would hazard the road, becoming bolder if several hours had passed with no incoming fire. Once three trucks and a couple of jeeps were rash enough to be bunched together on the approach to our HQ in the village. They were clobbered with both 88s and the regular artillery. A half-hour later when we were getting the wounded taken care of, the Germans let fly with a barrage of Nebelwerfers. "Why don't they give up; they must be fundamentally perverse," said Lieutenant McKenna. "They've lost the war; why can't they just lay low until our cocksucking diplomats sign some piece of paper." McKenna's language was degenerating; he was a skinny high-strung fellow and he became increasingly neurotic as the war dragged on and he remained still a lieutenant. All around him his fellow officers had been promoted to captain and major; his old sidekick from OCS, Lieutenant Jones, actually made lieutenant colonel and was a battalion commander. McKenna's sharp tongue became shriller as winter turned into spring and the war drew to its close. He felt demeaned by circumstance and dug himself ever deeper into his private hell. Most of the officers who had known him since Camp Gruber avoided him and when he began to seek my company they began to whisper that he was queer, though he never made the slightest advances to me. He was a special kind of war casualty and he wasn't going to be any better when he got out.

The final assault drew near. The air force increased its bombing of the road and supply network out in the valley. We moved out of our battered little town and down into the valley under the slopes of Monterumici. The last great artillery barrage of the campaign pounded away at the Germans' emplacement up on the crest above us. Corps artillery had been dragged up and added heavy stuff to our regular divisional guns. From the 4.2 mortars of the chemical warfare unit attached to our regiment white phosphorus shells scorched the tops of the enemy dug-outs with their horrid fierce fire. The Germans continued to fight back. Incessant mortar fire covered the slopes as the line compa-nies moved out and up. Tiger tanks with 88s were positioned just over the crest; they kept up an intermittent fire, constantly changing trajectory as they were shifted about. Casualties began to come back down the hill that first night; all the next day we remained pinned down. The next night we pushed on up with the battalion HQ only slightly to the rear of the line companies. That night I was nearly paralyzed with fear. Two times a mortar landed in front of me, then in back of me, and twice almost on top of me. Each time I clawed my way into one of the rocky holes the line companies had left behind as they made their terrible ascent the previous night. When we were a bit below the top we learned that Captain Lynch, A Company's commander, had been killed by machine-gun fire just as his company was ap-proaching a saddle to the left of the summit. He was a man of sunny temperament, gregarious and well liked, the best of our battalion's company commanders. Those of us who had been in the regiment long enough remembered his father, our origi-nal regimental commander, Colonel Lynch, who had been dis-missed and whose place had been taken by Colonel Fry, way back at Minturno before the real fighting war began. He loved his son and had been proud to have him in his regiment.

The second day was bad; the Germans kept fighting and we were pinned just under the crest of Monterumici. On the third day we made it. It was over. The line collapsed and we streamed up over the top. Just over the crest were two Tiger tanks which had been blasted to smithereens. On one of them two bodies hung out over the turret, torn apart by artillery and burned by the fierce flames of our white phosphorus shells. "Poor bastards," said Joe Isaac as we tramped by them. "Why didn't the motherfuckers give up? Look at 'em; it just don't make no sense."

We peeled off Monterumici down to the river below, streaming out onto the flat billiard table we had been aiming at for that whole long fall, winter, and early spring. It wasn't just a victory, it was a rout. We passed a bit to the west of Bologna, pushing forward at a frantic rate through the fertile fields of Emilia, headed for the Po and beyond. It was a festival for the populace. They took out the good things they had hidden from the Germans and filled our mess cups with Lambrusco, the fizzy red wine of the province. "Looks like Dr Pepper but son of a bitch if it ain't wine," said one of the boys from South Carolina. We chomped on their white bread with its smooth inside and shiny thin crust and crammed cheeses into our packs. Cherries and peaches were loaded into our helmets. We were conquerors in the fields of plenty. We never stopped; we just kept going north, drinking, eating, and chasing the Germans — drunk, exhausted, and victorious. There was no opposition at the Po; the engineers got us across in record time. The Adige was now our goal and Colonel Fry was on fire to get the whole regiment up there. The Germans had begun to put up some resistance but not at the spot where we crossed over and headed east toward Vicenza.

We did have quite a firefight as we edged our way into Palladio's town; there were machine guns and snipers in the side streets around the piazza. Three quarters of an hour after we had entered town Sergeant Mollin, the 81-mm. mortar sergeant from D Company, a friend of mine, passed by where Lieutenant Boatner and I had squatted with a radio and our maps in an alley behind the famous town hall. He made a V for Victory sign and grinned at me. "Allanbrook," he said, "I done it again. First man to get laid in the city of Vicenza! Fucked her standin' up just over behind that buildin' with the fancy front!" Lieutenant Boatner eyed me quizzically and I filled him in on Mollin's accomplishment. His goal throughout the campaign had been to be the first man to get laid in every town we entered. This had been carried out at some risk to life and limb, but it was a clear and unblemished record.

"I suggest we award him the Combat Infantry Badge with Pendant Penises," said Lieutenant Boatner. "See to it that you write up the proper papers for it when the current unpleasantness draws to a close. I must say, however, that I am amazed that a boy of your refinement should frequent such types. It must have to do with democracy and the draft."

"There are traditions and traditions," I said to the lieutenant.

8

AFTER VICENZA we had no more fighting, no more deaths, no more wounded. The town we were in the day the war ended — Marostica, a walled city up in the Veneto not far from Bassano — had already been cleared of the Germans by the partisans several days before we entered upon the scene. They were in charge: they had a headquarters and a city government set up and functioning in the crenelated town hall that flanked one side of the square. They greeted us as companions in arms; we ate *porchetta* (roast pig) and drank quantities of good white wine sitting together on trestle tables set up in long lines around the piazza. When the official news of the surrender came through on the radio they marched around the town, singing the "Internazionale" and shooting their Bren guns into the air. Our Cajun first sergeant never had gotten it straight as to who they were and what they were called. "Goddamn Protestants," he said. "All drunk and shooting off their guns." I knew they were Communists and drank even more with them the next day when we received an official communication from Allied Force Headquarters proclaiming that all of us fighting in Italy must be prepared for a new peril threatening from the East. By the end of the week an entire division had been hustled over to Trieste.

Our destination was to the north. A whole flotilla of 2½-ton trucks lined up in the square at Marostica on our third day there.

We drove out of town with loud whoops and volleys of Bren guns from the partisans. Mountains rose on each side of the river road we were following, higher and higher as we wound our way north to Trento and Bolzano. "It don't look like no Italy I ever seen," said Joe Isaac. Way off to the east as we entered Bolzano glimmered the picketed summit of Monte Marmolada, the evening sun catching the whiteness of its marbled cliffs.

Inside the city something was fishy. German staff cars went past, driven by Germans with German officers in full uniform. They saluted our convoy with perfect aplomb. "Don't them fuckers know the war's over," said our first sergeant. "We won, not them."

"It's just as I thought it might be," said Lieutenant McKenna. "Those cocksucking diplomats of ours have finagled a quick surrender and now the Germans are going to be real cooperative and we'll all work together to bury the hatchet. This stupid war is over and we're going to tie it up in a pretty red ribbon." His bitterness and his bile were well founded. The terms of surrender drawn up by Allan Dulles in his negotiations up in Switzerland left General Wolff in place in his headquarters in Bolzano. We were to work with him in any way that might facilitate the surrender of the German forces. He was an evil man, an SS general with a portfolio of horrors behind him. He had the gall to invite our Colonel Fry (about to be promoted to brigadier general and already assistant division commander) to a champagne party to celebrate his birthday. Fry had had almost two weeks of living with Wolff's arrogance. He ordered the general to appear on the street outside the ornate villa where the party was to have been held. He was then marched through the streets of Bolzano with a full field pack, all the way out to the prison stockade set up several miles outside town. Some of the troops in Fry's headquarters posted large and very legible posters upon which was inscribed HAPPY BIRTHDAY, GENERAL WOLFF. Much of Bolzano was sullen as it watched this drama unfold. The majority of its inhabitants were Tyroleans, German-speaking Austrians who felt in their guts that they had been trifled with after World War I, unfairly handed over to the Italians under the terms of the armistice. There were lots of Nazi party members among them and they had profited mightily from having the headquarters of Army Group C (a kind of regional German Pentagon) stationed in their town.

Our battalion HQ established itself not in Bolzano but high up off the road to the Brenner Pass in the pristine town of Siusi, untouched by the war, nestled snugly under the Alps of Siusi and surrounded by lush meadows and many cows. Its wooden chalets had balconies with red geraniums; its inhabitants were substantial and well fed. You arrived at the town after a tortuous climb up from the route leading to the Brenner. You rounded a curve and meadows and mountains of a celestial cast were suddenly in front of you. "Fucking never-never land. It looks just like the movies," said Joe. He was right; it resembled an over-scrupulous set for a rather expensive production of *Heidi*.

"Those are the Dolomites," Lieutenant Boatner told me. "We used to come up to Cortina over the other side there when my father was military attaché in Paris. The mountains are of a special geological structure, limestone I believe, that leaves them sticking straight up out of the meadows like cathedral spires."

We established our battalion headquarters in a perfectly appointed little hotel which faced upon the central square. We would stand out on its balconies and contemplate the scene before us, rubbing our eyes. Poor old Italy, desolate and ruined, was another universe, far away in the distant South. Siusi was a paradise and we gazed upon it with the eyes of innocence. This made it all the more disturbing when, in a week or so, we began to be aware of the serpents in our garden.

The morning of our second day in town a man who called himself Martin came up to our colonel and offered his services as an interpreter. "I am sure I can be of use to you, Colonel," he said. "I know not only English but perfectly well also German and Italian, which you will find useful up here in Siusi." I couldn't place his accent, but then I was hardly a sophisticate of Central Europe. The colonel, good Indiana boy that he was, accepted his services without a second thought. Martin's first suggestion was that we hang an American flag from the balcony which overhung the front entrance to our little hotel. "You will then be official, don't you think," he said. "The people in town will now see your authority." The two of them made a memorable tableau vivant standing on the balcony of the hotel, hauling up the Stars and Stripes together in the morning sunshine. He urged the colonel and the executive officer to move into a commodious chalet a few hundred meters distant from the hotel. "It is only appropriate, you are in charge," he said. He found a local lady to cook for them and stocked the house with French and German wines, asking only for a few cartons of cigarettes and some five-gallon cans of gasoline.

That first week was so pleasant that I gave no further thought to Martin though he was always around, in and out of the little hotel. A family who lived not far away had heard me playing Mozart on the old upright in the hotel and invited me over to try their Bechstein. It was such an un-Italian household. There were three girls: one of them very studious (I noticed her Latin and Greek texts on a table near the piano) and the other two serious music students. After I had played several preludes and fugues from the *Well-Tempered Clavier* for them they, at the gentle urging of their mother, played the great big Schubert F-minor Fantasy for piano four hands with surprising competence and no little passion. The father spoke a bit of English as did the daughter who was studying classics. He told me he was from "Bozen," which I suddenly realized was the German name for Bolzano, though, he was quick to add, his wife was from up here in "Seis" (Siusi). "It has been, how do you say, more tranquil up here in the Seisenalpe," he explained to me. "Down there at Bozen and in the valley there was much bombing and unpleasantness. It has been a hard time for us Tyroleans."

The second afternoon I visited them they offered refreshments: dark beer and slices of delicious lean pork, served with their own bread and homemade butter. I couldn't resist bringing up Martin's name. (Lieutenant McKenna, who was beginning to feel his oats as battalion intelligence officer, had been wondering who and what the man was. He clearly was not one of the locals.) There was a momentary pause in the house when I mentioned his name. The studious daughter began to speak with some heat but was interrupted by her father who said that they knew little about him. He had appeared six or seven months ago with only a couple of suitcases and moved into the hotel where we had our HQ. He seemed to have something to do with certain German officers who passed through town occasionally. "You understand, do you not," the father said in his stilted English, "that the war had to us up in this quiet town sometimes brought from many places people who want to be out of danger." He looked hard at me, his wife averted her gaze, and the girls launched into the Mozart four-hand Sonata in D, the one with the finale that sounds straight out of Offenbach.

What was Martin and who was he? No clear answer was forthcoming though by the end of our first week up at Siusi he began intimating to the colonel that we should be playing a larger role in the neighborhood. "A certain intelligence function is your prerogative as an occupying force, is that not so, my dear colonel," he said several times within my hearing at headquarters. We had instructions to cooperate with the Germans in these first weeks of the surrender but it was not obvious what role Martin played in this. Certain of our responsibilities were clearcut, however, and one of them, which was delegated to Lieutenant Boatner and myself, had to do with supplying necessities to a German military hospital a few miles from Siusi. The Germans in charge always submitted meticulous morning reports and were full of helpful suggestions as to the logistics of their supplies and medical needs.

One morning when Lieutenant Boatner and I were over there "cooperating," as the terms of the surrender document called it, it became clear that someone would have to ride down to Bolzano with one of their supply trucks to pick up some urgently required medical supplies. Lieutenant Boatner smiled sweetly at me; he had no intention of going himself and there was no available jeep and driver for me. "No fraternization, Allanbrook," he said. "Have a pleasant trip." I clambered up into the cab of a heavy squarish German truck, squeezing in beside the driver and an *Oberfeldwebel* (a sort of superior corporal). The driver was a steely-eyed man of a certain age and the corporal a blue-eyed blond with milky-white skin. He could have served as a model for the type of Aryan youth the Nazis portrayed in their textbooks on racial classifications. We departed with an alarming grinding of gears and a stench of black exhaust pouring out the back. I saluted Lieutenant Boatner as smartly as I could from the confines of the cab and he snapped his salute back at me with a bit of worry showing in his expression.

The road from Siusi down to the Brenner route was all precipitous descent and hairpin curves. We were in the Alps! As we emerged from one sharp curve and began down a long steep slope an acrid stench arose from the brakes. We began to pick up speed and the driver jammed his foot on the brake pedal. Nothing happened. He jammed it down again. Still nothing. "Kaput!" he muttered. "Kaput!" repeated the blond German next to me. The driver tried to force the shift into a lower gear but it popped out of its slot and rattled loosely. We were now proceeding at a considerable and increasing clip down a steep straightaway that culminated in a sharp curve a half mile or so ahead. The road was chiseled out of the mountainside: on the left was a sheer drop and on the right a well-constructed masonry wall. The driver did not lose his nerve; coolly and efficiently he began, little by little, to scrape the side of the cumbersome truck against the wall. At first we swerved and bucked but gradually, as he maneuvered for more and more contact, friction increased and the truck began slowing down, finally shuddering to rest with fenders and mudguards littering the roadway in back of us. All this time I had been leaning away from the right-hand side toward the center of the cab as the cab door was being torn off its hinges. When we had scraped to a dead stop the corporal and I were clutched in a tight embrace which could so easily have been consummated in death. Seized by the moment we remained silent for a bit. We had no common language, but we were alive; that we had in common.

Awkwardness and embarrassment descended soon enough as we scrambled out over the driver's seat. The right-hand door was a tangle of crumpled metal jammed against the stone retaining wall. We were a strange trio by the time one of our trucks chanced by. I became acutely self-conscious of being an American with two German prisoners in tow. We shook hands when we parted. I often think of that scrape with death and my fearsome embrace with that Aryan *Feldwebel,* so blond, so blue-eyed. It was the closest I ever was to a German.

Martin's case became murkier. Was he a German like the Germans we had as our prisoners? Or was he like so many of the people in Bolzano and Siusi, a South Tyrolean classified since World War I as an Italian citizen, inhabitant of the province of Alto Adige? Martin seemed not particularly interested in our responsibilities vis-à-vis the hospital or with the ordinary German prisoners we might have to deal with, though he would lend his abilities as an interpreter when called upon. He was a small man with dark eyes and a large nose whose face readily adapted itself to the wishes of the person he was talking to. He foresaw that the colonel would be intrigued with a particular nugget of information he dropped in his lap concerning the whereabouts of a very high Fascist party official from Milan. The colonel was at first puzzled as to his duty in such a matter but when, at Martin's suggestion, he called down to the division intelligence officer he was quickly made aware of his responsibilities and praised for his ferreting out of such characters. "He's on our list," he was told. "Send the bastard down to us and keep up the good work."

We were immediately sent out on what was to be only the

first of many similar missions. In two jeeps with Martin as our guide and Lieutenant McKenna as our leader, we pulled up in front of a large chalet. Nestled under a Dolomite at the head of a lovely meadow, it resembled an illustration from a storybook. Weapons in hand we thumped on the front door, rather nervous about the whole undertaking; we had never acted as policemen before. Martin had stationed himself down near the jeeps in such a way that when Signor Bellugi himself, short and fat with beetling eyebrows, opened the door he saw only the group of American soldiers in front of him. I used my Italian to ascertain that he was indeed Signor Bellugi. He poured out a stream of explanations as to who he was and how overjoyed he was with the Allied victory and what a blessing it was that he had been able to bring his family up to these quiet mountains of the Alto Adige. In the midst of these effusions he caught a glimpse of Martin down in the driveway. He stopped short. His face became pale and I became aware of his sweat; I could smell his panic. "I see you're working for them now," he screamed at Martin, and spat on his front steps. He made us no further overtures and we drove off with him. He was delivered to the proper authorities down in Bolzano later in the day. The colonel was delighted and congratulated Lieutenant McKenna on his valuable work in what was now, he said, seeing that the war was over, our most important task: counterintelligence.

Himmler's family was the next plum Martin offered us. They were escorted down to Bolzano by a contingent of MPs with several counterintelligence officers in attendance. The town affected not to notice that procession as it passed by, though it was sullenly aware of the presence of Martin and the colonel. They officiated on the balcony of the hotel as if it were a reviewing stand. It took a considerable time for the full import of Martin's having been an informer for the Germans to sink in. "Right now he's buying time," was Lieutenant McKenna's conjecture. "If he keeps feeding us names he gives himself a period of grace, and our boys down in Bolzano think he's the cat's pajamas."

The last of these expeditions that I participated in was bloody. Martin did not go along with us but he supplied us with the name of the victim, Major Carità, and gave us exact directions as to where he was hiding out. As I later learned, he was the head of the Fascist police in Tuscany. As the war drew to a close he and his colleagues acted like wounded tigers; their cruelty had not the bureaucratic efficiency of the Gestapo but made up for it in sheer sadism. Martin had let us know that the major had not brought his wife with him. "His family is back in Florence in their house at San Domenico, just under Fiesole," Martin told us with a certain relish. He took pride in knowing the details of his victims' personal lives. "He is here with his mistress. Look out; he is a passionate man with a terrible temper." Lieutenant McKenna was gung-ho for the mission. Whatever his shortcomings may have been when the war was still on he was now gaining a new respect for himself in these so-called counterintelligence operations.

Major Carità's chalet was well hidden from the twisty mountain road which passed below its driveway. When the six of us, in two jeeps, approached the house we found the front door, a massive Tyrolean affair with cast-iron hinges, wide open. We thumped upon it several times before we became aware of music coming from a gramophone somewhere in the rear of the house. It was never clear to any of us whether the major had planned this as a setup or whether what happened was gratuitous. It is possible he intended to lure us into his bedroom and to shoot at us as we entered in a kind of cinematic Grand Guignol. If this was his plan why was he in bed with his mistress? At any rate the moment we entered the door he did shoot at us, wounding Lieutenant McKenna slightly in his left arm. We returned his fire immediately, killing him outright while his mistress cowered to one side of the enormous bed. McKenna received a special commendation for the action; the mistress was carted off somewhere by the proper authorities and the town kept its own counsel.

Soon after this Martin's jig seemed to be up. Two counterintelligence lieutenants came up from Bolzano and had a long talk with him. They went through all of his papers and ripped open the linings of his two suitcases. It turned out that he had a variety of names and as many passports as nationalities. One of the lieutenants, a sharp-faced little man who enjoyed his job and let us know he had been to Princeton, filled us in. "This is quite a case," he said. "As you probably figured out, Martin, or whatever name he goes by, informed for the Germans, for the Gestapo, to be exact. And now, of course, he has been helpful to us. What you didn't know is that he saved his own skin by doing what he did. He's a Jew, after all." They carted him off that afternoon. The colonel was somewhat abashed at having been manipulated by the man but the town, according to my family with the Bechstein, felt that we had done what properly had to be done and that they were well off without such an informer in their midst. Whether this was because of his activities or because of his Jewishness was not clear. Soon afterward, some of us in the battalion were moved down to Bolzano and I was not present several weeks later when Martin returned to Siusi, a free man, cleared of all charges by the army intelligence people. It was a humiliation for those in the battalion who were still stationed in the town. It was not only Central Europe that Martin knew his way around; it looked as if America might well become his newfound land.

It was dreary down in the real world. We were set up in an electric substation a few miles out of Bolzano on the Brenner route. The bombers had left desolation everywhere. In front of us was the highway. Across an iron bridge over the Isarco River were the tracks of the railroad from the Brenner Pass, the principal supply route for the Germans in Italy. It had been bombed constantly for years but traffic had never ceased upon it despite all our efforts. It was another of the many many examples of the inefficacy of our incessant air strikes. There were multiple sets of tracks laid side by side, some near the river and others snuggled up against the steep slopes of the valley. They were all camou-

flaged with black asphalt so as to mask them from the air reconnaissance photos. "All them bombs and they never stopped the
trains," said Joe Isaac as we gazed upon the scene from the front
steps of our shattered electric substation. "For all the good they
got out of it they mighta just as well stayed at their nice warm
air base and jerked each other off." Also included in our view
was the most genuine medieval castle imaginable. It perched on
the cliff above the river and was equipped with the most spec-
tacular latrines; they were two-holers which stuck out of the
walls high up on the castle. "You could count up to twenty
before the shit struck," commented Joe as we contemplated our
surroundings.

Prisoner of war camps now became our business. There
was a big one outside Bolzano but we were not assigned to it.
Instead we were put in charge of a very special one which Lieutenant Boatner called our "bitches' sabbath." It was for ladies
only. There were two classes of prisoners: camp followers who
had plied their trade with the Germans all through the campaign and local bourgeois girls from Bolzano who had worked
as secretaries and administrative assistants in the extensive of-
fices of the German military headquarters. The first group were
not only German or Austrian; every nation in Europe was rep-
resented among them. They were united, however, in their scorn
of the second group. "You could, if you wanted to, think of
them in the same category as nice girls from D.C. or Alexandria
who got a job with the Defense Department beginning in 1942,"
Lieutenant Boatner said with his customary good sense. "However," he went on, "they worked for the Nazis and that monster,
General Wolff." They had been routed out of their proper Ger-
manic homes and trundled off to a set of dirty old Italian army
barracks to be lodged with the random whores of Europe. They
complained endlessly, professing their innocence and flaunting
their decency. They had the gall to petition for separate quarters.
I began to consider them as the real bitches and to enjoy the
epithets in a variety of tongues and dialects which the ladies of

pleasure threw at them. These latter were very jolly with all of us, volunteering their services and offering prudent advice concerning their kitchens and the general policing of the camp.

Toward the end of our stay in Bolzano we were ordered to transport all the prisoners to Verona and deliver them to the appropriate authority at Fifth Army headquarters by 0600 hours on a certain given morning. None of the officers wanted to go; they had established a well-appointed club for themselves in Bolzano and were intent upon enjoying the war's end. General Wolff had sumptuous tastes and once he was bundled off to his internment camp the officers inherited his villas and his extensive warehouses of wine, liquor, and comestibles from all parts of Europe. "You're in charge, Allanbrook," said Lieutenant Boatner. "The war's over and I'm not about to stint on my pleasures."

So it was that at 1800 hours one evening I was to be seen lining up an extensive flotilla of 2 ½-ton trucks, reading off the names of hundreds of women one after the other. They were each given a number as their names were called. The professional ladies were saucy but most cooperative. They called me all sorts of sweet names in a variety of tongues and several of the lewder ones among them made great bows of their lips every time the number 69 came around. What a delight when that obscene number descended three times on one of Bolzano's daughters. Who knows? — she might well have been a private secretary to an SS general.

As I look at photographs of myself in that year I realize how callow I was and how skinny. I weighed 123 pounds. There sits my tender face under the great iron basin of my helmet with four sergeant's stripes painted on the front of it. The whores, especially the older ones, appreciated innocence. (Look at that young boy who is in charge of our convoy!) After the war there might be some hope for a better world even for them. They would hardly be punished: their services had not been so culpable. The good bourgeois girls of "Bozen" were guiltier, but they had no sense whatsoever of this. They importuned me not to place them in the same trucks with the prostitutes but I refused; they were to pile into the vehicles in the order of their numbering. One of the "Bozen" girls was pregnant, very pregnant! I remember her number, 133, but not her name. She was desperate and received no comfort from her Tyrolean fellow workers. It was a sympathetic Hungarian whore, between thirty-five and forty with red hair, who pointed out to me a sober fellow who was helping her into the truck, holding her hand and trying to console her. "Ça doit être le mari ou au moins le père de la pauvre," she said to me in very good French. Another of my ladies, a German from Bremen, told me in English, "She is very near to having the baby. It is no time for a truck ride. Let her man help." I took action and told the man to get on the truck. The girl wept with relief and the man squeezed my hand in appreciation. The camp followers helped the two of them all that long night.

It was a tiring trip, down the narrow valley with the Adige rushing alongside, past Trento and then along the east side of Lake Garda. As dawn was breaking we wound our way into the square at Verona with me leading the way in a jeep. I saw the sign for the Fifth Army HQ over the door of a palazzo. A duty officer, half asleep, was at the desk inside. I showed him my orders and pointed out the door to the trucks and all the women. "What the fuck am I supposed to do with all them Kraut dames?" he shouted at me. I pointed out to him that the orders had issued in good form from his headquarters and that the prisoners were all here at 0600 hours on the day prescribed. "There is also a girl who is about to give birth," I said. "Call the medics." I saluted smartly, turned around and hightailed it for my jeep, leaving the Fifth Army in charge. I learned a month later, when the Hungarian whore showed up in the women's section of our camp in Modena down in the Po Valley, that the girl had had a fine baby boy and that a sympathetic medical officer had gotten her released to her man and that they planned to get married. "Isn't the world sometimes a good place!" was the Hungarian's comment.

Soon after this we left the South Tyrol and retraced our steps back into the long-suffering Italy we knew so well. We were assigned to an enormous prison camp just north of the city limits of Modena. In it were not only regular units of the German Army but also an unholy mixture of prisoners from all the nationalities and races of Central and Eastern Europe: Poles, Great Russians, Ukrainians, Bulgarians, Romanians, Slovaks, Czechs, Croats, etc. All of them had in some manner or another worked for the Germans, hence they were classified, all of them, as prisoners of war.

The German Army units were easy enough to take care of until their repatriation to their homes in Germany. But what order was to be unscrambled and dealt with in the midst of the Babel of tongues and the multiplication of ethnic passions present among the hordes of non-Germans? None of us knew anything of the horrors of the German occupation of half of the heartland of Russia. We certainly knew nothing of the hatred the Ukrainians felt for Moscow. We knew nothing of the Nazi Croat state in Yugoslavia or the one they had established in Slovakia. Even if we had been aware of these we would have had the same difficulty that Allied headquarters (AFHQ) was having in knowing to what extent each group was culpable of having either fought with the Germans or simply having cooperated with them. Some of our prisoners were conscripted laborers who moved up a slot or two in some dreary hierarchy of responsibility. Many had been coerced. Ukrainians had welcomed the Germans when they arrived and then, to their horror, found themselves being treated as members of a slave race. (Lieutenant Boatner, that well-educated West Pointer, commented on the etymological connection between *Slav* and *Slave*.) Some of the Ukrainians had been only twelve or thirteen years old when the Nazis had arrived. Some of them remained members of the Labor Corps; others moved up a notch, and some, the more serious cases, had become noncommissioned officers and even *Leutnants* in special German units.

History, terrible, bloody European history, dinned in our ears. They poured out their stories, preached of their rights as ethnic nationalities, spilled out their hatreds and their parochial passions. We had seen a very small piece of this up in the Tyrol but now there opened before our eyes a vast chaos, an expanse of misery and conquest that dwarfed in complexity our simple experiences of fighting every day up the rocky spine of the Italian peninsula. It was with chastened awareness that we now compared our campaign in Italy with the greater one that had taken the Allies from Normandy to Berlin and then compared all of that with the enormity of what had taken place in Russia. "We would have lost without them," said Lieutenant McKenna. "I bet you we'll have to fight them ourselves one of these days. Didn't your sharp little nose catch the meaning of that communiqué we received the day the war ended and one of our divisions was ordered over to Trieste?" He smiled his sly smile.

"That little motherfucker is too smart for his own good," said Joe Isaac, who detested McKenna. He had overheard our conversation. "He didn't get himself noplace during the war and he sees nothing but shit now that it's over. I don't like the way he looks at you, Allanbrook. Don't have nothin' to do with him." Some things Joe didn't think it was worth his while to understand and it was no use trying to din it into him. It isn't that he merely turned his eyes away from what was unpalatable; he felt that there was nothing that could be done about such matters. He was going to return to his beer joint outside Memphis, work a few hours a day, and shrug off the misery and the horrors that hovered around the edges of his awareness. Politics, nationalities, our unhappy crowd of prisoners, and McKenna — all were part of the terrible mess of the war, which was a conundrum not to be solved. He was an ethnic Syrian from Memphis, but had never had any troubles in his own native Tennessee.

Allied headquarters had no clean solution to our mixed bag of prisoners. Confusing orders arrived from them concerning the disposition of the Russians. Those Ukrainians who had

merely been enrolled in labor battalions were to be trucked to
the Russian authorities in Bruch, up over the Austrian border
above Udine. The trucks were to be left open on the trip and no
prisoner was to be prevented from jumping ship and hightailing
it off into the landscape. Lieutenant Boatner explained it to us.
"AFHQ knows the Russians lost thirty million people in this
war and that they are not going to have any particular mercy
for anyone who worked for the Germans. They also know that
Stalin is still our ally and that we won the war together. But why
should a bunch of boys be shot just because they were impressed
into a labor battalion at the age of twelve or thirteen? Who the
hell can solve that to everyone's satisfaction?"

It was a bizarre convoy. My trip with the ladies from Bolzano
to Verona was normality in comparison. The prisoners caught
on immediately. We smiled at them and shooed them out when
we stopped for a pee call. By the time we were near the Austrian
border there were only a few left. As we approached Bruch only
one boy remained. We stopped outside town and motioned him
to the woods that bordered the road. He wouldn't leave. As far
as we could understand him he said that he was not a Ukrainian
but a real Great Russian and that he wanted to see his Russian
comrades again. He insisted on going all the way into town with
us. I don't know what happened to him though I suspect he was
shot.

It was evening when we turned him over to the Russians in
their headquarters in the town. We must have looked somewhat
sheepish as we wheeled our empty trucks into the square. The
Russians didn't seem to care; they were drunk. It was as if a
party had been going on for days and days. What I have never
understood was the presence of numbers of German officers
drinking together with their Russian counterparts in cafés or
together in convivial groups around tables set in the square.
Russian privates were lurching around the streets and alleys of
the town. A group who said they were from Kazan hoisted a
barrel of beer up into the back of one of our trucks. They took

out the knives they had tucked in their pants and cut us hunks of bread and sausage. We drank and drank. Some the Russians gave us big hugs and one of them kissed me. The night passed and we departed Bruch in the morning.

AFHQ dilly-dallied for weeks over the question of what to do with those Russians who had attained noncommissioned rank in the German Army. Word finally came through: they were to be transported up to Bruch in closed trucks. When stops were made they were allowed to descend to attend to their needs, but only if accompanied by armed guards. However, we were not to shoot or to say anything if they took off for the woods. "'Yes my darling daughter, / Hang your clothes on a hickory limb / But don't go near the water,'" was Lieutenant McKenna's comment. It was a quiet and surreal convoy. Guns in hand we watched them as they climbed down out of the trucks: some of them actually stopped to pee before they took off into the woods. A few stayed with us all the way, perfectly calm. I wondered if they were trusties. Things were soberer this time up in the square at Bruch. The party seemed to have petered out. One Russian officer yelled at us and shook his fist but we merely saluted, turned the trucks around and headed back to Italy.

With those Russians who had attained commissioned rank with the Germans there was no compromise. The trucks were locked and had barbed wire across the back. We were to make no stops. Buckets were provided. Communication was strictly forbidden. While the previous convoy had been unreal, this one was a descent into hell. They knew it and we knew it. Joe Isaac for the first time in his life had nothing to say and neither did Lieutenant McKenna. The same Russian officer who had yelled at us on the previous trip regarded us now with grim satisfaction as we parked the trucks, unlocked the chains that secured the barbed wire and lowered the tailgates. Out they came and off they went, marched in single file down a narrow street that led off the town square, herded along by a whole platoon of Russian guards. Some of them could not have been more than sixteen. The Russian officer in the square made a V for Victory sign and ordered up vodka and schnapps. We tossed them off, saluted and left immediately. I think he expected us to stay and have a party. One PFC who was with us threw up as we pulled out of town. Joe Isaac thought he could hear the shooting begin as the drivers gunned the motors, anxious to get away.

9

Now began our preparations to return the Germans to their native soil and the first step in the process was to take all of their money away from them. Each soldier would hand over his wad of Italian lire. He was then given a token, signed by an American officer, which certified as to the amount he had turned over. This token was valid upon repatriation for an equivalent value in the appropriate local currency. Bales and boxes of lire began to pile up at battalion HQ, each tagged with the precise number of lire. Lieutenant Boatner would go downtown with me to the Banca d'Italia, situated near the Romanesque cathedral in the middle of Modena. There platoons of clerks were busy bailing great bundles of lire and stowing them away in boxes, separating the large-size 1,000- and 10,000-lire bills from the more modest amounts. By the third trip Boatner had had enough of it and I went by myself, depositing bags and boxes of the colored paper inside the doors of the bank.

By the third week of our financial exchanges we noticed that the amounts turned in to us began to be nicely rounded-off numbers: no more amounts such as 3,567,293 lire; now the count would always be a neat 3,000,000 lire. Elegant rows of zeroes. It had been discovered that the army post office would accept Italian lire as legal tender for the purchase of money orders payable in dollars back in the States. One lieutenant colonel who had been with us since Camp Gruber and was now a battalion commander, sent enough home to build himself a new barn on his Tennessee farm. "Hellfire," he said to Lieutenant Boatner, "This has been a long war and we might as well get some value out of it." The bonanza continued for a week and was abruptly terminated, though enormous wads of lire continued to stick to everyone's fingers; they served just as well as the AMG money (so unreal we all called it Monopoly scrip) for local purchases. Cigarettes and coffee were, as always, a more substantial currency; with them, at least, there was a genuine exchange, object for object. I did not indulge in the traffic, though when I left for Florence a few weeks later, Lieutenant Boatner insisted I pocket a goodly amount of the stuff.

The world had changed. The war had been real; I had gotten used to it. Now I felt myself an inhabitant of a never-never land. Nationalities, prisoners, and political guilt that seemed impossible to define paraded in front of me. Lives meant no more than money, and both were exchanged according to the whims and passions of the times. This postwar world had no substance and my interests now centered on the nightclub I had set up. The orchestra from the SS division played Strauss waltzes and souped-up arrangements from Cole Porter while I drank with my tough friends from Hoboken and Kansas City who helped me manage the place. They thought I was the real McCoy. We ran a happy island down there in the blue-painted cellar of the automobile factory amid the ghosts of defunct Lamborghinis: no past, no future, just a boozy present with limitless cases of Biscuit cognac and me the boss.

The summer continued with rumors that the division would be split up and that we would all be dispersed. Lots of the Germans had already been sent home, but most of us had to wait until the arcane point system would give us enough credit to be shipped home, a process that might well drag on for six or more months. One hot morning as I was leafing through a pile of mimeographed poop sheets my eye was caught by a bulletin announcing a special detachment to be set up at the University of Florence. This unit would allow selected enlisted men to study art history and related matters and was intended to help ease the transition back to civilian life for those soldiers who had spent time in the Italian theater and who also possessed the proper academic qualifications. That night at the club I told my two helpers that we were all going to go to Florence and study art history.

"Shit, man," said the tougher of the two. "I can sit in a room and look at pictures if they don't fuck with me the rest of the time. I got a lot of adjusting to do before I go back to KC and Florence might just have more to offer in the line of evening entertainment than what we got set up here." He glanced around at the local girls living it up on our garish dance floor while the SS Symphony pumped out big-band medleys orchestrated by some Hollywood hack back in the States and then rented to the U.S. Army Special Services for the delectation of the soldier population.

It was decided. I got in touch with the master sergeant up at division headquarters who was in charge of such things and told him to cut the orders for me and my two pals. (All business was now transacted by sergeants: an officer was needed only for the signature at the bottom of the order.) We were duly certified as having both the proper background and an abiding interest in the history of art and as being anxious to deepen our cultural appreciation of the country we had been fighting in for so long.

Lieutenant Boatner raised his eyebrows when I told him I was leaving. "Allanbrook," he said, "do you really think you can get away with studying Giotto and Cimabue with those two bums who run the club with you?"

"Sir," I replied, "those two always knew how to keep their noses clean, and after three years in the army so do I."

He shook my hand. "I'll miss you; I'll really miss you. We ran a good operations section. Don't get too cultural down there in Florence." He grinned and I grinned back.

Off we went. Special orders and special army transport. Down the straight road to Bologna, up the hills past Monterumici, over the Futa Pass on Highway 65 and on down into Florence. Goodbye First Battalion headquarters, farewell 350th Infantry Regiment. It was enough for me to have my 88th Division Blue Devil cloverleaf sewed on my shoulder, my four sergeant's stripes on my arms, and my combat infantry badge lined up next to the Bronze Star medal on my chest. When we got there we found that we three were different: we were infantry. All the rest of the special detachment was from air force ground personnel or quartermaster corps or other such outfits. They had not fought. Many of them already had degrees in art history or Renaissance literature. Not all, however; some were hard-drinking and high-living ground crews from the air bases down at Foggia who, like the three of us, had cottoned on to a good deal.

We were quartered in the Florence railroad station, in an administrative building out by the tracks, just behind and to the left of the main waiting room. It was comfortable enough: cots and plenty of hot water and showers. An ineffectual colonel had been assigned to us as our commandant. He tried to have us stand reveille but was soon persuaded that it was not in the nature of our task in Florence to perform such duties, that we were to be aided in our transition to civilian life, and that our responsibilities lay in the classrooms of the University of Florence.

There was lots to do and I tucked into all of it: classes in art history to be sure, but also the possibility of polishing up my French and Italian in language classes. I soon discovered that the conservatory offered private piano study. My two sidekicks attended the lectures faithfully and I wrote their papers for them. They were busy, however; they got together with some of the air force boys and set up a club down by the river on the Via Tornabuoni. We had plenty of cigarettes and coffee to finance it with, and some of our professors began coming to our parties. A good life began which lasted for almost five months. Florence seemed real: I was studying at a university and playing the piano, and in those first weeks by the Arno the war seemed to be safely over. Normality was reestablished and the Alps of Siusi and the imprisoned hordes back at Modena receded from view. Florence might have been a fancier Boston with the Piazza della Signoria substituting for Copley Square and the Uffizi for the Fine Arts Museum.

The Red Cross had set up its tents in the railroad station and had had the good sense to hire cultivated Florentine ladies to act as guides and counselors to soldiers who wanted to explore the monuments of the town. They all spoke fluent English and I soon became attached to one of them, Ada Boni, a dear and intelligent woman, blond and skinny, who gave me careful instructions as to what to see and in what order. One afternoon she caught my eye as I was passing through the station and motioned me aside. "This afternoon, my dear," she said, "this afternoon you are going to accompany me to my good friends the Maggioras. They live halfway up the hill to Fiesole, on Via Camerata, just short of San Domenico. We'll have tea with them. The mother, dear Ducky as they call her, is an American and I've already told her all about you. She's anxious to know you."

That afternoon we climbed onto the trolley and rode through the Piazza Santissima Annunziata, past the university, and got off just where the trolley turned around to go on back downtown. Ada explained to me that the *filobus*, the trackless trolley that ran all the way up to Fiesole, had not begun running as yet. "The war, you know," she explained. We climbed the road for a bit and turned off onto a pleasant shaded way that ran parallel to it on the right. We stopped in front of the grilled door of a small villa and rang the bell. A short lady with a roundish face and large saucer eyes opened the door. "Dear Ada," she said, "and this must be the American you've told us all about." She beamed at me. "I hear you're from Boston," she said. We walked through to a most agreeable living room. There were several landscape etchings on the walls, pleasant slipcovered sofas (rare in Italy), a well-sculpted bust of a woman in one corner, and a good-size Bechstein. "Henrietta will bring us some tea right in here in a minute," said Mrs. Maggiora. "It's too hot to be out there in the garden." She then turned and beamed at me again. "I'm from New Jersey, you know, but I haven't been back there for twenty-five years. That is a long time; there's been this war and then those other ones we had down in Albania and Africa." Ada looked slightly embarrassed but at that moment the two younger Maggioras entered, a girl and a boy.

"Dolly and Mummi," called out Mrs. Maggiora, "this is Douglas Allanbrook. He's an American from Boston and we're going to talk about all kinds of things." Dolly came forward and shook my hand; she was a reserved girl, with a round face somewhat like her mother's. "Welcome to Via Camerata," she said. "I am sure that all of this must be rather strange to you." She smiled modestly, but I could feel her gaze passing over my medals and my badges. "Not half as strange as I must appear to you," I replied, slightly embarrassed with the archness of my reply. Mummi, a year or so younger than Dolly, said nothing but shook my hand firmly. He resembled his mother and Dolly but with a more stubborn cast to his features. It turned out his English was not as fluent as his sister's. I played the first movement of the Italian Concerto for them. The tea party warmed up as I spoke of my classes down at the university and my maestro at the conservatory and of my studies before the war with Mlle Boulanger. The children knew the people I was studying with down at the university and had a friend who studied piano with my maestro. I had already learned from Ada that Carlo, the father, was an architect and a professor but she had not told me too much about the children. Mummi's passion was for philosophy while Dolly's was literature, especially English literature.

Time began to pass quickly when Ada glanced at her watch. I would have liked to stay longer and I felt that they would have enjoyed it but I hastened to say my goodbyes. When we reached the door Mrs. Maggiora suddenly said, "Carlo must know him.

He has never known any Americans except my family. You will come tomorrow to dinner and then you will talk with Carlo." The children looked pleased and I was happy to accept the invitation. "You will become fast friends with all of them," said Ada as we went down the hill to catch the trolley back to the station. "They are an interesting family, and you will learn a lot about Florence from them. Carlo, you know, is restoring the Santa Trinità bridge, which the Germans demolished as they were leaving. Such a time, my dear, such a time."

Supper was delicious that next evening: homemade tagliatelle followed by *petti di pollo* — chicken breasts — sitting on a bed of spinach. Ada had suggested I bring some coffee. (Working down at the Red Cross in the station she had seen that soldiers easily got hold of GI supplies. It had been years since the Maggioras had had real coffee.) Carlo was a serious man, slightly shorter than his wife, dark-eyed with a mustache over firm but sensuous lips. It was he who had invented the name Ducky, taking a certain delight, not entirely innocent, in mouthing the English nickname, though it soon turned out he knew very little English. It took all of my attention to follow his sometimes recondite discussions phrased always in a most elegant and pointed Italian. Ducky often seemed not to have the slightest idea of what he was talking about, and the two men in the family had long since given her up as a serious participant in their long and involved conversations, though Dolly, good daughter that she was, would attempt to bridge the gap. When the war came up in our dinnertime conversations (I soon became a regular guest at Via Camerata) Ducky would gush forth with all sorts of stories which often embarrassed the rest of the family but which I found most revealing as to the state of affairs up on that enchanted hillside just below Fiesole.

"Well, you know, Douglas," she said to me one night, "we have a dear friend in the villa just above the square at San Domenico, Mlle Charpentier. We will have her down for tea and you will meet her. She's a very nice landscape painter and she and her mother have lived up there forever. The mother must have been there since before the first war, and none of us ever did know who M. Charpentier was. Old Mme Charpentier always says what she thinks, and she used to make loud remarks about the 'sales fascistes' while sitting out in her garden, and of course you know there were always horrid little men hanging about who would inform the police about such things. There have always been lots of foreign ladies living up here, goodness knows, many of them English; after all, Queen Victoria had that big villa just under Fiesole."

She saw that her husband and Mummi were restive with her garrulousness and said to them, "We did have a war here and Douglas knows nothing about it." She turned back to me. "We had to hide Mummi from the Germans and Carlo made counterfeit identity cards. I used to be so frightened. The head of the Fascist police lived just down the road. At any rate, to return to what I was talking about with Mme Charpentier and the Fascists and the English ladies. The people downtown began worrying about Mme Charpentier and her anti-Fascist remarks, and their worries spread to all of the old foreign ladies who had been living up here since God knows when. So one day they appeared with trucks and carted them all down to the Bargello, right there in the middle of Florence. There they all were, stuck in one of those enormous old rooms with absolutely no privacy and skimpy little cots to sleep on. Mme Charpentier took it in her stride, glaring at the little men who would bring them their food and water and demanding that they be released. The biggest crisis was with one of the English ladies. She was very proper and could not bring herself to use the buckets that had been provided. Mme Charpentier tells of it all so charmingly. After four days she saw that poor Miss Smith was in agony. She held up her blanket in front of one of the buckets so as to shield the Englishwoman from public gaze, and said, 'Pour l'amour de Dieu, ma chère, faîtes vos devoirs.'" The family was embarrassed. Carlo, like many Italian men, was a bit of a prude when in the bosom of his family. Ducky was not to be stopped. "Well, you must know, Douglas, that some of the Germans weren't so bad. The German consul here loved Florence. He managed to save a lot of people, and he saw that it was folly to keep those old ladies downtown in prison and persuaded the powers that be that they were making fools of themselves. He was certainly worlds away from that beast, Major Carità, whose wife still lives just down the street. He was as bad or worse than the Gestapo those last months before you arrived and they had to leave."

Worlds came together. She had named the Fascist major we had shot up in Siusi, hidden away in his chalet with his young mistress and pointed out to us by our informer, Martin. I said nothing at the time but did bring it up later when a question arose at the dinner table as to the moral issues involved in accepting an invitation to tea from Major Carità's wife. The family had engaged in a debate during the war: when was it proper to work against one's own country? How far should one support the regime, and if one didn't support it should one be actively against it? The debate became more immediately relevant when the Germans and the Fascists began gathering up boys of Mummi's age and shipping them north. Mummi had been hidden off in the mountains upriver toward Arezzo, where the family had a small farm.

Ducky could not resist. "It got so you couldn't trust anyone, even Americans. My old friend Bobby — just think of it! We both went to the Sacred Heart Academy on Long Island, you know, and we both came over to Florence to be finished off, as we used to say. Daddy had bought a villa down there between the river and Volterra, and Bobby would often stay with us. Of course I married Carlo and Bobby married Franco, who began to rise and rise in the government. When this war came around he was way up in the party in some high position downtown, and she would give big receptions for all the bigwigs. Well, to cut a story short, after Mummi had been hidden away for several weeks I would meet Bobby down in the square at San Domenico (there was always an informer posted there just beside the church), and she would say to me in a very clear voice: 'Dear Adrienne (that's my real name, you know, not Ducky), dear Adrienne, where is that nice son of yours? It's been weeks now since I have seen him around.' Can you imagine it! — talking in that high little voice of hers and letting that informer know that Mummi wasn't at home, and we both went to the Sacred Heart together. How can I ever speak to her again? I suppose the war is over, however, and did hear just yesterday, Carlo, that her husband has just returned, so she's not alone anymore."

Carlo would have preferred to have our talk on a higher level, but it was difficult to stop Ducky once she began. Dolly told of the identity papers they had forged not only for Mummi but also for members of the resistance. Carlo's architectural training had made him a skilled draftsman and engraver. After Ducky's encounter with Bobby they had lived in constant fear of the Fascist police, and the villa of Major Carità, just down the road, became a focus of their apprehension. All Florence feared and detested the man; he was known as a torturer, and as the war drew on to its climax his cruelty increased. They continued to see Signora Carità, deeming it wiser to retain all semblance of normality. I couldn't resist telling them of the young mistress who was in bed with the major when we shot him. Carlo blinked and said nothing. "Well, I have heard," said Ducky, "that Signora Carità now has Allied officers in her house every day of the week!"

"Are we to visit the sins of the husband on a wife who may be perfectly innocent?" was Carlo's rejoinder to his wife. "Is Signora Carità as culpable as your old American friend, Bobby?" Ducky was flustered; her husband's tone was mocking, and Mummi then proceeded to phrase the question in terms of Spinoza's *Ethics,* and she remained quiet for the rest of the evening.

I had difficulty in following the arguments, but Carlo and Mummi would insist that I grasp the premises of whatever was being asserted; they were tireless teachers and I proved an apt student. After several weeks I became proficient in their philosophical talk, and Carlo pressed various texts upon me, including one which he wanted me to pay special attention to: it had to do with proofs for the existence of God. He had seen that I was not a believer, and he bent his considerable abilities to have me admit at least to the bare existence of God. He paid a great deal of attention to me; he saw that I was a composer and an artist, and urged me to use his study any time I wished. "You must have quiet and tranquility, dear Douglas," he would say. "I know. It is the same for my work." In our philosophical and theological discussions he would bend low over the table, his brown eyes intense, constantly demanding, "Mi spiego?" — "Am I making myself clear?" I had never thought of Italians as being particularly religious before. My witticisms with Lieutenant Boatner had always to do with the fact that the least religious country in the world had the greatest number of churches. Carlo, though philosophical in his discussions, was an unswerving Catholic. Later he did everything to hinder Dolly's marriage to a young doctor whom Carlo considered an atheist, and he and Ducky schemed with one of the Franciscans up at Fiesole to arrange a marriage for the girl with a well-heeled and properly Catholic spouse.

Ducky, dear American Ducky, had a rough half-hour with her family when I suggested to them that they would enjoy a friend of mine who was in the student detachment. He was a large black man from Kansas City, a Benedictine whose abbot had deemed it wise for him to do his army service and then return for his final vows. His name was Clinch, Sergeant Humphrey Clinch. "I'm sure we never had a Negro in our house in New Jersey," she said to no one in particular, though she looked hard at me as one of her compatriots.

"This is not New Jersey," said Carlo. "This is Florence."

"But Douglas," she said, now addressing me directly, "I'm sure your mother would never invite a black man to dinner."

"Probably not," was my reply, "but he's my friend."

"And Mama," said Dolly, "he's a Benedictine."

Ducky's scruples were brushed aside, and Clinch soon became a friend of the family up on Via Camerata. Mrs. Maggiora's American prejudice, once she got to know Clinch, melted away.

One evening, for my benefit, Carlo pointedly explained the Greek etymology of the word *Catholic*. "Καβολον," he said, "means 'according to the whole' and is transliterated into Italian through Latin as '*cattolico*,' or, to translate it into more philosophical language, 'universal.'" If the ontological proofs of God had not convinced me of God's existence, Carlo was intent upon my understanding that his church was universal; its fold included all of the human race, and his wife's American prejudices were paltry things when placed next to God's established church. At any rate, we were a happy family up there; affection was the bond and the universality of the church had little to do with it.

Downtown, death struck. It wiped out a man who was a bit older than the rest of us, perhaps thirty-three or thirty-four, Sergeant James Yarnell. He was a charter member of our club, drinking with us there two or three evenings a week. He had been stationed down at Caserta in Allied headquarters as some kind of clerk and had been a student of art history at NYU before entering the army. He was a small man with a prominent forehead, delicate in his tastes, a lover of men though most discreet in his behavior. He adored music; in particular he loved opera, and we would bellow out together, when drunk, arias and duets from *Trovatore* and *Butterfly*, even attempting on special occasions snatches from *Tristan*. He was well liked by most of us, though some of the more studlike air force people professed scorn for him.

One night had been particularly festive; we had gotten hold of excellent cognac and a last case of champagne from a German warehouse. Two or three of our instructors were present that evening, including Professor Ghisi, a garrulous old musicologist of some distinction. He offered us snatches from obscure Donizetti operas, and James and I retaliated with a bit of Zerlina's and Don Giovanni's duet to show we knew something besides the nineteenth century. We broke up around two in the morning and wandered on up the Via Tornabuoni, past the Baptistery and Giotto's bell tower, and on down to Santa Maria Novella and the railroad station. Once inside the station our eyes were caught by one of the wheeled contraptions which were used to replace lightbulbs high up on the ceiling of the station. They were about eight feet tall, square, with four wheels on the bottom and a small platform on top. There was a steep ladder affixed to one side. James and I had been belting out the Prize Song from *Meistersinger* as we entered the station, but once we saw the wheeled contraption we clambered up it, eager to try Isolde's *"Liebestod"* from a proper elevation. We began, arms entwined, to sing; others caught the infection and began to push our wheeled parapet around the expanse of the vast waiting room. It began to sway but no one paid attention; we were dizzy with drink. Then it happened — the tower under our feet tilted off its center of equilibrium and toppled over onto the marble floor of the station. I rolled over, arms and legs in a ball, but James, James landed on his high-domed forehead and never stirred again. He continued to breathe for several hours, but was dead by the time day broke.

A major from the judge advocate general's department came to investigate two days later. He gathered those of us who had been there together. He listened to all of our stories. "You must know," he said, "that those of you who were pushing that gizmo around the station could be held for manslaughter, and as for you" — he looked straight at me — "what the hell were you doing up on top of that thing at two-thirty in the morning? Didn't you have enough excitement in the war?" He paused and looked pained. "I suppose you were just a bunch of GIs tying one on. That's what I'll say. Let's wrap it up and call it an unfortunate coincidence, a genuine accident, and we'll strictly forbid any soldiers from handling or even touching any of the equipment used to maintain the Florence railroad station." And that was that: my last army death, uncalled for, gratuitous, and senseless. James is buried in the U.S. cemetery on the old road to Siena, along with so many of my other dead ones, who died by the hands of the enemy.

One of the sexiest of the air force boys, Bingo — though his whore down at the club called him "Zingaro" (Gypsy) — called out to me a couple of days later from his corner of the big room we all slept in. "What do you want, Allanbrook? He's just as well off dead. What kind of a life could a poor old queer like that have; what did he have to look forward to?" He was sitting with his fly open on his cot, contemplating his fat uncircumcised cock and diddling it gently up and down, crooning to it: "Baby boy, are you ever going to have one luscious afternoon when old Graziella peels you back and gets her lips around your sweet little head."

A major scandal the next month at San Domenico was occasioned by the bishop up at Fiesole, who thundered his imprecations against the ostentatious luxury evidenced in the preparations for the wedding of the daughter of a certain Signor Colasso. The Colassos were neighbors of the Maggioras and their daughter a friend of Dolly's. I had been presented to the family a few weeks before the incident of the bishop's injunction; they had invited all of the Maggioras for tea and aperitifs in their garden. Signor Colasso played the host with his American guest. He evinced a mild interest in my doings, but listened not at all as I told him a bit about our progress up the peninsula and of the hard times we had had in the mountains north of his city. He was a large man with froggish eyes and a firm paunch. He stared at me for a minute and then turned from the garden terrace where we were assembled and led me by the hand to the back wall of his seventeenth-century villa. He pointed to a small hole next to one of the graceful doors which gave out from the formal drawing room onto the terrace. "Hai visto la guerra?" he said. ("Have you seen the war?") "We in Florence suffered also." I noted Mummi's face as our host was saying this to me, and later, as we were walking back down to Via Camerata, he repeated to me the saying that I later heard so often when I lived in Naples — "Look out for a fat man; it's someone else's fat."

"Signor Colasso," explained Mummi, "made a fortune during the war selling shoddy cloth at inflated prices to our wretched army. He has a large factory over in Prato. Our soldiers were sent to Africa with shoes made of cardboard and uniforms made of cloth that rotted on their backs. Colasso's profits were enormous. He got his contracts from important members of the Fascist party and shared his gains with them, but plenty stuck to his own fingers. Everyone benefited except of course the soldiers, but who worried about them; they were of no importance."

A special loggia was already in the course of construction when I made my visit to the Colassos, and adjoining it a small chapel had been built in which the nuptial mass of the happy couple would be celebrated. Carlo had been involved in the design of these two structures as all efforts were being made to preserve the historic character of the villa. Ducky was agog with the dresses of the bride and the bridesmaids and the sumptuousness of the collation that was in store. The bishop put a stop to all of this, though it struck some of us that he waited an unconscionable amount of time to thunder from his heights up at the top of the hill. The message was carried down to the Colassos by the bishop's own confessor, a Franciscan, and was read from the pulpit the following Sunday: "So soon after the miseries of war and the sufferings of our people, it is to be deemed an immoral excess to lavish wealth so openly and with such ostentation."

In the inevitable family discussions of the affair Carlo confessed to a degree of culpability, in that he was a party in the construction of such unneeded and superfluous structures, though Dolly came to his defense. "But, Papa," she said, "you love Florence and always want to be sure it stays as it is and if there is something new you always fuss that it fits in with the old." Ducky offered the opinion that it was vulgar to spend that much whether there had been a war or not, an opinion which cut the ground out from any further moral discussion. I kept my silence; I liked both the justice of the bishop's pronouncement and the punch of his rhetoric. Such a satisfaction! It was like having your cake and eating it too.

I learned more about the Florentine church and the monks up at Fiesole from my friends the Steiner brothers. The older of the brothers was my instructor in French at the university; the younger was a painter. They were my first European aesthetes: cosmopolitan Jews who had fled Germany and settled in Florence. Hans, the elder, was a student of European languages and literature and adored music. He was thin and intense, with a sickly cast to his face. The younger brother, Fritz, was a simpler man, and not such a bad painter. They were both taken with the music I was writing and the way I played the piano. "What a pleasure," Hans would say to me. "How marvelous to really play and to write and not just talk about it, which is all I can do. And you are still so young!"

They lived on the other side of the Arno on the third floor, in an apartment which looked out over the Piazza Santo Spirito. "Look at the façade of Santo Spirito," said Hans to me one afternoon, pointing out his window. I had never paid it any particular attention; it seemed remarkably plain to me. If I had had to classify it, I would have called it "whitewashed Mexican." "Everything began right there," Hans continued. "Look at those two symmetrical curves framing the upright center like paired seashells, the round rose above the front door, the proportions of the flanking doors. All the Renaissance waiting to flower." He smiled at me. I looked and saw what he meant.

All of Western Europe was his province. He told of the first trip he and his brother had taken to Paris. They had scraped and saved, and descended from the Frankfurt train, two breathless adolescents, into the city they had read and dreamed of all through their younger years. "Paris is the quintessential amalgam of North and South. It has the strength of the North but it is everywhere tempered by southern grace — small wonder

Heine loved it so," he said to me. In our class at the university he turned aside one week from his grammatical teaching and had us parse and translate the great Baudelaire poems on the city, the *Tableaux Parisiens*. No parts of Europe escaped his gaze. I heard for the first time of Palermo's history and of the Norman king's cathedral at Monreale, and of the magic temples at Paestum, set in a meadow above the beaches just below Salerno. "Never look down on Naples and the South," Hans warned me. "There is so much there if you know how to look for it. Of course you have only seen it in the war, poor Naples. One day you will return." They had pictures which the younger brother had painted of Positano. They described it to me as a perfectly possible paradise. "You could live there for nothing, dear Douglas, nothing," said the younger brother. "So bright and clear, enclosed in its circle of mountains, and the water so transparent. Everything is healthy down there, unencumbered. Bodies to look at and everywhere flashing eyes!" Hans looked a bit abashed as his brother held forth. "Europe has been such a prison, dear Douglas," he said to me. "We have to remember what it was and to look again at what it is."

Florence had been kind to the Steiners. Friends had forged identity papers for them, and when the worst of the push toward the deporting of Jews began, the Franciscans up at Fiesole had given them refuge. They nodded their heads when I told them of the bishop's fulminations against extravagance. "He is a good man. He encouraged the monks to hide Jews up there; he found it a Christian work. He would present a perfectly bland face to the Germans and to the Fascist police when they got around to questioning him. He has a great gift of language. When the Germans left they took their revenge, however; they destroyed one of his diocese's minor extravagances. The monks made a most excellent liqueur which they kept in barrels in their cellars. The German officer up at Fiesole, on the morning they finally headed north, ordered all of the barrels brought out to the edge of the hill. He lined up his machine guns and filled the barrels with holes. A river of sweet nectar poured down from the heights and people scrambled out with cups and pans to retrieve it. Of course there were accidents. The Germans had also been careful to place booby traps in the most unforeseen places. A macabre story, dear Douglas, not without its ironies when now we see the bishop fulminating against the excesses of the wealthy manufacturer down the hill."

There had been no lovemaking since that night in Naples with Bianchi when the avuncular pimp had bedded the two of us like brothers in one large bed and the adolescent girl had done her duty. In the early morning she had clenched my flaccid cock in her fist. "Cos'è successo?" she had said. "What's happened?" Now, here in Florence, the death of James in the railroad station, my family and their talk up on the Via Camerata, my studies at the university, piano playing at the conservatory, and the sweet converse of the Steiner brothers contrived to keep Venus at arm's length.

At the club, Graziella, Bingo's whore, came in one night with a bruise on her left cheek. "He is so jealous," she said, looking at her *zingaro*. "He came early and found me with a client and hit me right here." She pointed to her bruise. Gypsy (we all teased him with that name) looked sullen, as if he were playing the part of a jealous Latin lover. Graziella loved pretense and had all of us typecast in a scenario straight out of *The Student Prince*. "It's wonderful to be in the midst of students," she said. She took out a pair of scissors and cut off all of our neckties close to the knot. "Che bello scherzo" ("What a good joke"). "Now you will all go back to the railroad station with the bottom of your *cravatte* missing and I will have a souvenir to remember each of you by."

On the way back, in the shadows by Santa Maria Novella, were, as usual, two children: a delicate sharp-featured boy and his little sister. They were perhaps twelve or thirteen years old. "Specialisti, Joe, siamo specialisti," they said as we passed by. My pal from the club up at Modena knew what was up. "Specialists, are they?" he said. "Florence ain't no different from KC. It turns some dudes on to get a blow job from a kid. Look at them poor little bastards puckering up their lips." He went over and gave the two children all the money he had in his pocket, and we all went home to sleep in the station.

The end approached. The Rector Magnificus, the dean of the university, made a speech about tradition, learning, Florence, and international goodwill, all couched in the most elegant Italian. Only a few of us could follow it. We received diplomas embossed with fleur-de-lis, and I received a special prize: a ceramic sculpture of a satyr playing a large phallic pipe. Up at Via Camerata the Maggioras presented me with the *Canzoniere* of Petrarch in an edition printed on fine paper and bound in leather. Mummi said to me as I thanked them for it, "Don't forget your Italian, and I will know English much better when you come again." Ducky wept, and I promised her that I would return. "You will go to see my sister in New Jersey. I have already written to her, you know. She lives outside Paterson." Carlo shook my hand firmly, but glanced sharply at Dolly as she kissed me on both cheeks. Across the river at Piazza Santo Spirito I played the "Waldstein" for the Steiners. Hans gave me a volume of Mallarmé, and the younger brother one of his small gouaches of Positano.

The trucks came on the tenth of December. Back down we went — south into the past, all the signposts of our bloody progress north hurrying past us in reverse order until at the end we would arrive once again at Naples, where it had all begun. We went across the Arno on a Bailey bridge and joined the Via Cassia at the city limits of Florence. In a few miles we passed by the military cemetery where James had been buried, next to all those from the 350th who had died earlier, before the war had ended. We drove along the ridges of the ancient Cassia, dipping into the valley at Poggibonsi and passing the towers of Monteriggioni on our left as we approached the wooded hills just short of Siena. We skirted the walls to the west of the city, catching just a glimpse of the zebra-striped cathedral crowning all that expanse of brick and tiled roof. On into southern Tuscany: the land grew more sere and the landscape to the east was delineated by the fine curve of Monte Amiata, speckled with the first snow of the winter. Up over the high pass at Radicafani, past Montefiascone with Lake Bolsena on our right, and then the long descent into the volcanic plain which stretches to Viterbo. The Cassia wound on through cuts in the volcanic tufa after passing outside the ruined walls of the ancient town, and suddenly we were approaching pine trees and Rome. The trucks dropped us off for the night at the army rest center at Foro Italico, that vapid cenotaph of Fascist megalomania. There we slept for the night in the dormitories built for the Olympic athletes — sterile structures in pale brick with massive stone copings.

The parking lot where we reloaded onto our trucks the next morning was dominated by elephantine men, frozen in stone and stupidly naked, fascism's heroes. One of the art history Ph.D.s who was on the convoy giggled as we drove past them; we were coming from Florence, and he had Michelangelo's *David* in mind. "They're engineered to do a lot of pushups but could you imagine them ever making love? They're equipped with appendages, not organs."

Ruins and bombed-out shells of towns awaited us as we proceeded south. There were the mountains on our left where I had been, and on our right the killing fields of Anzio and the ruins that marked the breakthrough from the beachhead. The plain narrows to a pass between the hills and the sea at Terracina, and soon enough my heart leapt as I caught my first glimpse of Gaeta off on its peninsula surrounded by the wintery-blue Tyrrhenian. We would round the corner into Formia, and there beyond would be the sloping ground leading back and up to Minturno; there was the lonely ditch where sweet Jack and Leonard had been shot in the back of their necks. More Bailey bridges across the Garigliano and the Volturno, and then we swerved and hugged the coast, passing between Cape Miseno and Cumae, ending the day sleeping in the same place we slept in on our first night in Italy: the Fascist barracks built on the shore facing the flat island of Procida, with Ischia and Mount Epomeo beyond.

The next day was a bad film played backward. It didn't seem possible at first; the war was over. We were told by a series of officious officers and sergeants, some of them WAACs, that no man would be allowed to board a transport without a proper distribution of objects in either the A or B bag. We howled at them when they found us out of order for not having in our possession either the requisite objects or appropriately labeled bags. "What about our medals?" asked one of us. "Should they be put in the A bag or the B bag?"

The next day found us, nevertheless, lined up on the dock, A and B bags by our side. We hadn't been given any time to see Naples; that very next morning we had been whisked through the tunnel under Posilipo and on down the Riviera di Chiaia, through the Piazza del Plebiscito, past San Carlo and on to the frenzy of the docks. Out in the deeper waters rode a brand-new aircraft carrier, virginal. It had never seen active duty; its hangar decks had been converted into geometrical fields of bunks stacked five high. "God bless America," said someone as we clambered aboard the shiny new machine, dragging our two bags after us, half of us with no hats and our uniforms every which way. Spit-and-polish marines stood at the head of the gangplank, showing us where to go. "Ain't they pretty?" remarked my friend the mortar sergeant. "So well fed and healthy, and such lovely skin tone." He blew them a kiss.

I made a beeline for one of the top bunks, remembering my twenty-five days on the Liberty ship two years before. There was lots of room above my head, and plenty of light to read by. To my horror "Semper Fidelis," the Marine Corps hymn, suddenly blared forth five feet from my left ear: there was a loudspeaker suspended from a beam in the ceiling. I descended from my

eyrie and a half acre away across the expanse of the hangar deck
discovered a marine corporal at the keyboard of a Hammond
electric organ. The instrument was rigged directly to the ship's
sound system. I told him I was a musician too, and asked him
if he was a chaplain's assistant. "What do you take me for?"
he said. "My duty pure and simple is musician to this ship's
company and I like to play." He launched into a medley from
Show Boat.

Supper came soon afterward, and it was good: fried chicken
and mashed potatoes with real butter, salads, pies, and strong
coffee. We hadn't had anything like it since we left the States,
and it was a lot better than anything we had gotten at Camp
Gruber. The ship began vibrating as I finished my pie. The marine corporal launched into "Semper Fidelis" again: he always
began with it. I got on one of the enormous elevators made to
bring the planes up top and rode it up onto the enormous expanse of the flight deck.

It was all over. I was leaving. It was a clear December evening,
and the ambient rays of the setting sun lit Vesuvius with a yellowish tinge, a color which shaded off into violet on the lower
slopes; houses on the shore below the volcano at Torre del Greco
threw back its light from their windows. From where I stood I
couldn't see Naples itself; my glance veered around to Sorrento
and the break in the chain of mountains which signaled the strait
between Punta della Campanella and Capri. That evening, my
war finished, my dead buried, ensconced on the deck of an enormous steel machine, no thoughts of what was past arose in me.
Some future was in front of me and I was along for the ride. We
went at a moderate rate across the Mediterranean, but when we
reached Gibraltar the captain announced to all on board that he
intended to break the world's record for an Atlantic crossing. I
was up on deck watching the wake of the ship as we moved into
the currents which course from the Mediterranean to the Atlantic. Minuscule Arab fishing boats rigged with lateen sails bobbed
below. The vibrations increased and we lunged out of the gates

of Hercules headed for America, leaving the fishing boats toss-
ing in our wake. We made it to Newport News in record time.
When I came down the gangplank with my A bag on my shoulder and my B bag dragging behind, a burly WAAC sergeant said
to me, "Come on, soldier. Pick it up."

There was snow on the ground in Massachusetts that day just
before Christmas when my father and mother came to pick me
up at Fort Devens. I had on a plaid scarf which my mother had
sent to me in Italy. She spotted that first in the crowd of soldiers
and rushed over to kiss me. My father stood still, overcome with
pride. I gulped. We drove home in the Ford, and when we arrived at Melrose Highlands everything had an appearance at
once familiar and disturbingly remote. It was like looking
through the wrong end of a telescope — chastening clarity and
microscopic dimensions: there was Melrose High School, there
was Main Street, there were my two sisters, there was Christmas
dinner with turkey and cranberry sauce, and the special etched
glass goblets trimmed with gold leaf from my grandparents'
fiftieth wedding anniversary, filled with cider. The war and Italy
were far, far away, and the trip from Naples to Newport News a
recent mechanical nightmare.

10

O F COURSE I WENT BACK. Seven years later, married but alone, after two years in the city, I sailed again from Naples. My friend Aldo and I had put Candida on the train to Turin in the morning. Bureaucracy, both Italian and American, had defeated us; it had not been possible to get her visa in time for her to accompany me. I kissed her goodbye in the huge old yellow stucco station (long since demolished) down in the lower level where the fast trains left for the North. There was a terrible passivity in her face. The American consul had told us only a week before that since I was leaving for the States all of the manifold documents we had prepared that summer in Positano were no longer valid; Candida now came under the jurisdiction of the U.S. consulate at Genoa, as her mother's house in Turin had become her official address with my departure and Turin was under the jurisdiction of Genoa, not Naples.

We had been married in June by the deputy mayor of Turin. Two days earlier he had been present at a concert I had given under the auspices of the U.S. Information Service with two American singers, and at the end he had spoken a few words about Italo-American friendship. "I had not expected my words to have such an immediate effect on the relations between our two countries," he said with a smile to the two of us as he shook our hands after marrying us.

It was sordid down by the docks. In addition to the general mess and hubbub that is part and parcel of Naples, the war's destruction was everywhere, though it was now eight years since the bombardments. Aldo and I sat together at an iron table in a café situated between the Chiesa del Carmine (tomb of poor Conradin, the last of the Hohenstaufen emperors) and the pier where the USS *Constitution* loomed over the hubbub of porters and taxis and departing travelers. There was terror in my bones. I had to leave. I had no money left. I was married, and I had to go back and earn my living. Aldo took my hand and looked straight at me with his silly big eyes. "So you leave all of this," he said pointing to the Neapolitan scene around us. "It's pretty awful if you look closely. You're going to a new life over there in America, a *vita nuova*."

Naples had been my new life, I said to myself, though I knew that Aldo, full of affection and poetry, was trying to cheer me up. He was an actor and very rich. Love, literature, and a "new life"! Dante wasn't much help. What about the other great poet the Italians liked so much, Petrarch? He wrote two cycles of poems about Laura and the second one dropped the word *life* — *In vita di Madonna Laura* — and was all about *death* — "In morte di Madonna Laura." I had dropped my Laura a year ago. She was out of my life, well and flourishing, and about to marry a rich count from the Veneto.

She wasn't dead; I was. She had loved me, and all I had worried about was her family's opinion. We had fucked underwater up at Cape Miseno and on the heights of Faito she had shoved me against the mighty mountain oak, but the moment Aldo, on the beach at Forte dei Marmi, had introduced me to my passive nymph I rejected my Neapolitan Bette Davis. A sudden linkage established itself in my mind, and I thought I was going to be ill. Aldo saw the color of my face and ordered up some Fernet-Branca, that enormously bitter potion used to settle the stomach in Italy. I swallowed it down and prepared to depart. There had been important hoots from the *Constitution*. I smiled, we embraced, and a ubiquitous Neapolitan porter took over, seized my ticket, shouldered my suitcases (my trunk was already in the hold), and guided me to my cabin down in the entrails of third class. I gave him a big tip.

I went up on deck as the tugs began warping the ship from her mooring. I could see the royal palace and San Carlo, and my mind wound up Via Roma when suddenly, all on its own, it swerved left into a very particular byway. I had expected a gentle reverie that would proceed all the way up to Capodimonte, a memory like a pleasing fiction which would weave a story out of my year up in that decrepit villa. The linkage fixed in my mind just before I had taken the Fernet-Branca was not so easily broken as my stomach's discomfiture had been. The war returned with all its fury. It had given me a medal and in my father's eyes it had made a man of me, but I was stuck in this present immediacy which made that moment in the morning with the teenage whore, up in that alley off the Via Roma, the mordant key to my present terror.

As the boat proceeded out into the bay it headed not for Capri and Punta della Campanella but in a more northerly direction out past Ischia: we were headed for Genoa to pick up more passengers before sailing on to New York. As we were clearing Posilipo I caught a glimpse of the Riviera di Chiaia and the hill going up to the Vomero. There so very recently, simultaneously with Erika's midnight hysteria, I had, as in a vision, heard Leonard's voice calling out as it had on that cold December night on the hillside outside Oran: "Allanbrook. Allanbrook." I had not answered then and never would or could. Was that voice, calling out my name, to be forever the guarantor of my loneliness, the only permanence granted or even possible, even though it had no substance and no existence except as a source of infinite regret? Was love to be forever linked with what was no longer and perhaps had never been? Eighteen years later, divorced from Candida, after I had traveled to Potenza and laid to rest forever my guilt concerning Laura and her family, I had, on my trip back to Faito, been bewitched by the clarity and the linkage of two experiences — Paestum at high noon and the word *essere* overheard at night as I sat by the sea at Elea, Parmenides' town. Rid of an obsession with which I had lived for eighteen years I wanted something in its place, something which would last. The Greek temples in Paestum had a beguiling look of eternity, standing there on the plain between the blue sea and the mountains, shimmering honey-colored in the glare of noon while just down the coast was Elea, the town where the never-ending talk about what remains and what passes away had been crystallized by Parmenides and where I overheard a student and his teacher talking of being and becoming. What a solace it would be if some timeless essence, clear and lucid, were standing in back of our time-ridden lives, if all of our shifting loves were grounded in some apprehensible reality.

Fully two thirds of the passengers on the *Constitution* that fall of 1952 were Italian-Americans who had returned to Naples and Calabria to see again the places where they had been born and to visit with their kinfolk. The youngest of them were middle-aged. They were on their way back to Bridgeport, Connecticut, and Revere, Massachusetts, and Dayton, Ohio. The few full-fledged Italians on the ship laughed at the way they talked and the native Americans ignored them. Not only could they not speak Italian — they had always spoken a dialect — but the very dialect was inalterably tangled with English and, in a kind of pathetic symmetry, their English was inalterably tangled with the dialect. They had not fared so well on their visits back to their native soil. They had returned to their villages proud of their Americanisms and their American dollars, but more often than not they had been condescended to. There was no place for them in Italy, and it wasn't that different back in Bridgeport. Caught between two worlds, they had no country they could call their own. (How different for their sons and their daughters: they were Americans. After all, it was dear Bianchi, an Italian-American from Rochester, who was with me, my American comforter, on that night in Naples with the girl, after Leonard's death.)

Until fairly recently my most recurrent dream has had to do with boats crossing and recrossing the Atlantic, always to and from Naples. There is uncertainty: What am I doing on board? Why am I going back? Which side of the Atlantic is where I am going back to? What have I left behind, and who is waiting for me? I become like those Italian-Americans on the *Constitution*: I have no home; I am an inhabitant of limbo. Some of this dream can be dismissed as the simple-minded nostalgia of "away-from-home sickness," all mixed up with its partner, "homesickness." Another part, more far-reaching, has to do with spending so much of my twenties first in the army, and then, after a few brief years at Harvard, five years in Paris and Naples. All of that lies on top of what everyone experiences, more or less vividly: the recollections of youth, though few recollections give rise to dreams with the clarity of my transatlantic one.

When work and marriages and children begin, the lights dim, the landscape becomes habitual. Despite the daily routine of being grown up and an adult the soul, in its own private place, peers backward toward the places and persons that formed it when it first left home, that shoved it into what it was going to be for the rest of its later life; yet, at the very moment that it recollects those times and places, it can't help jumping even further back to where it came from, to its original home. All that may be a general phenomenon and there's no one who hasn't ruminated more or less consciously upon such matters. If lives have stories, this is the soil those stories spring from; a composed fiction can only imitate and embroider upon what is given.

Comedies end with marriage; it is what brings down the curtain, and we follow with enormous pleasure the vicissitudes of Joe and Mary (or of Figaro and Susanna!) until the moment when their vows are secured and the end we knew was coming has been elegantly taken care of. No one wants to see their married life — if it is happy it is of no special interest, if unhappy it will turn out to be a squalid story. Our interest is entirely in the events which preceded the marriage, in the art with which it was all encompassed neatly in a circumscribed number of chapters. In the middle years there is no drama, death is not imminent, youth is past, and there's work to be done: children to be raised, music to be written, money to be earned.

I see Naples clearly now I am old. The middle years are over — a long plateau which the memory skids over. I am twice divorced, alone, and will be dead fairly soon. The recurrent dreams of my trips back and forth across the Atlantic stopped a year or so ago. I now see the city as it was the first time I saw it: the gateway to where so many were to die, though I lived. My view is from the deck of that British freighter, with Leonard, who was the first of us to die, and his death fixed a certain, inevitable path, ever present until the end of memory, which is death. When I look again at my Neapolitan years I see myself on the hill at Capodimonte, living in a villa with the Picabias, that sad and marooned couple shipwrecked up above the city while I sported in the Neapolitan waters like a callow dolphin. Laura dumped, I lived downtown with Erika, another shipwreck, alone up on the sixth floor of her dead parents' apartment. There I saw despair and decency going on, hand in hand, from day to day. There Erika trod the lonely path which woke me to my own future. She loved Candida and she loved me, and she gave us her parents' wedding rings.

Toward the end of November Candida finally got her visa from the American consulate up in Genoa. It happened only after my father wrote to one of our Massachusetts senators, Henry Cabot Lodge, who was chairman of the Senate Foreign Relations Committee and had clout with the State Department, which put pressure on the American consulate in Genoa. Her visa was issued in a matter of days. She arrived on the USS *Independence* on a bitter cold day toward the end of November. It had been a stormy passage. I waited and waited on the dock on the Hudson as passenger after passenger left the boat and made their way to the customs shed. She finally emerged, the last passenger off the boat. Blinking her eyes at the New World she came slowly down the gangplank to where I stood waiting, shivering in the elegant overcoat I had had my Neapolitan tailor make for me with the last of my fellowship checks.